6.00
cx 7↓

Spooke (64 - 216 95) 9-345

THE TALKATIVE PRESIDENT

THE TALKATIVE PRESIDENT

THE OFF-THE-RECORD
PRESS CONFERENCES OF

CALVIN COOLIDGE

EDITED BY

HOWARD H. QUINT & ROBERT H. FERRELL

THE UNIVERSITY OF MASSACHUSETTS PRESS *AMHERST*

Library of Congress Catalog Card Number: 64-21695

Printed in the United States of America

FOREWORD

CALVIN COOLIDGE was the contriver of the most persistent and transparent political hoax of twentieth-century America. He effected it by speaking to the American people twice weekly from his White House press conference forum through the medium of "the White House Spokesman." I was a party to the hoax. So were a dozen or so of my news colleagues. All of us were press conference regulars in the latter Coolidge years. I was assigned by United Press (now United Press International) to cover the State and War Departments, housed in the gingerbread building just across West Executive Avenue from the White House. In the State Department press room we were only a step away from the President's office in the west wing of the White House where the press conferences took place. Treasury reporters were not press conference regulars. The Treasury building, across East Executive Avenue, is a long block north and a long two blocks east from the White House Executive office. Consequently the Treasury men did not always come.

Mr. Coolidge could count his press conference well attended if a dozen reporters appeared. Press association reporters, representing all of the daily press in the United States and much of it throughout the world, were there, of course. We could not have imagined in the time of Mr. Coolidge the camaraderie and electronic gadgetry of the modern White House press conference. Neither could we have imagined the hell for leather spontaneity of the press conferences of Franklin D. Roosevelt. FDR fielded oral questions on the fly with no protection other than his quick tongue and those admiring New Deal newsmen who were always ready to laugh at FDR's not-so-sly humor or to drown out or divert a hostile questioner who sought more than a wisecrack as a response to a tough question. Two hundred or more of us would crowd into FDR's Presidential office where we once had met Mr. Coolidge in sparse company.

Questions had to be written and submitted to C. Bascom Slemp, President Coolidge's secretary, prior to a conference. Mr. Coolidge had no press secretary. The White House Secretariat, including a press secretary, was set up by Mr. Hoover in 1929. Slemp was a Virginia politician whose funereal appearance and melancholy air may have come of his lifelong effort to proselyte his native state, Virginia, for the Republican party. He winnowed the potentially troublesome questions.

The five, ten or twenty questions (each of us could ask more than one) that survived Mr. Slemp's scrutiny went to Mr. Coolidge a few minutes before we strolled into his office. The President would be completely relaxed. I always had the impression that he had not peeked at the questions before we arrived. The briefings and skull sessions which preceded the Eisenhower and Kennedy press conferences were not for Mr. Coolidge. If such anxious preliminaries had been part of the press conference operation, Mr. Coolidge would have abandoned the whole thing. The rugged man from Vermont liked his comfort.

Mr. Coolidge was a no-nonsense man. He sharply rebuked any who presumed to put an oral question. He seemed even to resent such spoken pleasantries as "Nice day," or "Pretty weather, Mr. President, isn't it?" as we were assembling in front of his desk. He was not to be trapped into responding to an uncensored question.

When questions were answered, we took notes conforming as nearly as possible to Mr. Coolidge's choice of words. From these notes we would dictate from the press room to our Washington offices whatever had been said but without attributing the remarks to President Coolidge. We hung everything on "the White House Spokesman," a device imposed on us by Mr. Coolidge and his forbidding servant, C. Bascom Slemp. The editors caught on quickly, of course, and in time so did the newspaper readers. Toward the end of Mr. Coolidge's administration, "the White House Spokesman" was being ridiculed by a great many newspapers. Mr. Coolidge seemed not to mind.

His press conferences were a forum for sly, wry humor, as the selections in Chapter I indicate. Moreover, the President often volunteered information. He liked to announce things at his press conferences—upcoming trips, nominations, occasionally major policy. He seemed to be proud of the Coolidge boom then resounding in Wall Street. Harry W. Frantz of the Washington bureau of United Press International recalls an occasion when Mr. Coolidge was asked at a press conference about credit and brokers' loans and responded so complacently as to cause a volcanic stock market upsurge in the succeeding several days. He liked the thought that his words skied stock prices.

I recall especially one unofficial encounter with Coolidge. One evening I had remained late in the press room. The sun was well down. I stood before one of the floor-level windows gazing carelessly across the lawn toward Pennsylvania Avenue. Dick Jervis, chief of the White House Secret Service detail, and three others were playing bridge behind me at a reporter's desk. From the corner of my eye I caught sight of a slight figure approaching the very window at which I stood. Another glance and I was sure. It was Mr. Coolidge strolling through the White House grounds. "Jiggers, Dick," I hollered, "here comes the President." Jervis and the others dove for hiding spots. I reached for the window shade and pulled it down just as Mr. Coolidge stopped squarely in front of the window. His face did not change expression as the shade came down. Neither did he come roaring into the press room to find out what was going on. The President just walked away. He never looked for trouble.

LYLE C. WILSON

In the preparation of this volume, we have benefited no little from the personal recollections of Lyle C. Wilson and Harry W. Frantz, who attended Coolidge's press conferences. We have deep obligation to John M. Buteau, John F. Murphy, Jr., and Kenneth G. Olson, Trustees of The Forbes Library of Northampton, Massachusetts, for permission to publish the press conference transcripts, and to the Library's Director, Lawrence E. Wikander, who has helped us at every turn. Violet Durgin and Stanley Greenberg of The Forbes Library staff also have been unstinting in their cooperation. We wish to thank the Research Council of the University of Massachusetts for its support of our project. The Director of the University of Massachusetts Press, Leone A. Barron, has given us enormous assistance; we wish herein to acknowledge our debt to her. Esther Blackmore has provided us with expert secretarial help. Finally, we wish to thank our wives, Eleanor Quint and Lila Ferrell, who probably never thought very much about Calvin Coolidge, one way or the other, until we started to work on this book. They have now heard all about Coolidge and have borne up nobly under the strain.

HOWARD H. QUINT, *University of Massachusetts*
ROBERT H. FERRELL, *Indiana University*

ix

CONTENTS

INTRODUCTION

CALVIN COOLIDGE, President of the United States from August, 1923 until March, 1929, never seemed a talkative man, and indeed made a reputation for being the opposite; but when he let down his guard, when he felt that what he said would not be subject to misinterpretation or used against him, he could be so talkative as to appear almost garrulous.

After Coolidge became President, the reputedly quiet man from Vermont soon realized that he had a sympathetic audience in his conferences with the White House press correspondents. He revealed a talkative streak. He met the press twice a week, on Tuesdays and Fridays. All questions had to be submitted in advance, and correspondents were forbidden to quote the President's answers or to attribute them to him. The President permitted, although usually with a show of irritation, occasional on-the-spot questioning. Once sure of his ground, certain that what he said would not be subjected to the repetition and speculation which presidential remarks always seem to provoke, Coolidge relaxed and began to enjoy himself with the reporters. These were meetings which he could control completely, yet where he encountered sympathy from his auditors, with the certainty that nothing dire would result. They were intimate dialogues, attended by a dozen or so correspondents as compared to the several hundred who jam the sessions which more recent presidents have had with the press. And they were entirely different from the meetings in his office with high-pressure individuals who wanted posts in the government for themselves or their friends or wished legislation pushed in Congress. With such ambitious people the President—as any sensible successor to Warren G. Harding knew instinctively—had to be exceedingly cautious.

The President obtained much free publicity from the press conferences. As he told reporters on several occasions, he himself could never have composed such skillful accounts of his administration for verbatim or background release to the country's newspapers. It was far easier, and much more effective, to meet the correspondents twice a week and let them do the work. Moreover, face to face with the correspondents, he was disarmingly friendly. He liked most of them; they, in turn, must have thought twice

1

before writing unduly critical accounts of the Coolidge administration.

The President ranged over a wide variety of subjects with a degree of expertise that historians of a later generation not always have appreciated. True, he had the advantage of being able to select from among the questions submitted in advance. But he did not have so great an advantage as may be thought over more recent presidents, who supposedly have had to face weekly press inquisitions with little protective armor other than the dignity of their office. For not only is the modern president presented beforehand with all varieties of questions which might be asked, but he is also supplied with answers by numerous experts from the various executive departments of the government. (He must, of course, remember the answers.) Moreover, he can depend upon certain reporters to ask him planted questions on which he is especially primed to speak. As one Washington correspondent, discussing the late President Kennedy's press conferences, put it, "Too many of the questions are lobs, set-ups and blooper balls, and there is too little effort to obtain any more than the most generalized information. I don't blame the President for knocking them out of the lot." What seems, then, to be a spontaneous and fact-crammed presidential response is frequently the product of intensive preconference briefing and the cooperation of helpful newsmen.

Although the range of the President's comments was wide, perhaps as much to the point is what he did not talk about. In some instances one seeks almost in vain, and in others totally so, for presidential pronouncements on such matters as the Harding scandals, prohibition, the Sacco-Vanzetti case, the Ku Klux Klan, labor unions, the movies, radio, welfare capitalism, the Scopes Trial, bank failures, the Florida real estate boom, and last, but not least, the New York Stock Exchange's rampaging bull market. When one compares what President Coolidge and, for instance, the historian Frederick Lewis Allen had to say about the twenties, it seems at times that they were not talking about the same era.

The press conferences remained carefully anonymous. In the fading and yellowed newspapers of the 1920's, one finds references to "the White House Spokesman" and to other sources coming vaguely from somewhere in Washington; most of them probably emanated from President Coolidge's press conferences. But from the news of the period, it is difficult to know exactly what he told the reporters about anything. For many years after Coolidge left the White House one could only discern his press conference statements through the opaque glosses printed contemporaneously in the nation's newspapers.

Now that the issues of the 1920's have subsided into history and most of the people involved are dead, there is reason to learn what the President really had to say, and such is the purpose of the present volume. The lack of any conference transcripts made a large gap in the historical record of the Coolidge Administration. And the Coolidge Papers deposited in the Library of Congress, containing presidential office files, proved disappointing to scholars. The President was an efficient writer of letters, but exasperatingly noncommittal. Like Franklin D. Roosevelt, he was brief and to the point, answering long epistles with a sentence or two. Public addresses and other speeches helped the historians scarcely at all, for the long years of politics had made Coolidge a master of platitudes—indeed, he relished repeating platitudes. When he left the White House, he took no steps to fill out the historical record. His *Autobiography,* which he marketed at five dollars a word, is not illuminating. His newspaper column was, to put it mildly, a bore. Coolidge died in January 1933; Mrs. Coolidge lived on until 1957 and the era of Dwight D. Eisenhower. Had she written her autobiography, it might well have revealed that life with Calvin was hardly a bed of roses. Although many of his bone-dry witticisms continued to circulate about the country, it was difficult to penetrate their screen to the man behind; and of course the Coolidge wit seldom revealed much of what the President really thought about public affairs. The Coolidge record —the straightforward, intimate historical record—was almost as barren as that of Harding, whose presidential papers have only recently been made available to scholars. Coolidge appeared as little more than a wispy, embarrassed, taciturn man from Vermont who, surprisingly, had a sense of humor.

Seeking records of the press conferences, one of the editors of the present volume called at The Forbes Library in Northampton, which possessed a sizable if miscellaneous body of Coolidge memorabilia—including the famous sombrero and chaps bearing the legend "C.A.L." which came from the President's visit to the Black Hills. Upon inquiry to the Librarian at The Forbes, Lawrence E. Wikander, a search began. Mr. Wikander turned up a wooden box addressed to The Forbes and sent out from the White

House in March, 1929. It held the typed ribbon-copy verbatim transcripts of all the Coolidge press conferences.

The present edition of the transcripts comprises approximately one-sixth of the press conference material from August, 1923 until March, 1929. We have selected what seem to be the more important Coolidge comments and statements, grouped them under appropriate topics (recognizing that overlapping was occasionally unavoidable), and provided explanation or identification when necessary. In a few instances, we have made editorial corrections for the sake of clarity. In no case, however, has the meaning of the transcripts been affected.

We believe that the reader of this novel material will obtain a fresh view of Coolidge. The President no longer will seem a small-boned, silent Yankee politician propelled into the White House by the accident of his predecessor's death and kept there by the delusion of American voters in the twenties, but will stand as a shrewd politician who demonstrated a surprisingly wide comprehension of public issues.

· I ·

A YANKEE IN THE
WHITE HOUSE

1 · Fundamental Vermont

Coolidge's countrymen may remember him more for his humor than for anything else. His was a dry wit, of course, never slipping into hilarity. Nor was it ever obscene. Lincoln was a master of the dirty joke; there is no record that Coolidge ever told one, though this is not to say that he did not or that he did not enjoy hearing one. In a way Coolidge's humor was like that of Will Rogers, his well-known contemporary. But Rogers, the professional humorist, worked carefully into his jokes, with a long windup before the "punch line," whereas Coolidge seemed to indulge in humor spontaneously. Coolidge never considered himself a jokester. His wit partook of the economy of Vermont—he doled it out sparingly, always with a straight face. And it had to have a purpose other than mere amusement.

Coolidge did not point his humor at anyone, nor did he expect his fellow citizens to be humorous about him. He had a very large sense of the dignity of his office. When Will Rogers once imitated the President's twangy voice over the radio, the President took deep offense, and Rogers became *persona non grata* at the White House.

August 24, 1923

An inquiry about whether Mr. [Chauncey M.] Brush is to be Chairman of the Shipping Board. Well, of course, he isn't. Mr. Brush was an old time friend of mine that I knew in Boston when he was one of the officers, and I think later, the President of the Boston Elevated Railway. He dropped in yesterday morning to pay his respects and we chatted of old times and I inquired how he was getting along in his

7

new project and, naturally, getting his opinion about some of my problems, particularly shipping, but it would be as impossible, I suppose, to get him to be Chairman of our Shipping Board as it would be as impossible to get one of our College Professors to be the head of one of our primary schools.

September 11, 1923

PRESS: Was there a Cabinet meeting today?

PRESIDENT: Yes, but there was practically no business transacted at the Cabinet meeting. It only lasted about 15 minutes, after which the world will soon know we had our picture taken.

October 2, 1923

One of the representatives of the Farm Bureau Federation, Mr. Silver, was in this morning. Brought me a box of very fine apples. I would advise all of you to ask him to visit you, if you can secure the kind of reaction that I secured.

October 5, 1923

I have an inquiry here on the subject of education relative to the statement that I made of approval of National Education Day, and whether I think more manual and industrial and outdoor training should be in order for all. I don't think you can make any hard and fast rule about that. It depends upon the locality and on the individual. I recall that when I was in college, one of the professors was discussing that problem before us and speaking of the need generally of athletics in education at the present time. But he said that he knew a man that had been President of the Massachusetts State College, I think his name was Goodnough, walked from Templeton to Andover, a distance of sixty miles, and carried his trunk on his back. He said that when he got there he didn't have any feeling for a course in football.

[*Coolidge's memory played him false. Massachusetts State College had a President James C. Greenough (1883-86) and a President Henry H. Goodell (1886-1905) but no President "Goodnough." The story, in any event, would not seem to apply to either man.*]

February 8, 1924

I have a great many questions today, but a great many I find are duplicates, triplicates, and other "cates."

March 11, 1924

I haven't made any final determination about the appointment of Commissioners in the District. I think at the last conference we had, I indicated the very unanimous endorsement that had come from the many different organizations in Washington of the two City Commissioners. I inquired of them if they would be willing to serve, if I should make up my mind to appoint them. Since then I have received a number of communications, not exactly in the nature of charges, but in the nature of protests that I thought perhaps I ought to clear up before I sent the names up, and for that reason I am obliged to take a little time to investigate the charges. I don't think they really amount to anything. It would be very unusual that Commissioners would be in office for three years without there being two opinions as to whether they functioned properly. I know that, because I was Mayor of Northampton [1910-11], and after I had given a very excellent administration for a year there was a division of opinion as to whether I ought to be re-elected.

April 18, 1924

I think this report that I am to attend the Republican Convention, from what I have already said, and make an address there, you will see is exaggerated. There will be plenty of members at the Convention prepared, I have no doubt, to make sufficient addresses without calling me and my assistance.

July 18, 1924

I haven't started any special work on my address of notification. I have gotten now just to the point where someone asked the man who had a reputation as a speaker how long it took him to prepare his speech, and he said he had been working on the speech all his life.

———

I don't think I can give any definition of the words "reactionary" and "progressive" that would be helpful. That reminds me a little of the old definition of "orthodoxy" and "heterodoxy." I think they used to say that "orthodoxy" was "my doxy" and "heterodoxy" was "your doxy." Sometimes the person is not well thought of and he is labeled as a reactionary. Sometimes if he is well thought of he is called a progressive. As a matter of fact all the political parties are progressive. I can't conceive of a party existing for any length of time that wasn't progressive, or of leadership being effective that wasn't progressive.

———

PRESS: Mr. President, will you take occasion to reply to the statement made by Mr. Davis, his address of acceptance?

PRESIDENT: Of course, I don't know about that. A great many times if you let a situation alone it takes care of itself. I mean that if I let this situation alone somebody may take care of it better than I can.

[*John W. Davis was the Democratic presidential candidate in 1924.*]

August 12, 1924

I don't know whether I will take the report of the Tariff Commission on the sugar schedule to Vermont with me or not. It is quite a voluminous document, I find. I shall take it with me mentally.

[*The majority report of the Tariff Commission maintained that the sugar rates of 2.20 cents per pound (1.76 per pound for Cuban sugar)*]

9

were too high. The minority report justified the existing schedule. The reports were submitted on July 29 and September 7. Clem L. Shauer, Chairman of the Democratic National Committee, was to accuse Coolidge of delaying the reduction of sugar rates. Shauer charged that several prominent Republican politicians were personally benefiting from the existing rates, among them Senator Reed Smoot of Utah, former Representative James Fordney, and former Ambassador to Mexico Charles B. Warren.]

August 29, 1924

PRESIDENT: I suppose the Washington baseball team is the one that represents the whole nation. The others have some local claims. That which comes from the city of Washington I suppose represents the nation in its entirety more than any other team. If it should be so fortunate [as] to secure first place, in that respect I suppose it would be more agreeable to the whole nation than that which could be secured by having any local team win the pennant. I don't know as I can make any statement about the present condition of our team that hasn't already been better made by someone else. I am not an expert on baseball, though I enjoy the game. I haven't made any plans yet about attending the World Series, but should that be the case I assume that it goes without saying that I should want to see the opening game.

PRESS: Mr. President, would it be permissible to quote that remark about baseball?

PRESIDENT: No, I don't think so.

September 16, 1924

I don't know as I can make any comment on the progress of the campaign, other than to say it is going on satisfactorily. I haven't any speaking engagements other than what are known. I think next month I am going to speak at Philadelphia on the 25th, and before the Holy Name Society here on the 21st. Those have no special significance. If I get cornered up by people wanting me to make speeches, and it is represented to me that on this occasion I am the only individual that can save the progress of civilization, and that unless I am to do it civilization is going to fail and I shall be responsible for it, when that proposal is made to anyone it is rather difficult for them to say they won't make a speech.

I don't know as I can comment any on the statement that I think Chairman Butler made in relation to my making speeches in the West. I have tried to make it plain that I have no plan about it. I shouldn't want you to be surprised, or to draw any particular inference from my making speeches, or not making speeches, out there. I don't recall any candidate for President that ever injured himself very much by not talking.

[*Senator William M. Butler of Massachusetts, a New Bedford textile manufacturer and Chairman of the Republican National Committee, was Coolidge's close friend and advisor. Appointed to the Senate in 1924 to succeed the deceased Henry Cabot Lodge, he was defeated for his seat in 1926 by Democrat David I. Walsh.*]

September 26, 1924

PRESS: Anything in the Cabinet, Mr. President?

PRESIDENT: Oh. No, there was no discussion in the Cabinet this morning, other than the report of [Agriculture] Secretary [Henry C.] Wallace that there had been a case of foot and mouth disease discovered in Texas. As soon as it was established, it was taken care of.

October 24, 1924

PRESS: Mr. President, what are the reports from Minnesota? I understand the latest report is that the Republicans are going to carry Minnesota?

PRESIDENT: I haven't any specific reports about any states. My reports indicate that I shall probably carry Northampton. That is about as far as I can go into details. That is based more on experience.

November 11, 1924

There is considerable speculation as to whether I am likely to change or not. I don't anticipate to change very much. I have tried in the conduct of my office to be natural and I don't want to change that attitude. There are two or three other people that have served with me in the conduct of the affairs of the United States that I should be pleased if they changed a little—that I have to change from saying "no" to saying "yes."

May 1, 1925

I don't know just why the Department has refused to issue passports to women in their maiden name, but I suppose because it has been the universal rule of the Department.

PRESS: Mr. President, Mr. Kellogg says it is up to the President. The regulations provide that the President can change it if he wishes to.

PRESIDENT: Well, it hasn't been brought to my attention officially. If it is, I will examine it with the State Department. I am sure the desire is to accommodate the person, keeping in mind that it should be such a document as will enable those who are to be visaed by notice of the passport that this is the person described in the passport. I don't know whether I ought to consult with the husbands of the married women about the rule or not.

[*Frank B. Kellogg, Secretary of State (1925-29), had been Republican Senator from Minnesota (1917-23). After serving as Ambassador*

*to Great Britain (December, 1923 to February, 1925), he was ap-
pointed to the Coolidge cabinet in March, 1925.*]

May 8, 1925

I have a couple of rumors. One is that the President is searching for a man to reorganize the Veterans Bureau and that General Hines is leaving. The other one is a question as to what I can say about the report that General Hines is about to retire from the head of the Veterans Bureau and that Colonel Arthur Woods is going to suc- ceed him.

I was thinking that perhaps this rumor was a mistaken rumor, and that they meant Major Haynes, the prohibition enforcer—which re- minded me a little of a story that Governor [Wm. C.] Sproul [Rep., Pa.] told when he came up to Northampton to celebrate with the neighbors my election as Vice-President. He spoke about some experi- ence he had with some of his friends in Pennsylvania. He went out somewhere to make some inquiries about a spaghetti factory, asked a man on the street if he knew where the spaghetti factory was, and the man said "no." Then the man followed him up the street a ways and said, "Perhaps you mean the noodle factory." And he said, well perhaps it was the noodle factory. And the man said, "Well, I don't know where that is either."

[*General Frank Thomas Hines, a native of Utah, had served in the Philippines and later in the office of the Chief of Staff during World War I. He was appointed director of the Veterans Bureau on March 1, 1923, succeeding Colonel Charles R. Forbes, who was involved in scandals which defrauded the federal government of millions of dol- lars. Major Roy Asa Haynes was appointed Federal Prohibition Com- missioner by President Harding on June 11, 1921. He was reap- pointed by Coolidge. Haynes had been an active prohibitionist for years.*]

June 2, 1925

This line, as I understand it, of the graduating class will move before me and I am to hand them their diplomas. I don't understand that I am to hand diplomas to any one except those that are actual graduates of the Academy. Now if someone wants to take a picture of the line and other scenes to present the life of the Academy, I am perfectly willing to have that done. The only embarrassment about it, as I say, is that perhaps one moving picture concern would have that and another wouldn't, but every motion picture concern is going to have the privilege of taking the picture of me and to make use of it in any legitimate way they wish in the ordinary carrying on of their business. As I said at the outset, I want always to help every legitimate concern in the United States. My only embarrassment is that there are so many competing concerns that those who didn't get the picture would say this is a kind of apple sauce. [Stenographer's note: Laughter broke out which continued during the next two or three sentences of the President and prevented accurate reporting of what he said. As near as could be heard the President stated that other concerns would then wish to make apple sauce, and that he would probably be deluged with requests to sample their apple sauce and he should have to say that the conduct of the public business wouldn't enable him to partake of it.]

[*On June 3, 1925, Coolidge addressed the graduating class at the Naval Academy and presented diplomas. Earlier, Secretary of the Navy Curtis D. Wilbur had given Metro-Goldwyn-Mayer permission to shoot on location and to film the President giving a fake diploma to actor Ramón Novarro during the regular proceedings. Coolidge objected on the grounds of "lack of dignity." The end result was that Secretary Wilbur stood in for the President at a special filming after the official proceedings.*]

June 16, 1925

I don't know of any developments regarding the [Potomac] bathing beach. Some provision of the law has been brought to my attention that I didn't have particularly in mind at the last conference that seems to raise a question as to the authority of anyone doing anything with the bathing beaches. Congress enacted a law abolishing the bathing beach that was contemplated for colored people and abolished also the bathing beach that was in existence for the white people. I should think under that statute it would be somewhat difficult to take any action.

———

I haven't had any report from the Tariff Commission on butter, or straw hats, or gold leaf. I have a report on cotton gloves.

July 21, 1925

The Secretary of War has not resigned. I don't expect he is going to resign, and I hope that for the sake of his peace of mind that his resignation will not be reported in the future oftener than once in two weeks. I don't want to unduly restrict the reporting, but I think that would be often enough.

[*Secretary of War John W. Weeks had been United States Senator from Massachusetts. He was defeated for his Senate seat in 1918 by David I. Walsh. A holdover from the Harding cabinet, Weeks had not been allied politically with Coolidge in Massachusetts G.O.P. politics. Weeks resigned in the fall of 1925 because of illness.*]

December 18, 1925

There isn't anything very definite that I can say about the Sesquicentennial Exposition at Philadelphia. I suppose I am booked for exhibition and that will probably be on the 4th of July.

13

January 15, 1926

Here is a question about George Washington. [Stenographer's note: The President pointed out the window.] His monument is still out there.

[*The twenties was an era of historical debunking; America's historic statesmen were cut down to size. Henry L. Mencken set the tone for this effort, and Gamaliel Bradford, William E. Woodward, and others singled out various statesmen for special biographical treatment. George Washington had an especially difficult time.*]

October 5, 1926

I haven't seen the book of Lindsay Rogers [*The American Senate,* N. Y., 1926]. It may possibly have been sent to me. I judge from this question that it is a discussion of the constitutional limits of the activities of the United States Senate. I think there was a British reviewer of books—supposed to be a great authority—who said he never read a book before he reviewed it because it might prejudice him.

March 11, 1927

I don't know whether I shall be able to go to the dedication of, I think this is Wicker Park, near Hammond, Indiana. A very large delegation came down this morning in a special train to invite me, so large that I suggested to them that I might make them a speech here and save myself the trouble of going out there, but they seemed to want to make speeches themselves down here, which they did, leaving me to make a proper response at some future occasion.

Rapid City, S. D., July 8, 1927

Technically, the President doesn't take much notice of state lines. I have come out here because I wanted to come to the West. But of course the President has the fact that there are state lines brought to his attention quite forcibly by the members of the House and the Senate.

———

PRESS: Did the Pine Ridge Reservation engagement escape your mind, or is that off?

PRESIDENT: It has not been definitely made. I want to go down and visit one of the Indian Reservations while I am here.

PRESS: How about Custer?

PRESIDENT: I think we shall go over there. I am not sure about that. It is a short distance, less than an hour's drive from the Lodge.

PRESS: You didn't say you were going to be initiated into a tribe at Deadwood?

PRESIDENT: Just because I belong to one tribe is no reason why I shouldn't belong to another.

14

PRESS: You will join the tribe then, will you?

PRESIDENT: I suppose so.

PRESS: You haven't found out your name yet, have you, Mr. President?

PRESIDENT: Well it is something about water; I don't know whether it is still water or what.

Rapid City, S. D., July 15, 1927

I was very much interested this morning to have a visit from a delegation of the National Woman's Party. They are engaged in working for the Lucretia Mott amendment to the Federal Constitution providing a larger equality as I understand it between women and men than they think now exists.

Rapid City, S. D., August 19, 1927

I expect to go to Yellowstone Park. In accordance with custom, I would rather you didn't publish the date of my going. You can get from Mr. Sanders the time. You will have plenty of time to get ready to go, those of you that want to go. And I understand that the telephone people are making arrangements for the accommodation of the press out there. I don't know where I shall be located. I expect, most of the time, on the hoof.

[*Everett Sanders, a former G.O.P. Congressman from Indiana, succeeded C. Bascom Slemp as Coolidge's secretary in March, 1925. In 1932 he became Chairman of the Republican National Committee, hardly an enviable post at that time.*]

October 21, 1927

It won't be possible for me to attend the World Series Rodeo, I think that is what they call it—at New York. Clyde Jones and I had a little rodeo of our own out on the south lot, which will duly appear on the screen and in the stills. I think that is about as far as I can go. I am no rodeo entertainer.

I shall not be able to go to the Army and Navy football game in New York. I wish I might go. I am interested in that game. It takes too much time to attend it. The last Army and Navy football game I attended—I guess it is the last one but one—it rained all the time. They had us seated out in the choice seats out in front, which were very choice in fair weather, but lacking anything but choiceness when it rained.

[*Clyde "Dakota" Jones invited Coolidge to attend a rodeo in New York for the benefit of the Broad Street Hospital. Coolidge, as noted, declined but, dressed in a cowboy outfit, did pose with Jones.*]

December 20, 1927

I don't know of any special Christmas pardons that are likely to come along. There may be some that are up for consideration in the Department of Justice. I am issuing pardons all the time, so that so

15

far as pardons are concerned every day is Christmas over here.

———

I mentioned the other day that any reports about what I was going to do when I finished being President were made entirely without consultation with me. I forgot to mention one report that is going around. I mention it now because I don't want to be accused of acquiring property under false pretenses. I am having sent to me quite a number of jackknives. I don't recall that I ever made any suggestion that after I finished my term of office I was going to engage in the occupation of whittling. I did some when I was a boy. I haven't applied myself to that for a good many years. I hesitate to spoil anything like a good newspaper story, but, as I say, I don't want to keep getting jackknives under false pretenses.

January 31, 1928

Nor have I any information on any supposed desire of President [*sic*] Hoover to stay in or leave the Cabinet.

[*Rumor had it that after Coolidge announced in the summer of 1927, "I do not choose to run in 1928," he really desired a draft, and that Secretary of Commerce Herbert Hoover's campaign to get the Republican nomination for the Presidency was not altogether welcome. Whether the designation of Hoover as President was humorous or sarcastic is difficult to say.*]

March 9, 1928

I have several departments making a study of the Alien Property bill. The Treasury Department reports to me that it isn't so good a bill as the one that they prepared, but I have not received their formal report on it. There is one thing in the bill that hasn't been overlooked. Three salaries have been raised.

PRESS: Could you say what they were, Mr. President?

PRESIDENT: I think they are two drafting clerks of the House and the Senate that have been put on the same salary as the Solicitor General of the United States, and some person in the Treasury Department. Those are all people that have access to the Ways and Means Committee of the House and whenever any bill goes through the Ways and Means Committee of any particular importance it usually has a way of raising somebody's salary. So you can see that the Alien Property bill has some merit in it. [Stenographer's note: laughter.]

PRESS: Was there any other feature?

PRESIDENT: I think that is the outstanding feature. [Stenographer's note: laughter.]

April 24, 1928

I haven't made any final decision, but I am rather expecting to make a Memorial Day address at Gettysburg. If I go up there, I don't know whether I would go by automobile or on the train. Would any of the members of the conference that might wish to attend have any preference as to which method of travel was adopted? Who is the head man of this conference?

PRESS: I have been over the railroad, Mr. President. I recommend auto.

PRESIDENT: Well, that might be an easier method of travel. I didn't know whether it would be as convenient for the members of the press that might like to go.

PRESS: The train makes one grade up there sometimes, and sometimes not.

PRESIDENT: With the press aboard, I take it that the railroad would be solicitous in getting us there.

May 1, 1928

I am thinking of going out to the circus grounds this afternoon at the invitation of Mr. [John] Ringling. I have some things to do here in the office, so I won't be able to stay for the show. I think he has one or two very interesting animals, or fish, I don't know which, or sea elephant, or something of that kind. I don't know whether that is the only thing you can catch with a hook and line, or whether you scare [spear] it. But he thought I might be interested in that animal.

[*When Coolidge arrived at the circus, he inquired to see the sea elephants "to ascertain whether they could be caught with a hook or had to be speared."*]

May 4, 1928

I haven't had a chance to talk with Colonel Starling very much since he came back from his visit to Swannanoa [North Carolina]. About the only thing I got from him was that it seemed to be a very fine place and he thought it could be adapted to my use during the summer. Of course, there are quite a good many other places that have got to be advertised. I expect to hold a conference gratifying the local desires in that respect.

[*Colonel Edmund W. Starling, head of the Secret Service detail which guarded Coolidge, warmly admired the President.*

Every spring during his administration, Coolidge received innumerable offers of hospitality for the summer from people and localities all over the United States. Some of these offers, he suspected, were real estate promotions.]

Superior, Wis., July 17, 1928

Mr. Sanders has suggested to me that while I have been a candidate for office in a great many previous campaigns for a good many years, with the exception of the fall of 1908, and have been constantly elected to something, that this time the only thing I was a candidate for was retirement and apparently I am going to be successful in that.

———

I have had a very pleasant visit with Secretary and Mrs. Hoover. The press was out there yesterday morning and after they came away we had lunch and the Secretary and I went fishing for a short time in the afternoon. He is a more expert fisherman than I am. I can't tell just when I shall accept Mr. Hoover's resignation. I expect to do so very shortly. There are some things in relation to his Department that have to do with the Pacific Coast that I want him to look into a little, so it will be some time after he gets out there before I shall accept his resignation.

PRESS: Have we authority to quote your remark about Mr. Hoover's being a more expert fisherman?

PRESIDENT: No,—no.

Superior, Wis., August 7, 1928

I am expecting to go over to Duluth some day. I think they are planning a sort of a drive for me around there. I don't know just when I shall go. I have been so busy out at the Lodge catching fish— there are 45,000 out there—I haven't caught them all yet, but I have them all pretty well intimidated. They have had to restock one lake.

Superior, Wis., September 4, 1928

I think the press already knows that I am expecting to attend the Fair—tomorrow, isn't it, Mr. Sanders?

MR. SANDERS: Yes, tomorrow afternoon about 2:00 o'clock.

MR. YOUNG: It isn't likely you will say anything tomorrow at the Fair?

PRESIDENT: No. I am just going as an exhibit.

September 14, 1928

I think the idea that I might go hunting in Kentucky arose from the fact that the bird dog that was given me in Superior, I had Colonel Starling send down to a friend of his in Kentucky, who is a very fine trainer of dogs. I presume that all the hunting I will do in Kentucky will be done by proxy through this dog.

December 11, 1928

Mr. Bok is giving the bird sanctuary as a tract of land at this place. He is dedicating it as a bird sanctuary and putting up these bells to interest the birds in music.

[*The philanthropist Edward Bok constructed his "singing tower" in Florida, and persuaded the President to go down to dedicate it. Coolidge performed the task with no evident enjoyment.*]

February 12, 1929

I am having rather more trouble in getting out of the White House than I had in getting in. There is a very large accumulation of things that a President acquires while he is in the White House. Most of them are of no intrinsic value, other than the fact that they have been associated with the residence of the President in the White House for some considerable time. It makes me desire to keep them. The packing of them up is a good deal of an operation. I think we have already reached something like over 150 boxes.

March 1, 1929

Perhaps one of the most important accomplishments of my administration has been minding my own business.

2 · The Press Conference

THE COOLIDGE press conference marked the beginning of serious presidential meetings with the press. Before Coolidge the Presidents of course had taken precautions with reporters, but their relationship with the press had been spasmodic and not always effective. Sometimes the Presidents simply had sought to overawe. The youthful William Allen White was highly annoyed when he sought to interview William McKinley. The President, according to White, stepped up on a pedestal and turned to marble. Theodore Roosevelt had good press relations, but no regular meetings. He dealt with the press in a highly personal way; if a correspondent strayed from friendship Roosevelt would cast him into outer darkness. William H. Taft was always awkward with the press and sometimes downright hostile. Woodrow Wilson gave the press a certain attention, even to the point of instituting regular press sessions, but dropped the idea during the war. Trying to be as helpful as possible, Warren Harding saw "the boys" regularly during his brief term in office—and on some occasions was too helpful for his own good. It remained for the careful Coolidge to put press conferences on a schedule, to solicit press backing for his administration, generously giving them news and hoping that on their side the press would respond with sympathetic stories. Usually they did so. In *The Nation* of March 16, 1927, Frank Kent noted, "Since Mr. Coolidge entered the White House he has had more solid press support than any other President. Frequently he has through the Spokesman expressed his appreciation. It would be strange indeed if he did not feel it."

Coolidge had his tart and sharp side, and could be rude if he wished. He was, however, always friendly and considerate with reporters. His friendship was not merely tactical. He enjoyed talking to reporters and revealed a loquacity altogether unexpected of the man whom the public had dubbed "Silent Cal." The press conference became, one suspects, a place of relaxation, where the President could meet men who were not asking for jobs or seeking influence of one kind or another. To be sure, the reporters had their own needs. But the needs were of a sort that Coolidge could easily gratify. And the President was sympathetic with these men earning their living. It is remarkable how kind he was to the reporters and how willing he was to allow for their convenience. Naturally he laid down his ground rules, but if reporters played by them they found no more helpful person than the man who was the source of their livelihood.

When the reporters entered the room, Coolidge would rise from his chair behind the big presidential desk and carefully deposit his cigar in an ash tray. As Lyle Wilson recalls, the press would wait in suspense while he leafed through their questions. Sometimes varicolored paper was used to enable the reporters to identify their own questions. The President occasionally would silently read the questions and let the slips flutter one by one to the desk top without answering them. When the last bit of paper had been discarded, he would look the reporters dead in the eye and say, "I have no questions today." The reporters would march out.

When Coolidge finally adjourned his White House Press Association in March, 1929, the remarks of gratitude to his friends of six years were in no sense perfunctory but reflected one of the most pleasant associations of his presidency.

———

September 21, 1923

I am reminded that when I came here I did a good deal of wondering whether I would be able to be helpful to the members of the press in these conferences that we have, and especially as to whether I wouldn't find it more or less of a bore on my part and, perhaps, not particularly pleasant. I haven't found it that way at all. In fact, I have come to the conclusion that I rather look forward with pleasure to having you come in twice a week, in order that I may talk to you, give you a little of the idea I may have of what the Government is trying to do, and satisfy you, insofar as I can, on the questions that you ask.

November 13, 1923

The class doesn't seem to be so inquisitive this morning as it sometimes is. There isn't a very large crop of questions.

November 20, 1923

I notice some of the representatives of the press take advantage of the opportunity to sit down. Any of you that wants can have my chair.

PRESS: Mr. President, does that go for anybody but newspapermen?
PRESIDENT: No.

———

Another inquiry about trips in the near future. The members of the press here seem determined to get me out of town, if not to New York some other place. I haven't any present intention of leaving Washington. Very likely when Congress gets here I shall be even more busy than I am now, and perhaps in the course of a month or two I might like to get away for a little while. But I haven't the slightest plan now. You know I remarked to you once before that I saw a great many rumors that President Harding was going to go to a great many places, usually accompanied in the same issue of the newspaper with the statement that he cancelled it. I don't want to prevent you from having all the news you can, but I would rather it would be of a little different nature from that. It is rather ineffectual to start on a trip and have to cancel it.

December 7, 1923

An inquiry as to whether I was gratified with the reaction to my message. I was very much gratified, of course. A great many telegrams have been coming in with very kind comment. Also on the part of the newspapers. It is in a good many instances flattering. Perhaps you had prepared them.

PRESS: Mr. President, what type of people do you hear from on this?
PRESIDENT: Well, very general and promiscuous. Different people. All kinds of people seem to be sending in telegrams.

February 29, 1924

Here is an interesting suggestion. A news story in the *Washington Star* this afternoon hints at some drastic and mysterious action which the President proposes to take within the next few months. Would it be consistent to ask if the Chief Executive has in contemplation any radical departure from his present policies? I don't think any radical departures now occur to me. While I don't want to disagree with so good an authority as the *Washington Star*—I haven't the report before me, it is a report of a report and sometimes there is a variance in those things—I think you would be warranted in prophesying, if any of you want to prophesy, that I have at present no expectation of any drastic and mysterious action. I think it is rather foreign to me to have drastic and mysterious action. I suppose that is why this is news. It is somewhat different from what I have been doing and perhaps from what you gentlemen have led the public to expect of me.

March 4, 1924

I haven't yet been able to make up my mind about a successor to Mr. Denby. I sometimes sit here at my desk and wish that I had the information at my command that is represented by you men. If I had all that information of the country and the men in it, as you do in your combined experiences, I could reach out and pick out a man for any place that the Government might need one to serve in, and that brings me to the suggestion that if any of you think of the right kind of a man for the Secretaryship of the Navy, and I am perfectly serious about this, though it might seem offhand as a little unusual, I should be very grateful to you if you will drop me a line or give the name to Mr. Slemp. I am searching the industrial world and the commercial world to see if I can find a seasoned executive that can take up the work of the administration of the Navy Department. It is difficult to find a man who meets all the requirements, and I don't expect to find such a man, but I do think I can find one that meets the majority of the requirements, and that is about all we can hope for. As soon as I find a man of that kind, I shall, after appropriate inquiries, submit his name to the Senate. We want a man of course of ability and character, and if I can find a great merchant, or if I can find the head of a great industrial or manufacturing establishment that would meet the requirements that I have in mind, I shall submit his name. There are some engineering problems involved now on account of the oil leases, but they are not predominant; they are somewhat accidental and other talent could be called in to give advice on those. However, it may be that if I could get hold of the right kind of an engineer that it would be helpful under these circumstances.

[*Edwin N. Denby, Secretary of the Navy, was a holdover from the Harding cabinet. Denby's ineptness, particularly his role in transferring control of the Naval Petroleum Reserves to the Interior Department, caused the Senate to request Coolidge to remove him from the cabinet on February 11, 1924. Coolidge firmly refused to accede to the Senate's pressure, but Denby voluntarily resigned later in the month. Coolidge replaced Denby, not with an industrialist or merchant or engineer, but with the highly conservative Curtis D. Wilbur, Chief Justice of the California Supreme Court.*]

March 7, 1924

PRESS: Did the newspapermen make any suggestions, Mr. President, or give you any aid [regarding a successor to Secretary Denby]?

PRESIDENT: Well, I think some of them have been suggestive. I haven't got quite as many as I expected. Perhaps it isn't so easy as it may have appeared to pick out the right kind of a man.

March 14, 1924

I can't give any statement regarding the selection of Chief Justice Wilbur as Secretary of the Navy, other than what the press already has. The suggestion came that he would make a good Secretary of the Navy from a newspaper source. That is a very good recommendation always, as you would probably be willing to admit, and after careful investigation it seemed that he was qualified by his experience and training, his character and ability, to undertake that work.

May 13, 1924

I have here another inquiry that I hesitate some to comment about, though perhaps I can with the understanding that there is not any undue prominence given to it, or any undue emphasis placed upon it. It is an inquiry about my going to the circus. It is no doubt an experience that all of us look back to with a good deal of pleasure. The first circus I ever went to was in Ludlow, Vermont, a railroad station about 14 miles from Plymouth.

June 13, 1924

I haven't made any plans yet for a summer vacation. As I have indicated before, I will do the best I can to arrange one for you.

July 29, 1924

I haven't any plan about what I shall do after the notification exercises—for the period after that. I shall have to wait and see what develops. I shall watch with my usual interest to see what you do after that. On that I may base my subsequent determination of what it is necessary for me to do. However, I don't look on that with any apprehension, and I shall hope very much to thank you. I hope that I am not remiss, however, in feeling appreciation for those who have been solicitous for my welfare, and who have exhibited kindness toward me. This brings to my attention the great kindness that I had from those who perform the White House Press Association duties, and their associates. Perhaps this is a good time to express the appreciation that I feel for the great kindness you have always exhibited towards me.

August 8, 1924

I think that sometime after my notification I may go up to Plymouth. My boy lies there, and naturally my wife and I would like to go up there. My regret about that is that there isn't any convenient place in that vicinity for the members of the press. Within 10 or 12 miles is Woodstock, which is a most delightful place and well-known summer resort with a very fine hotel. It is a matter of 40 or 50 minutes run in an auto.

[*The Coolidges had two sons, John and Calvin, Jr. The latter died on July 7, 1924, of blood poisoning resulting from an infected toe. The loss of their younger son was the greatest tragedy in the lives of Calvin and Grace Coolidge.*]

September 26, 1924

Mr. [Cornelius] Vanderbilt who started some newspapers in California dropped in to see me. I knew him when he was one of the reporters here in Washington. There was no special significance to his visit, other than that he came back to call on me, as I hope any one of you would who came back to Washington and started some newspapers and expected to start some more.

November 7, 1924

I haven't any legislative program that I can announce at the present time. Naturally that brings up the old question of whether I ought to deliver my message to the Congress to the newspapermen before I deliver it to the Congress. I think that you usually get the best of that.

January 23, 1925

I don't know what I am going to put in my inaugural address. I suppose that will be a standard question from now until the address gets into the hands of the press. If any of you think of anything that ought to be covered in the address, I should be obliged to you if you will suggest the subject to me at any time.

April 10, 1925

Here is an interesting suggestion that there isn't very much on the horizon and would like to have me give some suggestions about news. I don't know what I can do about that. I want to help everyone I can. That inquiry about Secretary Weeks suggests to me that if you wanted to dig up a newspaper story about newspaper stories that have been published and didn't prove to be true, it makes quite a long story. Since I have been President three members of my Cabinet have resigned and one has died. I don't know how many of them the newspapers have resigned for me and how many reports have come that they were about to resign or had resigned. Perhaps some of you that have enterprise and enjoy research would like to look over that list and write a newspaper story about it, if you are short of some kind of copy.

I am glad to have any questions asked about anything. I don't want anybody to hesitate about asking questions. That is what I meant by my suggestion, I think at the last conference. I don't want to cut off newspaper discussion about anything. But it isn't helpful for me to keep talking about certain foreign relations unless there is some development that warrants some statement on my part. I didn't really want to keep rehashing practically the same thing, because it irritates foreign countries oftentimes and they wonder why the White House keeps making statements that don't appear to them to be very helpful.

April 17, 1925

It wouldn't be possible to make any change in the rules that govern the conduct of a conference between the newspaper association and the President. Every one of you men who come in here to the conference know what those rules are and the need to observe them carefully. I speak of the question that has been propounded here relative to quotation. If anybody has any doubt about it, let him consult with the Secretary of the White House Press Association, who will give him all the information he desires.

June 23, 1925

PRESIDENT [addressing a reporter]: Are you taking down in shorthand what I say?

PRESS: Yes, sir.

PRESIDENT: Now I don't think that is right. I don't think that is the proper thing to do. Who do you represent?

PRESS: David Lawrence.

PRESIDENT: Well, I wish you would tell Mr. Lawrence that I don't think it is the right thing to do. I will see to that myself. . . . I don't object to you taking notes as to what I say, but I don't quite throw my communications to the conference into anything like finished style or anything that perhaps would naturally be associated with a Presidential utterance. It would interfere with me very much if I understood that it is to be taken down in shorthand here and then used outside for such purposes as anyone might want to use them. What I say here is not to be taken down in shorthand other than that which is taken down by my stenographer for my purposes. Otherwise it greatly interferes with my freedom of expression and my trying to disclose to the conference the things that I have in mind, which quite naturally, if they were to be used verbatim, I would want to give considerable thought to and perhaps throw into a little different form of language.

I don't know as I can say very much about my vacation. I expect to spend a considerable part of it trying to amuse the newspapermen. [Stenographer's note: laughter.] There is a friend of mine who lives in Lynn that is a large newspaper distributor, Ralph Bauer, who is going to have some kind of an Essex County Newspapermen's gathering at his place in Amesbury, that I shall take the liberty of suggesting being increased by inviting all the out of town newspaper correspondents that happen to be attending on the President. I think you would like to go up there. He has a farm and it is a very interesting place, not very far from the residence of Whittier, if you would like to look at his old home where he wrote *Snowbound.* You better get a copy of Whittier and read *Snowbound* before you go there. It is a fine piece of work and it is the piece that brought Whittier into prominent notice. You will see there the old home in which he was living the time that the theme of *Snowbound* took place.

January 5, 1926

This is the first meeting that we have had since the New Year came in. I forgot to wish you collectively a Merry Christmas. I am very glad to take this opportunity to express my sentiments as desiring that you may all have a Happy and Prosperous year and also to express my deep appreciation of the care and candor with which you handle the news that affects me personally and the administration of the Government. I am sure it is very gratifying and must be very pleasing to those in whose employ you find yourselves, and very satisfactory to the public in general.

March 12, 1926

Mr. Strother, who had something to do about arranging and compiling in conjunction with Mr. Slemp that book that Mr. Slemp issued, was in this morning and brought me in a presentation copy of it. Glancing at it I see that it is very well indexed and there is topically arranged in the book things that I have said in relation to a great many subjects. I think your offices ought to provide each one of you with a copy of that book.

PRESS: Would you autograph each copy?

PRESIDENT: Yes, I would be glad to, and whenever you want to know what my position is on any subject, if you will just glance at that index it will very quickly refer you to a place in the book where you can learn what I have said in relation to a very great many different subjects.

[*Coolidge was referring to a book edited by C. Bascom Slemp,* The Mind of the President. As Revealed by His Own Words *(N. Y., 1926). White House literary secretary French Strother had written an article, "A Week in the White House with President Coolidge,"* World's Work, *LXVII (April, 1924), 575-90.*]

March 23, 1926

I want to express my gratitude to those of you who went up to Plymouth with me. It was a real satisfaction to have present those of you who had been so intimately associated with me here, and it was a real help to me in bearing the burdens that I had to bear there. I want especially to thank you for the many tributes that were paid on that occasion to my father. I am sure that he was worthy of all of them. It was a great satisfaction to see the appreciation in which he had come to be held by those of you that knew him and knew me, and especially the appreciation that was expressed in the many messages of condolence that came to me.

[*Colonel John C. Coolidge had died on March 18.*]

April 20, 1926

Congressman Treadway was in the other day to suggest two places in Stockbridge—I think one is the Woodward place—that is the Woodward that was connected with the Woodward and Lothrop Store here in Washington, and the Patterson place on the Lee-Lennox road—as possible places for me to occupy during the summer. I have taken those under consideration and of course have a good many places offered. I am very glad to have the press report on all of them. While I can't occupy more than one place during the summer, it is very nice to have brought to the general public's attention the availability of all these different localities for other people that are seeking places to go during the summertime.

CHARLIE MICHAELS: Would they get such good rates?

[*Allen T. Treadway was Republican congressman from the Western Massachusetts 1st District. First elected to the House in 1912, he was for years a G.O.P. wheelhorse. Charles Michaels was the New York* Times *correspondent. Coolidge heartily disliked Michaels, who irritated him with needling questions.*]

July 6, 1926

I don't know how many of you are thinking of going with me up to the Adirondacks, as many as can I hope. Those who go I shall see up there. Those who stay in Washington I shall not of course see, and I wish to take this opportunity to express my amazement at the constant correctness of my views as you report them to the country. It is very seldom that any error creeps in. I don't know how that could be done. I wouldn't be able to report as correctly the views of any one of you. I don't know how you get before the country so clearly and so well my views as you do. And I also want to thank you for the consideration with which you have always treated the Presidential office during the time that I have been President. It has been very helpful to me in the transaction of the public business and I think very helpful to the country in coming to a comprehension of what the Government is trying to do, how it is trying to function, what efforts it is making to benefit the condition of the people. I hope those of you that stay here or go to some other part of the country will have the opportunity to have as pleasant a summer as I expect to have and as those who go with me I know will have.

White Pine Camp, Paul Smith's, N. Y., September 14, 1926

MR. [CHARLES] GROVES [*Boston Post*]: Mr. President, I have been asked by my colleagues to express our very great appreciation for your courtesy and consideration during this summer. The newspaper work of course has its difficulties and this has been an important assignment, important to us, important to our newspapers, and important to the public. But your consideration has been constant and I think that the little matter of the trip to Plymouth is an example of the fact that you had our comfort in mind. And especially do we appreciate the manner in which you have ordered the activities of this office, the fact that you have held your conferences regularly twice a week and that you have brought your guests, your important guests, down here so that we might see them at this office instead of chasing them all over the country. And I am sure that I express the feeling of the correspondents when I say that we are very very glad that you had a pleasant summer and that your health has been maintained, and we do appreciate everything that you have done for us.

PRESIDENT: I am very much gratified to know that. I know the difficulties that the members of the press usually have on summer vacations. In fact, it is a tradition of the Presidential office, with the old heads in there like Mr. Forster, that whenever the President goes away on a summer vacation that it is always very difficult for the members of the press that go with him. Usually there isn't much for them to write about and they are sent there by their paper and are supposed to furnish copy, and they have to resort to a good deal of fabrication and fable. Of course there is always some of that that goes on. I don't think it is particularly important, though it is important that the Presidential office should be correctly represented to the country and the attitude of the Presidential office should be accurately interpreted. But that isn't a personal matter that the President, I suppose, cares very much about. But I regard it as rather necessary to the carrying on of our republican institutions that the people should have a fairly accurate report of what the President is trying to do, and it is for that purpose of course that those intimate conferences are held. Now, I don't regard, as you men know, that it is at all necessary for the President to give out a verbatim statement of everything that may be discussed here, but rather to leave it to the different reporters, because they are reporters, and a great many times can do those things on the whole better than the President could do them and leave it to them to make their interpretation. That of course is where the art of reporting comes in. I have found the interpretation of these press conferences given to the country on the whole accurate, and I think helpful to the country and fairly satisfactory to me. I think you have done rather better than I could have done, if I had undertaken to sit down twice a week and dictated a statement to be given out. As I have indicated once or twice before, if I did that I would become a reporter and I don't know what would become of the occupation that you gentlemen now have. I don't want to compete with your business. I am sure that we all had a very pleasant time up here and look forward to having another pleasant summer next year.

December 21, 1926

I expect to have the press conference Friday afternoon, not being able to provide by Executive Order for the members of the press to have a half holiday. I have exercised my authority in behalf of the press once or twice. I think you will recall that at one Gridiron dinner I suggested that the press here was so efficient that I thought their salaries ought to be raised. How many have found a favorable response? Those of you that have, I would like to have you raise your hands. [Stenographer's note: No hands were raised.]

MR. WILE: Wouldn't it be a good idea to investigate their income taxes?

PRESIDENT: I am afraid my influence with the press is not very great. [*Frederic William Wile had his own news syndicate.*]

April 22, 1927

I have had called to my attention lately the fact that some of the press are beginning to get a little careless about quoting the President as the result of these conferences. It seems that it is necessary to have eternal vigilance to keep that from being done, and to caution the members of the conference against that. Of course, it is a violation of the understanding to say that the spokesman said so and so, and put in quotations on that. I think, by the way, that it would be a good plan to drop that reference to these conferences. It was never authorized in any way that I could determine by the President. It has been used from time to time, but it has been used so long and there has been so much reference to it that one might as well say that the President said so and so, or the White House spokesman or the official spokesman said so and so.

PRESS: Mr. President, do we understand that the term spokesman is not permissible?

PRESIDENT: It has never been authorized and has been used in a way that it is perfectly apparent that when the word is used it means the President. Now, that need not have been done, but it has been done, and having been done I think it would be better to drop that. . . . What I said about quoting the President in relation to the use of the term as spokesman wasn't said for publication. It was just said for the information of the conference. That part of the conference we will consider carried on in executive session.

PRESS: Have you any formula to suggest?

PRESIDENT: I think your ingenuity will provide you with one. The only thing I am suggesting is that you observe the rule of not quoting the President.

May 17, 1927

Here is an inquiry relative to the use that might be made of questions that are submitted to me and which I do not discuss. I had supposed that the rule about that was that questions that were submitted and not discussed would not be discussed in the press. I don't mean by that that it isn't perfectly proper of course to discuss the substance of the questions, but I did understand that it was the rule that if a question were submitted to me and was not discussed by me that no report was to be made, one way or the other, about the fact of the submission of the question.

May 31, 1927

I am expecting to go down to review the Fleet, as the press already knows. I have conferred with the Secretary of the Navy this morning about making arrangements to take care of the press. They will be taken out from some appropriate point and either stay on the boat that takes them out or go on one of the battleships. I use battleship only in a general term—one of the ships of the Fleet that will be located at that point to give them every possible assistance in properly reporting the review. I hope we may have good weather and that the press anticipates the enjoyment of it as much as I do.

———

Here are two or three questions that perhaps could be answered more desirably by reference to Mr. Slemp's book—what is the title of that?

PRESS: *The Mind of the President.*

PRESIDENT: The Class is perfect.

Rapid City, S. D., June 28, 1927

I hope you are all enjoying this climate and the surroundings here as much as I am. There are a great many things to write about here in the Black Hills, and I am going to make this suggestion to you for what it may be worth. We shall be here for some weeks, and I think you will find that at the end of your stay here that your work will be more satisfactory if you take up some particular thing and write a very good story about it, and at a later time pass on to something else, rather than try to include almost everything in one story.

Rapid City, S. D., July 1, 1927

I am having a little party at the Lodge on the afternoon of the 4th of July, partly so far as I am concerned in the celebration of that national birthday and personally in celebration of my own birthday. I should like to have the newspapermen and the photographers come out. The band from Terry, Montana, is going to visit me on that afternoon, and also the mounted Boy Scouts of Custer. I think that is the only troop of Boy Scouts that are mounted anywhere in the United States. I expect now that it will begin about 1:30 in the afternoon. I think that hereafter if it is agreeable to the press we will call this conference at 11:30 instead of quarter to twelve, and that will give me a little more opportunity to get home for lunch.

September 13, 1927

I want to congratulate the members of the conference that were able to be with me in the Black Hills and commiserate the rest of you that were not able to be with us. We had a most enjoyable season out there—very pleasant to me—and there was such a diversity of happenings that I think the newspapermen found sufficient material nearly every day on which to make a story. I heard very little complaint about that. I haven't seen the official figures of the amount of space that was sent out from the Black Hills. I think a computation was made of the space that went out from White Pine Camp. Of course, I stayed in the Black Hills considerably longer, but I judge the amount of material was certainly as much as that of a year ago.

PRESS: I understand it was 2,150,000 this year and about 600,000 more than last year.

PRESIDENT: Well, I stayed away a much longer time. Last year I went away on July sixth and came back about the same time as this year. This year I went away three weeks earlier.

February 3, 1928

There are quite a good many of the members of the conference that don't seem to be able to comprehend just what these conferences are held for. They are not in any sense interviews to be given out by the press, or statements. They simply furnish a background, so that if people who are writing for the press desire to write on a certain subject they may have the proper information with which to write their story. They ought not to be referred to as statements from the White House and there ought not to be any reference to the fact that there is a newspaper conference here. Constant practice of that kind by the men who write for the press hamper me very greatly in the help that I might give them. Every time I make a statement that is of any particular importance as news, those who undertake to write a story about it give it out as though it was a statement that I had made or an interview that I had given, so that I had to refrain from saying anything that might be reported along that line. So I suggest to you that you exercise more care about that and remember that these are not interviews and not statements from the White House, but simply information that I give to the press in order that it may intelligently write reports and comments about the subjects that I dwelt on.

April 6, 1928

You will notice I have a new addition to the conference. Another dog has come in. That is a dog that is very much attached to my wife and he is very disconsolate in the absence of his mistress, but he has been willing to come over here.

May 11, 1928

It was brought to my attention today that the *National Zeitung* of

Berlin on the 21st of April printed what they said was an article by me. I never wrote any such article and never authorized it. It was an entire fake. Yet it had a heading on it which was signed "The Editor," saying that it was my article. I tell you that so if you see it none of you may feel slighted because you didn't get the fake.

PRESS: Could you tell us what the story was?

PRESIDENT: It purported to be some statement by me about American conditions, international relations, and so on. I didn't read it.

Superior, Wis., July 17, 1928

The members of the press have been out to the Lodge a couple of times and I think now probably from their own observation they will be able to report that the mosquitoes are not very deadly. Did any of you get bitten by mosquitoes yesterday? [Stenographer's note: no answer.] Then there must have been some error in the reports that have been sent all over the United States that mosquitoes eat every one up, and it might be a graceful thing if the press would report that as a result of personal investigation the mosquitoes have entirely disappeared. That is an old story that always goes the rounds when I go into the country. The newspapermen have nothing to write about for the first two or three days, so they elaborate on the mosquito stories. I don't care anything about it particularly, but when people have been kind enough to put at my disposal a very beautiful and enjoyable place, as I have had the advantage of having for the past two or three years, to have reports sent all over the country that it is a very bad place and uncomfortable for anyone to live in, it can hardly be very pleasing to the people that own the place, and if the press could report that which is the fact, that the mosquitoes have entirely disappeared and that the place is very beautiful and very enjoyable, I think it would be a courtesy that perhaps is due to the owners of the property.

Superior, Wis., September 4, 1928

And I believe the newspapermen and picture men are coming out to the Lodge tomorrow morning. It may be a little wet out there in the dew. You better bring some rubbers along with you to keep dry, if you are coming out early in the morning.

October 2, 1928

Ambassador Houghton hasn't resigned. I don't know whether he intends to resign, and of course any speculation about a hypothetical situation of that kind while it might not be premature on the part of the press, which always delights in speculation, would be quite premature on my part. I have all I can do in dealing with facts and realities and leaving the press to deal with hypothetical situations. They are much better equipped to do that than I am.

[*Alanson B. Houghton, a prominent industrialist, served first as*

Ambassador to Germany (1922-1925) and then as Ambassador to Great Britain.]

November 16, 1928

I am working on my Message to the Congress. I have made some progress on it. There isn't very much legislation, so far as I have been able to discover, that is exceedingly pressing that is new. We have some of the old problems that have been left over from the various messages that I have sent in before and such surveys of the country as I have received from reports of various departments indicate that the country is in very good shape. I want to get the Message done so that it can be early in the hands of the press and that leads me to make a suggestion that is born of my past experience, that the advance copies that are given out are given out exclusively for the use of the press. But each year they turn up in the hands of the people that are in no wise connected with the press like legislative agents in Washington, brokerage offices in different cities, so that I think the news reporters or news agents to whom my message is to be given here for press release ought to warn people to whom they may send it that it is exclusively for newspaper use and not for general distribution before it is presented to the Congress. It is almost a slight on Congress to have a message generally distributed promiscuously around the country before it goes to the Congress itself. For the purpose of assisting the news distribution we make these early deliveries of the message. I hope this year it can be kept confined exclusively to news services and not fall into the hands of others.

March 1, 1929

Nothing special took place at the Cabinet this morning. I took occasion to thank the members for the service they had rendered to the country and to me, expressed my regret at severing my relations with them, which have been so pleasant and agreeable, and I think a paraphrase of that kind would be about all I could say to the members of the conference. You have been, I think, quite successful in interpreting the administration to the country. I have known that I wasn't much of a success in undertaking newspaper work, so I have left the work of reporting the affairs of my administration to the experts of the press. Perhaps that is the reason that the reports have been more successful than they would have been if I had undertaken myself to direct them. It has been a pleasure to have you come in twice a week and give me an opportunity to answer such queries as you wished to propound. I want to thank you again for your constant kindness and consideration. I hope you will find the years to come as pleasant to you as I have the years that are gone by pleasant to me.

3 · Life as President

A PRESIDENT'S personal life has always been treated as public property—he quickly discovers that he cannot move about like other people, that his smallest decisions prove interesting to his fellow Americans. He learns that he could make dedicatory speeches 365 days a year were he to accept all of the invitations tendered him, that the President becomes a special personage, and the conveniences and ease of private life are things of the past. Never again can he achieve privacy. Even in retirement Coolidge discovered that people would drive past his Massasoit Street house in Northampton on Sunday afternoons, just to get a glimpse of him. Sometimes they tiptoed up to his windows and peeked in, to see how a former President sat in a chair or ate his dinner.

Coolidge accustomed himself to presidential life with a mixture of patience and annoyance. He found some White House visitors too curious about his personal affairs, and treated them with scant courtesy. Yet when it came time for the press conference and the reporters needed copy of some sort or other, perhaps about the President's daily life, Coolidge was willing to oblige. Once in a while he had to ask for more privacy, notably in the case of his son John who, whether attending Mercersburg Academy or Amherst College, found himself hounded by reporters. The President told the press conference that John was a boy like any other boy, and that press coverage of his school days should not be of interest to the nation nor would it help him.

August 21, 1923

An inquiry about when we intend to move into the White House. We are going to get in as soon as we can. It is possible that we can come over this afternoon. We would like to go in quietly, not without observing the befitting dignity of moving into the White House, but with as little ostentation as possible, on account of the circumstances, of course with which you are familiar, that surround our taking up our residence there.

August 28, 1923

Inquiry about an invitation to the Johnson Morgan Memorial exercises at Durham, North Carolina. Like all other invitations this was a peculiarly attractive one, but I had to give a negative answer. I want to be here to take up the details of this office, to work them out with the different departments, in order that I may prepare myself as quickly as possible to carry them on to the best of my ability. Now I wouldn't be able to do that if I accepted invitations taking me away from Washington. It seems to me that what the country most needs now is stability and confidence and reassurance, and in a knowledge that things are going on smoothly and as well as can be hoped, and that they can build on the present foundation with an assurance that there isn't going to be any violent change in it or recession from it. For that reason I don't want to stir up a lot of political speculation. That can wait. I don't want to limit you, in serving your constituents acceptably and interestingly, but there are certain limits that are always to be observed. There are many fine men in the service of the United States. Remember, if you can, that they are entitled to credit. They are entitled to my confidence and require support. Don't suggest, if you can avoid it, without your knowing it an absolute fact, that I am going to change or displace them with somebody else. That may come some time or other, but you owe a little to the men that are trying to cooperate with us in carrying on the Government, to see that their work has proper public appreciation, and the assurance that it is properly appreciated by me.

September 18, 1923

I am not quite certain whether you have saved an hour this morning or lost half an hour. Generally the meeting of the Cabinet lasts until about one o'clock. Not always. We never know. Sometimes it takes two hours and sometimes not more than 20 minutes. I presume you know how a Cabinet meeting is held. The President sits at the head of the table and asks each member along down whether he has anything to present to the President or the Cabinet for consideration. Oftentimes you go clear down through the list and each one says, "Not anything this morning." Of course that generally means rather a short Cabinet meeting.

September 21, 1923

I am reminded too that my boys have returned back to school. They are just such boys as some of you have, I have no doubt. I hope that they can remain there at school without much of anything in the way of publicity. When they are here anything that they can do to be helpful, or that we can do, we are glad to do, but I sent them up to Mercersburg, which is a very excellent school. They have always been in the public schools at Northampton and would have been there now, had we remained in Massachusetts, but there is no one in Northampton now, but my housekeeper. I wanted them to be under more supervision than that, so I sent them up there in order that they might be out of Washington and have that opinion, which I think boys are entitled to have, of privacy in their school affairs. Dr. Irvine has been very helpful to them up there, and I presume that if you make any application to him, or any of your associates, to get any story about the boys up there, he will have to tell you that we very much prefer that they be not subjected to publicity while they are there.

[*William M. Irvine was Headmaster of Mercersburg Academy.*]

November 27, 1923

An inquiry as to whether I have any plans for Thanksgiving Day. Why, of course I have. I thought I made that very plain in considerable detail in a proclamation I made some time ago. You will be perfectly safe in following the terms of the proclamation for information about what I am going to do. I think I advised the people to assemble in their usual places of worship and in their homes for a suitable observance of Thanksgiving Day, and that is the way that I hope to observe the day.

PRESS: Mr. President, will your sons be here?

PRESIDENT: No. They only have one day in the school where they attend, so that they will not be able to come down.

December 4, 1923

An inquiry about a report of Major General Beach as to the safety of the White House. I haven't seen any report of that kind. I think there was some reference to it in the newspapers. Whether he has made an official report that would properly be characterized as representing the White House to be unsafe or not, I do not know. I have much doubt whether the report would go to that length.

PRESS: Mr. President, the report was that of Major General Beach to the Secretary of War. If my memory serves me correctly, he said he called that to your attention.

PRESIDENT: I am not going to dispute a gentleman and an officer. I don't have time to read every communication that comes into the office, although I look at every communication that comes to my desk with the care which it deserves. But that hasn't come to my attention. The White House is an old building, but I think it is fireproof to the roof. Whether it is unsafe in any way, I don't know. A man who was there with President Cleveland told me that they found during his term there was an accumulation of books and old papers and documents, which you know come to be very heavy, placed up on the third floor, that was causing a sagging of the floor. There may be something of that kind there now, some water tank, or something of that kind that makes a crack in the wall.

[*Major General Lansing Haskins Beach was Chief of Army Engineers.*]

December 21, 1923

I don't know as I have any very definite plans for Christmas. I think Christmas Eve that some of the church choirs, or one church choir, is to sing carols at the White House—outside the White House—in which they will be joined by some of the citizens of Washington. I believe also the plan is to have a church service, a union service, which I think is to be held in the church that I attend, on Christmas morning, where I expect to go. And I think I am to press some buttons to light a Christmas tree down on the Ellipse. I think, also, I am to start some kind of a celebration in California. You men that represent the California press perhaps can tell us what that is. I think something is to be opened. What is that? Any California men know?

PRESS: Is it Pasadena?

PRESIDENT: There is something out there. It seems to me it is a water works or a town, or something of that kind.

February 1, 1924

I am very much disturbed to hear of the illness of President Wilson. I met him most pleasantly when he returned the first time from France and landed at Boston, where a public reception was tendered him. I made an address in which I extended the welcome of the Commonwealth, and I have always recalled with a good deal of feeling that when I was chosen Governor the second time, though he was very ill, he sent me a message of congratulation. So that learning of the probable nearness of his end, it is a matter that touches me deeply.

[*Coolidge, who warmly welcomed President Wilson after his return from Europe, was never an isolationist. On the League of Nations issue in 1919-1920 he was a mild reservationist.*]

April 1, 1924

I haven't any plan about a summer White House. I rather imagine that we will stay here, if that is agreeable to you, a very large part of the summer. Perhaps all of it. I don't know. I will do the best I can, though, to get a trip for you. But it is easier to transact business of the Government here than it is anywhere else, and the White House with the large open space around it and the grounds is fairly comfortable in the summer. We didn't find any great inconvenience last August, after we came here. It is not nearly so warm in the surroundings here as you probably know it is in the street. You see a marked difference.

May 24, 1924

I have an inquiry about the chlorine gas treatment which I took. According to what they told me down there it affects different individuals in different ways. You sit down in the room where it is. You get a slight effect from it. It affects the eyes of some people. It did not affect mine that way. The first two treatments I felt immediate relief. The third treatment, which I took yesterday, they put in a considerably stronger dose for that treatment. I did not like the immediate results. It made my throat smart. I thought I felt an irritation; but this morning, when I got up I found myself quite free of the cold, and the treatment was practically a complete success. I was not suffering so much from my cold as I was from being tired out. I am working rather hard and get tired out, so I thought I had better go home and rest up, which I advise all of you to do.

Plymouth, Vt., August 22, 1924

I don't know that I can comment on the benefits that I have received from my vacation. It is naturally quite a relief to be up here for a while. While we had as you know a remarkably comfortable summer in Washington, yet the altitude there is low and the atmosphere is very much different from what it is here. We have about a 400 foot elevation here and we are quite a distance north of Washington. They say it is a good plan for a person to go back as often as they can into the atmosphere in which they were born and brought up. I always get refreshed by coming up here. Naturally I feel rested and revived.

I haven't paid any particular attention as to what we were having to eat. I think there is a story isn't there about the man that illustrated the perfect digestion. He said that as for himself he had no digestion. And I assume the cooking up here has been so good and so natural that I have eaten it without thinking about it.

PRESS: Have you weighed, Mr. President?

PRESIDENT: No, I haven't.

October 21, 1924

I hardly expect to go to Northampton to vote, though I haven't made up my mind fully about that. I should go there by all means, if I could go without the necessary train attendants that always have to go when the President goes anywhere. I have to take so many people with me that if it takes any kind of a journey, why for myself and Mrs. Coolidge it is a good deal of an undertaking, and of course there is a considerable expense to the Government. I may go, but I haven't decided yet.

39

November 4, 1924

PRESS: What are your plans for this afternoon?

PRESIDENT: None, except what I have every day—to do the work that comes to my desk here. Of course, in the evening I shall receive the returns over in the White House as they come in. I don't intend to sit up very late about it.

PRESS: How late?

PRESIDENT: Well, I usually go to bed about 10 o'clock, though for the last two or three nights it has been much later. I didn't wake up until 8 o'clock this morning, so perhaps that will entitle me to stay up later tonight.

December 19, 1924

I expect we shall observe Christmas at the White House about as usual. My boy John is coming home from college. I think he will be home on Sunday morning. I expect the observance of the holidays will be about the same as usual. The only difference, which will be apparent to all of you, is that three of us will be present rather than four, as in the past. I expect Mr. and Mrs. Stearns will be at the White House at that time, and on Christmas eve I am expecting that the Choir of the First Congregational Church will sing at the north portico of the White House the same as they did last year.

[*Coolidge's wistful comment refers to the death of his son, Calvin, Jr., in July. Frank W. Stearns, owner of a well-known Boston department store, was a political mentor of Coolidge, and probably the President's closest friend.*]

December 23, 1924

There hasn't been anything done about the unofficial side of the inauguration, or as to a parade or a reception. Some of the people that came in to see me yesterday did tell me that they had seen and known of many inaugurations here in Washington, and that it was the general consensus of opinion that that which was held four years ago was on the whole the most satisfactory of any that have been held. Of course sometimes we suffer badly on account of bad weather, trying to have a parade under very adverse circumstances, so I am going to make further inquiries before anything is done about a parade or a reception. I haven't felt very favorably about having a reception. If they want to have anything of that kind it will be better to call it a ball. That as you know has not been very attractive to me, though I approve of people that like to dance dancing as much as they wish.

PRESS: Mr. President, does that mean that if the people express a preference for the ball it will meet with no objection on your part?

PRESIDENT: No. But if they are going to have a reception or a ball, I should judge it would be more agreeable to those that want to go to have a ball.

PRESS: Mr. President, do you mean by that a charity ball or something of that kind outside the White House?

PRESIDENT: Well, you can't have a ball in the White House. You couldn't get anybody in there, not even the newspapermen. Those who had the picking out of the people that should be invited to a ball in the East Room would have some trouble.

PRESS: Would you attend the ball, Mr. President?

PRESIDENT: You mean if they have one? I don't think so.

January 23, 1925

I haven't any plans for speaking away from Washington after the first of March. I am going out speaking just as little as I can and keep the public peace. The pressure on me is great at all times. There were eight delegations in yesterday forenoon and asked me to make speeches, but it is very difficult for me to get out for that purpose.

February 10, 1925

PRESS: Mr. President, while we are on the subject of inauguration would you mind telling us whether in the matter of the ceremonies there will be any relaxation by you?

PRESIDENT: I don't know just what you mean by relaxation. I want all the newspapermen to come. If any of you want to parade I will be glad to have you. Do you want any more relaxation?

PRESS: Mr. President, I think the inaugural committee of Washington does in the sense that it wishes the parade to be somewhat more elaborate and more informal.

PRESIDENT: I think it will work out rather satisfactorily. I appreciate the compliment of people that want to come and join in a parade, but unless we set a limit to it somewhere there is almost no place to stop; it creates confusion and always more or less disappointment; and I would rather have the disappointment in relation to a short parade than to have it in other directions. I want the public to participate insofar as they can, in the inaugural. Now, as they did four years ago, they have the advantage of amplifiers, so that many thousands can hear the delivery of the message, which naturally I think is quite important, that couldn't in years gone by hear at all. That will be helpful. Some of the men in the Congress tell me that the inaugural four years ago was, on the whole, the most satisfactory that they have had. They didn't have any parade at all, but I thought it would be appropriate to have a parade, particularly of the Army and Navy and such Governors as want to come and participate in it, bringing with them their party, which I thought would be very well limited to 100—50 I thought at first, but the committee thought 100, so it has been put at 100. That will give the people who will assemble along the line a chance to look at the Governors of the various states and those that may come with them.

41

March 3, 1925

I shall take the oath of office tomorrow on a Bible that was given to me by my grandmother. That was the family Bible to which I referred the other day. Someone wrote in and wanted to furnish a Bible that George Washington had used, and I wrote thanking them and saying I had this family Bible and preferred to use that. It will be opened at the first chapter of John, which happens to be the first chapter of the Bible that I can recall reading. My grandfather was ill for a long time before he passed away and I used to read that chapter of the Bible to him when I was a small boy not more than four or five years old.

April 14, 1925

Here is a suggestion that instead of shaking hands with people that come here to the White House, that they be assembled out on the lawn and I go out and make them a speech. I don't view that with much approval. I do not at all dislike shaking hands. It brings me into a personal contact which you can't get any other way. I am sure that the people that come to Washington are much more pleased with an opportunity to pass through the line and shake hands with me, even though it is a rather formal and distant method of greeting, than they would be to gather anywhere and have me say a few words to them. I also know that it takes me less time and is easier for me. I rather like the handshaking. I can't give up more than 15 minutes or half an hour each day to it, but I can take care of a good many people here in that length of time.

June 9, 1925

It is customary I suppose for those who are interested in those things to look into the possible inherited background of Presidents. Some one has dug out a tradition that my family, the Coolidges, came from a place in Normandy. The French spelling was Colynge. I have seen on the screen within a short time a picture of a castle in that town— I can't tell the name of the town. Now I assume that that meant that we had a Norman background, which as I indicated yesterday was a Norse or a Norwegian background. I have got so many backgrounds of one kind or another that I am pretty purely American, having I believe a little tinge of Indian blood in me. I simply speak of the Norman background as of a little interest on account of the Norwegian gathering yesterday. I have got several others that I don't need to dwell on—Scotch, and, Colonel Hennessey says, Irish.

[*Coolidge was returning to Washington after a visit in Minnesota. Michael Hennessey was the author of a eulogistic and superficial book on Coolidge:* Calvin Coolidge, From a Green Mountain Farm to the White House *and of* Four Decades of Massachusetts Politics, *an equally mediocre book.*]

September 8, 1925

I have got two or three questions here about my son John. I have already suggested to the press that I didn't regard his actions as necessarily to be reported in the press, but of course if the press wants to report them there is nothing I can do about it. I don't object to it especially, but I don't think it is particularly a good thing for the boy. I don't think it is a particularly good thing for the other boys in the country. There isn't the slightest foundation for the report that appeared the other day that he is going to West Point.

PRESS: Annapolis, Mr. President?

PRESIDENT: No, No. There was a report that made a categorical statement that he was going to West Point. That was followed in the course of two or three days by another that he was going to the Naval Academy. Either one of those could have been verified by simple inquiry at the office, if there was a desire to find out the truth. There was no foundation that I know of for either suggestion. He is going to Amherst College. I don't think that that is a matter of enough public importance to justify any newspaper notice. He is doing the same as some hundreds of thousands of other young men that are going to take up their studies again when their school opens.

November 3, 1925

I have somewhat expected that my father, Colonel John C. Coolidge —he likes to have the C put in. I don't know whether he thinks he might become confused with his grandson. He likes to have it put in, and it doesn't take up much more type. I have asked him to come and **stay during** the winter at the White House. I spoke to him about it when I was up there last summer and have been in communication with him relative to it, and I received a letter this morning from the Attorney General [John Garibaldi Sargent] saying that my father was yesterday at the bank meeting at Ludlow and seemed to be in good spirits and was getting on comfortably. But the winters up there are very cold. The house is heated by wood. I thought it would be much more comfortable for him if he could come and stay at the White House. I rather think that he will come. That is for him to decide. I want him to consult his own wishes about it, of course, and stay wherever he thinks he will feel most comfortable and have the greater peace of mind.

[*John Garibaldi Sargent, a native of Ludlow, Vermont and a graduate of Black River Academy, which Coolidge attended as a youth, had been Attorney General of Vermont (1908-12).*]

I don't recall now whether I have had an invitation to go to Louisiana next year. It seems as though someone came in and spoke to me about going to New Orleans. I would like to go down into the South, especially Louisiana, to go to New Orleans, because I have never happened to be there. I have been in most of the states of the Union, as far South as South Carolina. I haven't visited Florida. I judge from the current news reports that Florida is not in need just at the present time of additional guests, but I should like to go down there very much. It is a wonderful country. I haven't been in Louisiana or Mississippi. I have been in Texas. I think those are all the states of the Union, with the possible exception of North Dakota, Montana and Idaho. When I went West once, I went over the Santa Fe and back another way, and another time over the Union Pacific and came back over the Canadian Pacific, so I didn't get into Idaho and Montana. I don't think I have been in North Dakota. The other states I have been in. But I haven't any plan about going South. It takes a considerable time to get down there and back. I think it is very doubtful if I can pay a visit to that state during the coming winter.

February 9, 1926

I haven't any expectation of making a visit to Plymouth in the near future.

PRESS: May I ask how your father is getting along?

PRESIDENT: My father is not suffering any pain. Mr. Stearns went up to see him at my request. He was up there Wednesday and again Thursday. He said father was cheerful and contented and not suffering any pain, but of course is confined to his bed. I speak to him over the telephone nearly every day.

March 12, 1926

I don't know about the necessity for legislation relative to the observance of the Sabbath in the District of Columbia. So far as my observation has gone the Lord's Day seems to be very well observed here. It may make a difference about one's opinon on that subject as to where you spend your own Sabbath. I usually spend mine going to church. I don't go outside much. Such observation as I have made seems to indicate that the observance of the Lord's Day is fairly good in this district, though the laws here I know are not quite so strict as they are in Massachusetts. I think the tendency of legislation has been rather toward liberality of Sunday observance, so far as legislation goes, rather than towards more strict laws. I recall that when I was Governor of Massachusetts I signed a bill permitting the playing of baseball on Sunday, not professional baseball and not baseball where any admission is charged.

March 16, 1926

The condition of my father seems to be about the same. I suppose he is gradually growing weaker. There doesn't appear to be any noticeable change. Some days he is a little stronger and brighter and takes more nourishment, and other days he seems to be weaker and doesn't take much nourishment and doesn't converse much with anyone unless they speak to him.

[*John C. Coolidge died two days later.*]

March 26, 1926

I hadn't thought anything about what would be done with the farm at Plymouth. I suppose I shall keep it. That isn't the place where my grandfather's grandfather, Captain John Coolidge, settled when he went to Plymouth, but it is one of the five farms he owned when he died and it is my understanding that he died there. It has always been in the family, ever since. I expect it will remain in my possession. I am undertaking to provide for it to be carried on as a farm for the next year.

March 30, 1926

There is no intention, so far as I know, to make any appeal for gifts of Colonial furniture for the White House. Congress passed some law in relation to that a year or two ago. The details of that law I haven't clearly in mind. If you want to get any information as to just what it is proposed to do, you will get it if you read that law and then assume that it is intended to carry out its provisions. I think it provided for the appointment of a committee or commission to pass on articles of furniture that might be offered to the White House. I don't think there is any intention of attempting to refurnish the White House with Colonial furniture. Some of the rooms on the second floor would lend themselves to that, but for the rooms on the first floor such furniture would probably not be altogether desirable. Of course, that all depends on what the particular piece of furniture is and that is why the Commission has been appointed to pass on it.

PRESS: Have any pieces of furniture been sent in so far?

PRESIDENT: I don't think so. I recall there was quite a good deal of newspaper discussion about it last summer. The source of it we didn't know and I don't know now what the source of it was. It was put out without any knowledge on the part of myself or Mrs. Coolidge. In fact, I don't think Mrs. Coolidge has anything to do with furnishing the White House anyway, except entirely unofficially, and except as a friend of the White House and in that respect.

June 11, 1926

I haven't given any thought as to what Mrs. Coolidge and I can do about a place to live while the White House is being repaired. The Director of Buildings and Grounds, Major Grant, says we shall have to move out; that the repairs will take from six to ten months. I confess that I regard that as a very painful operation. I have resisted as long as I could the suggestion that the roof should be repaired. Colonel Sherrill was telling me it ought to be done three years ago, and I have finally come to that conclusion. It will be necessary to work clear down to the second floor in the White House, so there would not be any opportunity for us to live on the second floor while the repairs are going on. That is due to the peculiar construction. Instead of resting the floors on the foundation, some of the floors are hung on the bridge work that goes up over to make the roof, so that when the roof is taken off there isn't anything to support the floors. They have to come down at the same time. I want to get some place as close as I can to the White House here.

PRESS: When do you contemplate having the work started? This year or next year?

PRESIDENT: I thought that perhaps after the Congress adjourns next March. That would enable us to use the White House for the usual winter social functions. Then we could move out. Congress would be away from about the first of March to the first of December undoubtedly—that is nine months—and during that period I should think they ought to be able to make the repairs.

PRESS: Did Major Grant think it safe to live in the White House next winter?

PRESIDENT: I think it is fairly safe, but it is a developing situation. The weaknesses are constantly getting greater. No one can tell just when the roof will fall in if it is left as it is, or perhaps it would not actually fall in at all, but the timbers are cracking and the weakness is very apparent. I had it examined by a member of the House, who is in the contracting business, a couple of years ago. The results of the examination and plans of the examination in reports that were made by the Engineers of the Army were sufficiently terrifying, but I knew the tendency of military men to think that it is necessary to take down the whole White House in order to fix a chimney, so I had a man in private life, or civil life rather, make an examination, and he rather confirmed the views of the military engineers. So that I very reluctantly came to the conclusion that it was necessary to have this done.

[*At this time Ulysses S. Grant III was a Lieutenant Colonel, not a Major as Coolidge states. Lieutenant Colonel Clarence O. Sherrill was Coolidge's Military Aide and his first appointment as President.*]

White Pine Camp, Paul Smith's, N. Y., August 10, 1926

I hope you all enjoyed your stay over in Vermont. I find it is helpful to me to go back once in a while to see that I am not forgetting how people earn their living, how they are required to live, and what happens when those who have harness breaks, or one of their shoes need some repairing, sit down and mend it. You can go out and do some work on fences, do such odd jobs as are necessary to keep the house in repair, and in general do such things as are necessary for the ordinary American citizen to do. There is always a little danger that those who are entrusted with the great responsibilities of business and Government may come to forget about those things and disregard them and lose the point of view of the great bulk of citizens of the country who have to earn their living and are mainly responsible for keeping their houses, farms and shops in repair and maintaining them as a going concern. I find it very helpful to go back and revive my information about those things, lest I should be forgetful about it and get out of sympathy with those who have to carry on the work of the nation.

White Pine Camp, Paul Smith's, N. Y., September 14, 1926

I sometimes tell people that I have one distinction. I suppose I am the healthiest President that they ever had. I am sure that the outdoor life has refreshed me, invigorated me, and been very beneficial. I have about the same amount of routine work to do wherever I am. I do it under a little different surroundings and get a new reaction from it, all of which results in giving me the benefit of a change.

[According to Coolidge's biographer, Claude M. Fuess, the President suffered a heart attack in the White House. Possibly this attack influenced his decision not to run again for the presidency in 1928. Fuess talked to Coolidge's physician. ("Reminiscences of Claude M. Fuess," Columbia University Oral History Project, 1962.)]

November 30, 1926

I don't use the radio in the White House very much. My wife uses it a great deal. I am most usually in the evening engaged in some kind of work that keeps me in the library. My wife likes to knit or something of that kind and while she is knitting she turns on the radio. She uses it a great deal. I haven't heard any complaint about interference. That may be due to the peculiarities of Washington. We are almost always getting our radio from the local radio station, which of course is sufficiently powerful so that outside interference wouldn't come in except in a slight degree.

_____

Then we turn to a somewhat lighter subject, one that interests me a little. We have received a present of a tame racoon.

PRESS: Edible, Mr. President?

PRESIDENT: That depends on your taste. I haven't much of a taste for racoon meat. Some people like it very much. But I have established him here in the south lot in suitable housing and he seems to be enjoying himself very much. There is another development in the south lot that I do not think has been suitably reported in the press. While we were away at camp this summer a swarm of bees moved into one of the hollow trees in the south lot and has been engaged during the summertime in making honey that is edible. Again, I don't have very much of a taste for honey. It never seemed to agree with me very well. When I was a small boy about three years old my grandfather's hired man visited his people and brought back quite a supply of honey. I ate so much of it that it disagreed with me violently and I have never enjoyed the flavor or even the smell of it. But I am interested in its production. I am quite interested to have what is known as a swarm of wild bees take possession of one of the hollow trees in the south lot.

PRESS: Is this racoon very young?

PRESIDENT: I think he is. I don't think he is quite grown yet. He is very playful, very interesting, and seems to be very well trained and well behaved.

PRESS: Have you a name for him, Mr. President?

PRESIDENT: Perhaps you can advertise for one.

Rapid City, S. D., June 17, 1927

I have a very fine location out at the State Game Lodge. I think most of you have been out there. It is just exactly what I like. I had a fine and pleasant trip across the country. I was very much interested in seeing the country that I was able to see on my trip out. Some of the people that came down to the station I wasn't able to see very well because about the station there is a great cloud of dust that comes up. That is because the ground around there is used to bring freight in for shipment and take freight out, and the soil is pulverized and soft and oftentimes I would go out on the back platform to see the people that were standing at the station and all I would be able to see when I got out there was a cloud of dust. I couldn't see them and I suppose they couldn't see me.

I was also sorry I didn't know when we went through Madison, Wisconsin. I understand there was quite a crowd down there to pay their respects to our party. They were only able to see the train go through. I didn't know when we were going through there, otherwise I should have been most anxious to get out on the back platform.

––––––––––

The trout that I caught yesterday were rainbow trout. I never happened to catch any of those before. They are a very good game fish to catch and very good fish for the table. I thought my first fishing trip in the hills was attended with very excellent luck.

[*According to Colonel Edmund Starling, Coolidge's "excellent luck" was enhanced by the fact that Rainbow Creek, where the President fished, was stocked with trout which could not escape from the area because steel mesh nets had been sunk across the stream both above and below the Lodge at which he was staying.*]

Rapid City, S. D., June 24, 1927

I don't know whether I have changed any in weight since I have reached the Black Hills. I am heavy enough. I don't desire to get any heavier and, perhaps, running through the fields may reduce my weight a little. If it did, I shouldn't regret it at all. I find the general effect of this climate and surroundings to be good.

Rapid City, S. D., July 29, 1927

I doubt if I can continue horseback riding after I get back to the capital, and I don't know what I shall do about taking the horse that was presented to me back with me. I enjoy horseback riding, but when I am in Washington it takes too much time to get my boots on and off, change my clothes, and then my horseback riding experience was all in the country, about what it is around the Lodge. What we have in Washington I didn't find very satisfactory with the necessity of crossing a road every little while and looking out for automobiles.

Rapid City, S. D., August 16, 1927

I think I remarked the other day that undoubtedly I shall have plenty of opportunities to work, some real and a good many fanciful. My college has just chosen a President, a young man as college presidents go, very promising, and I doubt very much if they are contemplating making any change. I should presume that the United States Steel Corporation would need an executive head during the next year and a half, which would probably prevent their waiting for my services, even though they thought that was desirable.

[*Coolidge had just announced that he would not seek re-election in 1928.*

Arthur Stanley Pease served as president of Amherst College from 1927 to 1931. A distinguished classicist, he had previously headed the Latin Department at the College.]

Rapid City, S. D., September 2, 1927

PRESS: Is it your plan Labor Day to come to the office?

PRESIDENT: I think so. Yes. You see mail that is sent up here from Washington for me to look after would be here on Labor Day the same as any other day. Very likely I shall observe that, as I do other days, here in the office.

September 13, 1927

The changes that have been made in the White House are very slight in that part that is occupied by my family and myself—practically no changes until the third floor is reached. A new roof was put on, as you know, and the third floor was made over. Of course, it is in very much better shape. It is more convenient and modern than it was before those changes were made. It leaves the White House now in first-class condition—practically fireproof from top to bottom, and leaves it of course entirely safe.

November 11, 1927

I am expecting to be present to confer the Hubbard Medal of the National Geographic Society upon Colonel [Charles] Lindbergh, I

49

think that is on Monday evening, and I am having a lunch Monday at 1:00 o'clock for those who have made transoceanic flights either in whole or in part. That is the only entertainment that I have in mind to provide for them.

Superior, Wis., June 26, 1928

I haven't been listening over the radio to the convention at Houston. I was out this morning up and down the river and forgot that the convention started today. I recall now that it does, and I think Mrs. Coolidge has had the radio on. But the radio there is over in the Lodge and I have scarcely been there this morning since I got up. Our dining room is across the bridge in another building, so when I came back from being out on the water I went into the dining room and haven't had a chance to listen to the radio.

[*The Democratic Party's National Convention nominated New York Governor Alfred E. Smith for the presidency.*]

September 4, 1928

My son John has no definite future plans. He has started for home and will look for employment. He hasn't taken any yet. He doesn't hold any public position. It might be just as well for him if all his goings and comings were not published in the press.

En route to Washington from Northampton, November 6, 1928

I don't expect to make any statement. Election day is a day when the people of the country speak. It will be particularly becoming for the President on that day to keep silent and let the people do the speaking.

Of course, I don't know whether I shall return to Northampton to live. That is my place of residence and likely to continue to be. I moved some of my bricabrac and things that have accumulated that we don't use up to Northampton today, because I suppose after the 4th of March I couldn't very well keep it in the White House. It has to be kept somewhere.

· II ·

THE UNITED STATES
AT HOME

4 · Office of the President

THE PRESIDENT of the United States is expected to be broadly informed not only about the presidency and affairs of state but also about the passing scene. Whatever he says is not only regarded as news, but as authoritative. At a press conference he may be asked anything and everything within the bounds of propriety and, on occasion, outside it.

Coolidge took up a wide range of subjects in his meetings with the press and frequently revealed a breadth of information and an expertise both in politics and in government affairs. At the same time his press conferences showed the President's intellectual limitations. From them, for example, there is very little evidence that he was ever really interested in ideas for their own sake. Abstract speculation was almost completely absent in his dialogues with the White House reporters. But, then, few American presidents have had this quality of mind, nor has it been expected of them.

President Coolidge's periodic reviews to the press on the duties of the President, the problems of government, and the state of the nation usually were replete with pedestrian generalities. They reflected a way of looking at government and politics that is completely out of fashion today, so great a change has occurred in American life. Yet when the President addressed himself to the merits of a specific piece of legislation, for example, the flood control bill, his analysis of the issues could be penetrating. For even if one disagrees with his point of view, the President often showed a mastery over detail that every truly successful politician must possess. And Coolidge, if nothing else, was a highly successful politician.

The President's political adroitness was perhaps best demonstrated by his handling of the Harding heritage. It is a familiar story—one of the most poignant of tales of the presidency—that in the early hours of the morning of August 3, 1923, in Plymouth Notch, Vermont, old Colonel John C. Coolidge went upstairs to tell his son Calvin that he was President of the United States. When Coolidge took the oath of office in the family parlor of the small, plain house at 2:47 A.M., he inherited a political mess from his predecessor. With wily patience, the new President managed to clean up the scandals of Teapot Dome and the Veterans Administration without giving the public reason to believe that the Republican Party had been responsible for them. He allowed Congress to take the burden of investigation; senators on the investigating committee had a field day. Coolidge's only major maneuver was his response to the refusal of Attorney General Harry M. Daugherty to resign. With exquisite care Coolidge allowed the public feeling against Daugherty to wane and the whole issue to become stale. Then he expelled the Attorney General. It was masterly political work, almost equal to Daugherty's own maneuvers to make Harding the Republican candidate in 1920. In handling the Harding heritage the President managed, in short, to put himself above the ruckus and to emerge untouched, untarnished, and in full armor for the 1924 presidential campaign.

August 21, 1923

An inquiry about the attitude towards the release of so-called political prisoners. I should be very sorry to see the United States holding anyone in confinement on account of any opinion that that person might hold. It is a fundamental tenet of our institutions that people have a right to believe what they want to believe and hold such opinions as they want to hold without having to answer to anyone for their private opinion. On the other hand, when persons holding opinions, whatever they may be, undertake to go out and influence others to commit acts that are contrary to the law of the land, why then, of course, they come within the purview of the law of inciting riot or advising the commitment of crime, or conspiracy, well-recognized criminal actions not at all related to the holding of ideas. When that has been the case, and especially in time of war when there has been any overt act against the administration of the Government, then people who engage in that activity become fit subjects for punishment. I recognize that we have allowed their punishment for some time and I shall do everything I can to extend a reasonable clemency on the part of the Government.

September 14, 1923

An inquiry also as to what is going to be done, as a result of the opinion of the Attorney General [Harry M. Daugherty] that there is no executive authority to use the armed forces of the United States to enforce prohibition without authorization of Congress. I haven't, at the present time, any ideas that I am going to ask Congress to use the armed forces of the United States for that purpose. I should doubt very much if it would be wise. I can conceive a time when it might possibly be desirable to use some boats of the Navy, or something of that kind, if it is shown that there is need for it to prevent smuggling, but I should do that with a great deal of hesitation. I do not think that the carrying out of police regulations ought to be put as a burden on the Army and Navy of the United States. That ought to be done by the regular police forces of the National Government and the regular police forces of the state governments. It is very seldom that any state government calls on its National Guard for any kind of police action, and it ought to be very seldom that the National Government should call on the Army or Navy for any manner of police action.

September 25, 1923

PRESS: Mr. President, can you impose an export duty on anything?

PRESIDENT: I think there is a Constitutional prohibition against export duties. That is my recollection, that the Constitution says that no export duties shall be imposed. I wouldn't want to be too certain about that offhand, but that is my recollection.

October 19, 1923

Another inquiry as to whether the Navy's interests are adequately protected in the lease of the Teapot Dome. I haven't any detailed information about that. My judgment about it would be based on the confidence that I had in President Harding and Secretary Fall. I think there is some suggestion pending in Congress for an investigation. I don't know whether it will be carried out or not, but that should reveal, if it is carried out—well, it is going on now, I believe. Yes. That, of course, will reveal the facts; so that, so far as I know, there is no action that could be taken by the President relative to it.

[*Albert B. Fall, Secretary of the Interior, had been a Republican Senator from New Mexico and a close friend of Harding prior to his ascendancy to the presidency. An arch Southwestern conservative and*

55

a pronounced anticonservationist, Fall was eventually to be convicted of bribery, fined $100,000, and sentenced to a year in jail. He was the first Cabinet member in the nation's history to be given a prison sentence for malconduct in office.]

November 2, 1923

I have here a quotation from a decision of the Supreme Court that is relative to ships bringing intoxicating liquor into port, and the inquiry is relative to a prospective treaty with Great Britain. Now, no definite information has been received about that. It is expected that Ambassador Harvey is to bring some proposal, or some answer to our proposal, when he returns. It has been so stated in the press. Just what the nature of the proposal might be, we don't know. There has been talk about a twelve mile limit, and talk about an hour's journey. Which one of these, or a combination of them, will be suggested, is not certain. The question here is raised as to whether this treaty would be in conflict with the Constitution or the present Volstead Law. Well, that, of course, depends entirely upon the terms of the treaty. I think I stated the general principle at a prior conference, which is that the Constitution and the treaties made thereunder shall be the supreme law of the land. That works out practically in this way, as I understand it; Congress, of course, has the right to make laws, which, when made in accordance with that Constitution, are the supreme law of the land. Our Congress has passed the prohibitory law, and that, at the present time, is supreme. But it has also the power, on the part of the treaty-making power, to make a treaty. Now, if the treaty is made subsequent to the passage of the law, the treaty should, insofar as there was any conflict between the two, supersede the law. Then it would be open to the Congress, as I understand it, at any later or subsequent time, to re-enact a law, or to make one that was different from the terms of the treaty, and then the newly made Congressional law would be the law of the land. That is, you have a sort of concurrent power between the treaty-making authorities and the law-making authorities, and the one that has acted last is the one that is binding.

PRESS: Mr. President, some of the editorial writers seem to think that the proposed treaty would contravene the Constitution—not the Volstead Law, but the Constitution itself. Do you believe it within the power of the Government to make a treaty that would contravene the Constitution itself?

PRESIDENT: Of course not. The only power the Government has to make a treaty comes from the Constitution, and there wouldn't be any question about it, for any treaty that might be made, that was contrary to the provisions of the Constitution, would be absolutely void.

[*Col. George B. Harvey, conservative editor of* Harper's Weekly, *was largely responsible for launching Woodrow Wilson into politics.*

56

He subsequently split with Wilson, supported the Republicans, helped bring about Harding's nomination in 1920, and served as Ambassador to Great Britain from April, 1921 to December, 1923.]

November 6, 1923

An inquiry about the Veterans Bureau investigation. Now, it is difficult, of course, for me to comment on the details of an investigation that is being made by a committee of Congress. Perhaps it would be almost enough to say that the Congress had provided for this investigation, authorized it, and directed it to be made by that Committee. It is not to be made by me. The Committee will make their investigation, and after they have heard all the evidence, they will make a report. When that report comes in, I suppose it may call for some action. Sometimes reports do. From the evidence that appears to be coming out, I suppose this report will call for action. But when it is finally made, then such action as the Committee determines, and such facts as they develop, will be taken under consideration, and appropriate action will be taken.

November 16, 1923

An inquiry also about extending clemency to the remaining political prisoners. I don't exactly like the term political prisoners, because I hope we do not have any such thing in this country, but I use that term because you know what it means, I know what it means, and the public knows. I am having an investigation made, and when I get the results of the investigation I am going to act upon it. I think I may be able to get a report on it within a short time. I am not exactly certain just when it will be.

November 20, 1923

An inquiry about a pardon for a German spy. That has never come to my attention. If it did, I should try to deal justly with it, as I should with any other request for a pardon. I wouldn't feel quite so sympathetic about it. But if there was a good reason for executive clemency, of course it would be extended. I should doubt very much the suggestion here, that the War Department has made a recommendation. I doubt very much if that would be made unless it was a case of disease or something of that kind, or the finding of new evidence, but it is perhaps not profitable to speculate on something of which you have no very great knowledge. I notice the name is Lowderwicz. It doesn't look so German as some other names I have seen.

November 30, 1923

An inquiry about the authority of the President to pardon. I don't know that there has been any direct decision of the courts about that. There are quite a number of opinions of the Attorney General on it from time to time. There are different kinds of contempt. This, I think, was a proceeding under a criminal contempt, which perhaps would make it more plain that the President would have the power of pardon. If it were a civil contempt, then perhaps the President wouldn't have. I spoke of it when it first came up, in relation to my experience as Governor of Massachusetts when there was, it was my impression, no authority on the part of the Governor to pardon in contempt cases. That is an action of the court for the purpose of giving the court authority to administer its business. A person may be called before the court to testify. If he refuses to testify then the court has authority to imprison him until he does. Now that isn't a crime in any way, and that he should be kept in confinement until he testifies, or if he doesn't come to send the sheriff after him and bring him. That is not on the criminal side of jurisdiction at all, but if a criminal contempt is committed, which I understand was claimed in this case, then it brings it on the other side of the court.

December 11, 1923

No decision has been made in the matter of appointing a judge for the Eastern District of Missouri. I should have made those appointments during the recess, except for the opinion of the Attorney General that, as they did not occur during the recess, they could not be filled. It is necessary for me to confer with Senators in relation to these appointments, and members of the House, because it is to quite a degree the source of my information. There is another matter that I think the press might stress somewhat, and that is my desire to appoint men of the highest character and most marked ability for service on the Federal bench. I am willing to have come to me—I welcome the suggestions from political committees and from those who are known to be in political life or holding political office about appointments to the bench. In other cases, suggestions of that kind might be almost entirely determined by them. But in the case of the bench I should look for something more than that. I have to have the assurance of the approbation of the bar, the assurance of the approbation of the general community as to the standing, character, ability and learning of men that are to be appointed to the bench. So that political recommendations, while they are helpful and will be given due consideration, cannot be entirely the determining factor in making appointments to the United States' bench. It is of signal importance that those places be filled by men about which there can't be any controversy. I don't mean by that that I should permit a man that from all the evidence I could secure was perfectly well qualified to be disqualified because he happened to have some enemies that might be willing to resort to tactics that I could not agree with or didn't seem to be supported by facts. But it is very important to put on the bench men

58

about whom there can't be any question, and I shall try, in my selections, to be guided by that principle.

January 8, 1924

An inquiry about the Cabinet meeting. We took up the question that has been under consideration and been talked about in Government circles; that is the inability of the Government to keep good men and high class individuals in their employment. That is rather the natural thing, as you would know from your own experience. People go through the various grades and so on, both in private employment and public employment. Some of the young men that are here today will be the editors and proprietors of newspapers in the future. So that probably some of the newspapers are complaining that they can't keep high class newspapermen in their employ, that are hired out to other occupations. Of course, that is the experience of every institution that has in its employ people of high class ability and character. They are sought for by others, and they graduate out. As I said to the Secretary of War [John W. Weeks], his Lieutenants become Captains, his Captains Majors, and so on up, and that is what happens in Government. But there is, I think, a real need to consider a better scale of remuneration for experts, because you can't carry on experiments and scientific investigation if your labor turnover in that department, or the employment turnover runs up to a very high percentage. I think there is a very great need of paying experts in the Government, on account of the higher scale that is prevalent outside of Government employment perhaps, larger remuneration.

January 18, 1924

Here is an inquiry about the lease of the Teapot Dome Naval oil reserve. That is under investigation, I think, by a Senatorial Committee, and of course no action is contemplated by any other arm of the Government so far as I know. It wouldn't be natural to take any action until the Committee had made their investigation, in order to find out whether anything develops that would appear to warrant any further investigation or action by any other part of the Government.

January 22, 1924

I have here several inquiries about the Teapot Dome. As I indicated at our last conference, that whole question is under most careful and searching investigation by the Senatorial Committee. The Department of Justice at my direction went there yesterday to observe and to see what evidence might disclose, on account of certain rumors which came to me. That is all that can be done at the present time—to observe the course of the investigation up there and to proceed in accordance therewith. I don't suppose it needs to be stated that if any irregularities are disclosed, or any misdeeds on the part of any one, they will be subject to investigation by the Department of Justice, and such action taken as the laws of the country require. I want it to be understood in making that statement that I am not making any accusations against any one, or have any opinion about the outcome of the investigation. Rumors and so on are flying around. Of course, wherever that occurs those people are summoned in before the Committee and asked to give their evidence. It may be that before the Committee finishes those hearings that discrepancies and so on that now exist will be completely cleared up. But in the meantime the Department of Justice will watch the situation and be prepared to take whatever action is warranted by the national laws. That observation applies generally. As I have already stated at previous conferences, I can't indicate that the Department of Justice is proceeding against this man, or that man, or the other. To do that would probably tend to dry up sources of information that would be necessary to have as evidence. You know evidence is very difficult to secure. It has to be done by secret investigations, and the Department of Justice I imagine, of course I myself, if I happened to know about those things, couldn't disclose them other than to say that an investigation of any alleged wrongdoing will be made; and the direction it is taking, or anything of that kind, necessarily has to be withheld. Otherwise, it would defeat the ends of justice.

January 25, 1924

Here is an inquiry about some Cabinet meetings in 1921 and 1922. I don't recall that the proposal to make the lease of oil lands was ever discussed in the Cabinet, before I became President. I don't say that it wasn't. But I don't recall. I think I should have recalled, had it been discussed at any length, or been referred to.

PRESS: Mr. President, were you present at all of those meetings?

PRESIDENT: Substantially all. Of course I was away in the summer of each year and once in a while I would be away speaking somewhere. I was away in August, 1921, and August and September, 1922. Sometimes I would be out of town on a trip to Chicago, or St. Louis, or somewhere.

I have here a number of inquiries about the Senate investigation into the oil leases. My position about that is as already indicated, that the Department of Justice is observing the course of events there and will very carefully review any testimony and take whatever action is necessary to protect the interests of the United States, and to punish any infraction of its laws. There seem to be two questions. I have already indicated them. One, and perhaps the most important is to undertake to punish and bring to justice anyone that is guilty in this situation in any way that is a violation of the criminal laws of the

United States. Now I don't want to be understood as jumping at any conclusion. I am very loath to believe that any one has been guilty of any criminal intent, but it is very evident that evidence has already been given up there that requires explanation. It requires investigation, and it points toward a criminal action. That of course will be investigated by the proper authorities to see whether any criminal action will lie. You can't start a criminal action on mere rumor. It requires, of course, substantial evidence, which can be produced before a Grand Jury and which can later be produced at trial. That will be taken care of, it goes without saying, if anything of that kind appears. The other matter is to see whether the United States suffered any injury by leasing these oil lands. That is a separate question and while it might be of considerable importance financially, it isn't the main question here. The main question is whether there has been any criminal wrongdoing. If the lease that has been made doesn't seem to be a proper one, why of course, appropriate action would be taken either for its annulment—I don't know of any other action that could be taken. In either instance every proper action will be taken to protect the rights of the United States and its property, and to protect the citizens of the United States against criminal wrongdoing.

I didn't know that any work had been stopped in the naval oil reserves. I am very sure that if that has been stopped it has been stopped by those that hold leases there, if that is the meaning of this question. I am certain the United States Government has taken no action in that direction.

January 29, 1924

PRESS: Mr. President, would you care to express your views specifically on the Senate resolution calling for Secretary Denby's resignation?

PRESIDENT: No, I don't care to discuss that.

———

PRESS: Mr. President, has any report been received from the Interior Department as to the wisdom of the leases?

PRESIDENT: To me?

PRESS: Yes, sir.

PRESIDENT: No. No report made to me. Of course it must be kept in mind that this investigation is being carried on by the Senate and up to the time that the suggestion came that there was grave suspicion of corruption there was very little question I think being made about the wisdom of the leases. Of course when the question of corruption or fraud comes up that vitiates everything and throws a question over the entire transaction and puts a very different light on it from that in which it was viewed before the question of fraud or corruption arose, and that is the reason why I have never made any inquiry about the validity of the leases. That question will now come up, of course, because the United States Government quite naturally will want to recover any property that may have been disposed of if it was in any way tainted with fraud or corruption. My statement of Saturday night was clear and definite that I propose to take action for those purposes, and to have action taken in the courts.

February 8, 1924

The Attorney General is returning from Florida in accordance with his own plan. He has constantly sent word that he will return at any time. He went down to take Mrs. Daugherty down, and because he himself was very much tired out. He took a good deal of work with him, which I understand he is finishing up down there, and for that reason is returning.

[*Because of his association with the major scandals of the Harding administration, Daugherty was hardly the man to move against others practicing governmental malfeasance.*]

February 15, 1924

Another inquiry about a rumor that former Secretary Fall and Secretary Denby started negotiations looking toward leasing coal fields in Alaska on similar lines to those followed in the Teapot Dome lease. I don't recall that any report of that kind ever came to me. I haven't at present any information about it. I know, of course, that there is criticism about the conduct of affairs in Alaska, though I had understood that the visit there last summer of Secretary Wallace of the Department of Agriculture, Secretary Hoover of the Department of Commerce, and I think Secretary Work of the Department of the Interior, had fairly well cleaned up any questions that were at issue. They had an opportunity to secure firsthand information and were working along the proposal for the development of Alaska to the best possible advantage.

[*Dr. Hubert Work, a physician from Colorado, was another carry-over from the Harding cabinet. At first the successor to Will Hays, who served only a year as Postmaster General, Work replaced Albert B. Fall as Interior Secretary after the latter's resignation amid the exploding Teapot Dome scandal.*]

February 19, 1924

The Attorney General has not resigned and there was no discussion of him or his office in the Cabinet either before or after the meeting.

I haven't given any special consideration to the selection of a successor to Mr. Denby.

I don't know just how far I can go hereafter in giving out any information about the oil lease cases. I am willing at all times to give the press anything I can give without embarrassing the cause of the public service. Now it is very seldom that that would be the case, but it is especially the case in the prosecution of cases in court. I don't imagine that those who may be defendants in these cases feel that their case was helped by supplying the details of their defence to the press, nor would the case for the Government be helped by supplying to the press the details of the Government's case, what it might think about the law, or what facts it had to present. I imagine though, that the press will be and is in possession of all the facts, and can advise itself about the law. But I think it would be better for the men who have charge of that, I mean Senator Pomerene and Mr. Roberts, to assume responsibility for giving out information. That doesn't mean that you won't get what you can from any other source. It is perfectly proper to do that. I prefer, though, that they should take the responsibility of giving what they can to the press other than doing it myself. They will stand in the same relation to these cases that the Attorney General stands to the other legal requirements of the Government. They are public officers, appointed under statutory provision and confirmed by the Senate, and that resolution or statute gives them full authority to prosecute these cases. I give you that as a preliminary, in order that you may understand hereafter if I don't have an opportunity to say much about the cases.

[*Senator Atlee W. Pomerene, an attorney, was a Democrat from Ohio. Owen J. Roberts, a prominent Philadelphia corporation lawyer and a Republican, was appointed to the Supreme Court in 1930 by President Hoover. Roberts completely overshadowed Pomerene in the oil investigations.*]

March 4, 1924

I have only had a telegram and a short note from the Attorney General since he left Washington. He sent me a telegram on his arrival in Chicago, saying that he was writing to me and sent me a note telling of his work up there and his expectation that the grand jury would report an indictment, which the grand jury did, and that he was on his way from there to his wife, who is ill in Miami. Those are the only communications I have had from him.

March 25, 1924

I don't know who will have charge of the contempt proceedings in the case of Harry F. Sinclair. I suppose they will proceed in the usual way that those cases proceed. I don't recall ever having noticed one of those cases before. I suppose the general way is to certify to the District Attorney of the District of Columbia, who then takes charge of it. I haven't any definite knowledge about it.

[*Harry F. Sinclair, a millionaire oilman, was one of the principals involved in the Teapot Dome affair. For refusing to testify before the Senate Investigating Committee, Sinclair was fined $1,000 and sentenced to three months in jail. Later he received a six-month sentence*] *for contempt of court when it was discovered that his private detectives were shadowing the jury. He escaped conviction, however, on the more fundamental charges of bribery and conspiracy—a miscarriage of justice, many people believed.]*

April 1, 1924

I haven't been able to reach any decision about appointing an Attorney General. Of course what I am trying to do there necessarily is to get a $75,000 or $100,000 man for a salary of $12,000. Now that isn't at all impossible. I expect to be able to do something that is substantially in that line.

PRESS: Mr. President, I think it would interest the country to know what your judgment is as to a $75,000 or $100,000 man.

PRESIDENT: What I mean by that is that a man in private practice might be able to secure that income. The Government of the United States is constantly served in that way by men, especially undersecretaries, men of capacity and of experience who are here in Washington at a very large sacrifice because they love the service. They are attached to it, not only because of the fascination of it, but because of a patriotic desire to serve the country. Of course when you come to members of the Cabinet, I don't need to designate any of the present members by name, you just think of them yourselves, you can understand whether the United States Government is getting the worth of its money in hiring those men for $12,000 a year and an automobile.

PRESS: Mr. President, have you any idea when the appointment might come?

PRESIDENT: Well, just as soon as I can find someone. It is difficult to canvass the situation in a hurry. I have to consult with a good many men and make a great many inquiries. If I wanted someone in Chicago, why I would have, perhaps, to send out there and get that person to come on here, then I would have to make inquiries in the town, make investigations, and find out what their connections are, and talk with a number of Senators and Representatives about it to see what they know. All of it takes time, but it is not a problem that will be by any means impossible or very difficult to solve. It takes some time to do it.

PRESS: Mr. President, may I ask whether geographical requirements are being considered?

PRESIDENT: I don't think that is highly important. What I want is a man of character and ability that will take that office and administer it in accordance with the well known standards of administration of the Attorney General's office, and if that is done it doesn't make very much difference whether the man, if he should return home, would go to Florida, Oregon, New England, or the middle states, or to the

Pacific coast. There are certain balances that we like to maintain. Sometimes that can be done, and sometimes it cannot. What I am looking for is the man, rather than looking at geography.

June 3, 1924

I don't know that I shall have any special message to the Republican National Convention, other than to suggest to them that they make their own choice of Vice-President. I think that was the course that Roosevelt adopted in 1904. It seemed to work very well then, and that is the course I am going to adopt in the coming Convention. The delegates will assemble from all over the country. They know what the general feeling of the country is better than I can judge of that, and I very much prefer to have them make the choice of a candidate for Vice-President, than to undertake to make one myself.

June 6, 1924

I have two or three inquiries here about the Vice-Presidency. I made a statement about that Tuesday, in which I undertook to announce that I had no candidate, and I adhere to that statement. Any reports contrary to that statement are, as perhaps some of you men know, without foundation. I usually keep my word for at least four days, and I can tell four days before the Convention what I am going to do. A good many very excellent men are mentioned for the Vice-Presidency. Many of them are perfectly acceptable to me, but I am not undertaking to approve one above another. Let the Convention select the man that after deliberation they think is best equipped to meet the situation. If I was going to pick out a candidate, I should want to go to Cleveland and talk with the various delegations when they come in, and find out what they think the requirements are, and what the sentiment is in the neighborhood in which they reside. In that way, I presume I could make up my mind what would be best. I am not as you understand making the slightest criticism of anybody, nor am I undertaking to promote any candidate. I am sorry that there are any reports that I am picking a candidate, and if there are any more of them they will be without any foundation.

July 29, 1924

I don't know as I could add anything to the sum of human knowledge by discussing my first year in the White House, and I don't know as I would be a very good judge of what would be considered as the outstanding feature. There are so many things that might be said about it, so many different ways of looking at it. I don't know what you would call the outstanding feature. I suppose it is my nomination for the Presidency, if you want to talk about political matters, and considering what the question refers to. Whether my work here has made any difference in the sentiment of the country would be something about which you could judge better than I, as you were more in touch with it before I came here.

August 22, 1924

I haven't thought about my annual message. I have an inquiry here. I suppose I shall see that about twice a week now—about what I shall put in my annual message. You can generally expect that I am advocating today the same things I have yesterday, unless you have an official announcement from me that I have changed it. I keep seeing in the papers that I have changed my position about something or other, which is all new to me. When people come to me about certain bills I refer them to messages to Congress and statements I have made. Sometimes they go out and seem to indicate that I have changed my mind. Of course there is a continuity of action where something is started today, and which would require supplementary action tomorrow.

November 4, 1924

I don't know that there is any comment that I can make on the election or the campaign that isn't perfectly obvious to all of you. I have conducted a campaign that I think will not leave me anything to be sorry for, whether I am elected or not. I don't know of anything in the conduct of the campaign that I have been responsible for for which I shall have to make any apology. I have been very much pleased with what has appeared to be the high plane on which my party have presented their case to the American people, the freedom from expenditure of large sums of money, and on the publicity that has been given and the care taken in relation to the collections and the expenditure of the campaign funds. They have at all times been under the supervision of chartered public accountants, so that practically on a minute's notice the National Committee were ready to have a certified oath-bound statement made in relation to the election expenditures by disinterested and chartered public accountants. I don't think a campaign was ever before conducted in that way. From all the indications that have come to this office I think the result of the efforts on our part are going to meet with success. A part of that success is due to you gentlemen who are here in the room and have done more to interpret me and my policies to the country than I could do myself.

January 2, 1925

There is nothing I can say this morning in relation to the call on me of Lord Cecil. It was that ordinary call of courtesy that is made by foreigners when they come to town, I suppose to satisfy a mutual desire to see what kind of people each of us may be, mutual curiosity perhaps in order that he might see what I looked like and that I might see what he looked like. We chatted about various things that I chat about here in the newspaper conferences. Nothing new developed. I usually inquire, and did of him, if the situation was clearing up in Europe, if there was a prospect of stability. He thought there was. That is as we long know over here. He wanted to know if I could give him any message, and I told him I didn't know of anything other than that he might say I was pleased with the friendly relations that exist between this country and his country. That is rather barren, I am afraid, of news, but there wasn't much of any news in the call.

April 14, 1925

I don't know of any special proposal about legislation to give the President power to transfer and consolidate various bureaus of the Federal establishment. I hadn't given that any special thought, because I had been interested in the reorganization bill which has never been acted on, and which I suppose will come up for action in the next Congress, which takes care of that kind of work. Now, looked at from its business side, of course the work of the Government has to be constantly supervised and checked up like the work of any business. Otherwise, it runs to seed. I don't know whether any of you happened to hear the story about the sentinel that was posted in the Garden of the European emperors, and finally someone undertook to inquire why the sentinel was posted at that particular place. Careful investigation revealed that more than 100 years before that there had been a rose bush and that bush had a very handsome flower on it and the empress wanted that flower protected. So the sentinel had been posted there to protect that flower, and nobody having looked into the matter the sentinel was still on duty years after the rose bush was gone. Now, unless you keep constant supervision over any kind of business, newspaper business, or the business of running the Government, it will run to seed and you will have men trying to function when the reason for their functions no longer exists. So that we have to keep constant supervision over the executive department and, of course, at this time we haven't yet finished up all the work of getting rid of our war activities. We ran into a great many activities at that time that are not needed in time of peace. While those are mostly closed up, yet it is a good idea to be constantly watchful to see if we are trying to carry on any activities of government that are no longer needed. While I am constantly engaged in this general idea, I haven't at the present time any specific plan about it, nor am I doing anything more than would be the ordinary routine of the executive department.

Swampscott, Mass., July 28, 1925

I am not familiar enough with the details of the work that the Federal Trade Commission does to go into any specifications in relation to it, but I should think there was a very broad field of useful activity in which they might engage which is set out in detail in the act establishing the Commission. They come upon that condition that is chronic in relation to commissions that are established to do something that the legislative body doesn't know how to do. Now that is no criticism on the legislative body. There are matters of legislation and control that are of such an intricate and technical nature that legislation doesn't appear to fit them, and there is a belief on the part of individuals and the public—I am speaking generally now—that there are evils that ought to be remedied and the established remedy is to provide a Commission to do that. It has been my understanding and experience in public life that a commission would be established and the legislature would go home thinking that that question was never going to bother them again. Well, these evils that are complained of are more or less chronic in the carrying on of business affairs and the relationship between different individuals of the community. While the commission may help to solve the problems, it isn't able usually entirely to eliminate them. Then the legislature comes back the next year and somebody gets up on the floor and says the commission is all right but it is the personnel. He wants to abolish that commission and appoint new members, then the evils will be entirely eliminated. That is the way things of this kind work. Well now, I don't expect that commissions are going to cure entirely all the evils of our relations, whether they be industrial or social. I think they are helpful. It isn't always possible to get the members of the commission, when it comes to be tried out, to be one that functions perfectly. But I have a good deal of faith and confidence in the state commissions here in Massachusetts and in our Federal commissions. I think they serve a very useful purpose and are very helpful, and I think the Federal Trade Commission can perform a very helpful service. Now it may be that there are practices that ought to be changed. It may not be doing some things it ought to do. As I say, I can't discuss the details of their work because I am not familiar with them. But I should be very much surprised if there wasn't a very large volume of work that would appear to be profitably performed by this Commission. It isn't very popular in the business life of the nation, but I don't regard that as a fatal criticism of it. It is in the nature of a business policeman. While perhaps it does things it ought not to do, and refrains from doing things it ought to do, I don't think it has reached that stage where it can be said it isn't any good.

[*It is generally agreed that the men whom Coolidge appointed to the Federal Trade Commission, particularly the reactionary William E. Humphrey, changed the character of the Commission from one that sought to some extent to police the business world to one that literally removed all government restraints upon it.*]

December 18, 1925

I don't know enough about the workings of the school board of the District to know whether it is feasible to have them elected or not. I recall about that what was an interesting incident to myself. When I studied geography I was very certain that it said in the geography that there were certain elections held by the people of the District, and when I was candidate for Vice-President I came through Washington and some of the local newspapermen here inquired of me whether I was in favor of elections in the District, and I told them that I thought they had local elections here now. I didn't happen to be correct, but it came about by reason of what I had remembered of my geography days. It seemed very curious to some of the newspapermen who were considerably younger than I, that I must be very much mistaken about it. I don't know what could be done. I want to have the schools of the District up to the very best condition. Whether they could be improved by having an elective school board—that is the direct question—or not, I do not know. And I haven't any mature views about the matter of general suffrage in the District. I can see a great many difficulties. Of course I am pretty well committed to local self-government, and having people elect their own officers. But of course I have also had it brought to my attention, though not in any discussion of what ought to be done here in the District, the rather sorry plight of the national government of one of the countries abroad. It has no jurisdiction whatever over the local police. It is never certain whether it is going to have police protection. It is in a certain city and it is there rather as a matter of suffrance. Now, the United States Government couldn't submit to anything of that kind. It has to have absolute authority to protect itself and pretty nearly absolute authority over local police, and in order to have authority over local police it has to have pretty general authority over the government of a locality. This of course is a Federal city set apart for the carrying on of the business of the United States Government. Pennsylvania is interested in it, the States of Washington and Oregon are interested in the Government here in the District of Columbia no less than Maryland and Virginia. And those states are interested in it no less than persons that live here. So it makes a difficult and complicated question, and unless there appear to be very serious abuses of some kind or another I should be rather inclined to let the present method of government go on. They tried local government here one time with an elective Mayor, I think, and then they went back to the present system.

April 27, 1926

It is stated here that there are two radio bills pending, one that would establish a separate Commission in connection with the Department of Commerce, and that is pending in the House and has been passed, and the Interstate Commerce Committee of the Senate has reported a bill to establish a new bureau to have entire jurisdiction over the radio regulations. I haven't in mind the various provisions of either of these bills. I think it would be a wise policy to keep the supervision over radio or any other regulatory legislation under some of the present established departments. Otherwise, the setting up of an independent commission gives them entire jurisdiction without any control on the part of the Executive or anywhere else. That is the very essence, of course, of bureaucracy, an independent commission that is responsible to nobody and has powers to regulate and control the affairs of the people of the country. I think we ought to keep as far away from that as we can, wherever it is possible. Of course that isn't possible in relation to courts. It wouldn't be possible in relation to some of the regulation of interstate commerce, the supervision of railroads, and so on, which is of a highly technical and also judicial character. But I should very much prefer that any future regulatory legislation be put under some of the present departments. If it is commerce, why under the Commerce Department; if it has to do with labor, under the Department of Labor. So that, I should think that the House bill was more nearly in accord with that theory and would be more acceptable to the public. It certainly would be to me, for that reason.

White Pine Camp, Paul Smith's, N. Y., August 3, 1926

This is the fourth [third] anniversary of my being President. The country has made a great deal of progress in the past three years. It hasn't been so noisy as it has at some other times, but judging from the general condition of the country it has been fairly successful.

Three years ago the German reparations problem had not been solved. The French still occupied the Ruhr. That question has been taken care of.

Our own problems were those that arose as a result of the war. Of course after the cessation of hostilities and during the almost five year period from November, 1918, until August, 1923 the questions became almost entirely, so far as our country was concerned, economic. We had our great war debt, which has been steadily reduced. We had high taxes, which have been reduced by two acts of Congress. And we had the question of keeping Government expenditures as low as possible. Those questions have been met very successfully.

The business of the country for the past three years has been, I should say, on the whole, better than any other three years. Of course there was a very large business during the war, but it was a business that was paid for by using up the capital of the country. The business of the past three years has been paid for in the ordinary business way, out of its earnings. We have been gradually recovering from the depression, and to a considerable extent, due to the reductions in taxes, there has been a decline in commodity prices. They don't stand so low now as they did in the middle of the deflationary period, but they are considerably lower than they were three years ago, which means that the people are able to purchase the same amount of commodities at a less expenditure of money, and this notwithstanding the fact that wages have not decreased, but on the whole, so far as there has been a change, wages would show a trifle of an increase over what they were three years ago.

There are some parts of the West where a full recovery has not yet been made. Mr. Ford told me that in North Dakota and in Nebraska business showed some falling off due to crop failures on account of lack of rainfall. Last year there was a considerable crop failure in Nebraska, and this year in parts of that state and in the Dakotas there has been dry weather, so that they have suffered from failure of crops. The textile industry has not been very good for the past few months, but it has been showing signs of a recovery, especially during the month of July. The metal industries and the automobile industry apparently are first-rate. The railroads of the country are doing a larger business than they ever did before and are practically all recovered and on their way to recovery from the strain they underwent during the war. They are a very large purchasing power when they are prosperous and able to finance themselves and put in the improvements and the extensions that are all the time required for the purpose of meeting an increasing business, and it goes a long way toward making all the business of the country productive and prosperous.

We hadn't resumed relations with Mexico, so far as sending an Ambassador there three years ago. Judge Payne and Charles B. Warren were in Mexico as Commissioners working out a plan for an adjustment of claims and for a recognition of the Mexican Government, which took place after I became President, and Mr. Warren returned there as our first Ambassador. We have adopted such legislation as the new immigration law, the Railroad Labor law. I have mentioned the two tax bills, they were important, we have ratified a great many treaties, the Senate has voted to adhere to the protocol of the Court of International Justice, and a great deal of other legislation that I can't recall offhand. Perhaps you gentlemen will recall some that I haven't. But the main thing is the general result, which has left the country in a flourishing and prosperous condition.

PRESS: Did you mention war debts, Mr. President?

PRESIDENT: No. The war debts have been settled. That of course is a very outstanding feature of the last three years. Those are the greatest international financial transactions that were ever entered into between different nations.

I feel that we are making some progress towards further agreements for limitation of armaments. We negotiated a treaty concerning the sale of arms. That doesn't change the present treaties, so far as we are concerned, that were entered into at the Washington Arms Conference, but very slightly. There are some changes, but they are practically the same thing that was entered into there in their main outline.

As I was about to say, a Government can't always secure the prosperity of the country. The best it can do is to create conditions under which the country will be prosperous if it adheres to sound business practices. I think that has been especially characteristic of the past three years; the caution and wisdom on the part of the business interests of the country in not becoming involved in overextension, in manufacturing a lot of goods without first knowing where they were going to secure a market, and in not borrowing a lot of money, but rather attempting to finance their own needs themselves. That has left the country in a condition that is basically sound.

There was a reaction in the prices of securities last winter that was entirely healthy and on the whole, I believe, beneficial. The recession in prices that took place at that time has been very largely made up in the last six or eight weeks. Levels on the whole are not quite so high as they were last winter. But that is not a matter that affects very much the sound business condition of the country.

Movements of freight are very large and the output of our manufacturing establishments taken as a whole is large.

I wouldn't want to be understood as indicating that the economic and material prosperity of the country is the only thing that ought to be considered, but it is so necessary to a consideration of other things that it is a fundamental consideration. We are not able to make much progress in other directions, unless we have sound business conditions. I feel that in addition to our material prosperity we are making progress in educational ways and in the general moral standards of the country. We have been troubled by some crimes of violence, but I think that has not been so large as that which has been inflicted upon the country in the succeeding period that has followed other times of war. Nor do I mean that we are in such perfect condition that we don't need to do anything more. There are a great many more things that we ought to do, and it is going to be necessary to put a good deal of effort into maintaining our present position.

[*Judge John Barton Payne was a member of the U. S. Commission to adjust American claims against Mexico and to bring about diplomatic recognition of that country. See "Vexations of Imperial Power."*]

January 28, 1927

I should doubt very much if it would be at all practicable for the President of the United States to go into conference with the President of Mexico. International relations are not conducted by that method. I think ever since someone attempted to conduct negotiations directly with George Washington, which he refused to do and referred them to the Secretary of State, it has been recognized that the foreign relations of this country are to be conducted through that avenue.

April 15, 1927

There isn't any division of the Cabinet over the policy that is being pursued in China. I don't think that would be possible in my Cabinet. The way I transact the Cabinet business is to leave to the head of each Department the conduct of his own business. While, of course, matters are taken up in the Cabinet and everybody is asked to give their opinion, yet I have never considered that it was for one member of the Cabinet to have any very great weight in trying to indicate to another member of the Cabinet how the latter member should conduct the affairs of his own Department. What I am telling you is a general principle. It hasn't any application at all to this matter in hand, because there isn't any division in the Cabinet. All members of the Cabinet have agreed that what the Secretary of State is doing ought to be done. Of course, it is done under the general direction of the President and with his approval. I noticed in a headline recently the statement that Mr. Hoover disapproved of what the Secretary was doing, thinking that identic notes ought not to be resorted to. It is my recollection that Mr. Hoover was the warmest advocate in the Cabinet of identic notes, pointing out what is evidently the condition, that if each of the countries concerned—and it was the common concern of all—went ahead on its own initiative it would fail very much in the influence it would have if they all adopted their identic policy, which is of course the policy.

There is another matter of general concern, and that is this—that when our relations with a foreign country are in the condition that our relations with some of the Chinese are in at the present time, it is in danger of being quite harmful if the press resorts to speculation about the attitude of this Government. It probably would be very comforting to any opposition that this Government might have in China, and I don't think there is very much there, but what opposition there is there would be comforted if they were told that the officials of this Government were in violent disagreement about what ought to be done. So that while I know that the press oftentimes has to speculate some and draw deductions of positions when our foreign relations are concerned, over a matter that is somewhat delicate there is grave danger that anything of that kind may do considerable harm and ought to be resorted to only on occasions when the press is pretty certain that it is going to be right. In this case it has no foundation whatever.

While I am on that, I might state again that Mr. Kellogg isn't going to resign. If he does resign, Mr. Hoover will not be appointed Secretary of State.

April 19, 1927

I didn't speak of Mr. Hoover's abilities the other day. I had rather assumed that that would be assumed by the conference. His reputation is so well established in this country, and indeed abroad, for ability and executive achievement that I doubt very much if I should be able to shake it even if I wished to. Certainly, I have no desire to do that and shouldn't want to be thought so lacking in appreciation of a man of his abilities as to think that he wasn't well qualified for any position in the Cabinet that he would be willing to accept. Of course, the place that he is in now is one of great importance and of constantly increasing importance, not only on account of our domestic commerce, but on account of our foreign commerce, which under his direction and encouragement has very greatly increased and shows promise of further increase in the future.

May 24, 1927

I haven't seen the suggestion that is referred to as having been made by Ambassador Herrick that Lindbergh be sent to fly to various European capitals. There would be some difficulty about arranging that through Government action. I had seen some reports in the press that he was contemplating flights to different portions of Europe. The more we learn of his accomplishment in going from New York to Paris, the greater it seems to have been. That is something that grows on us the more we contemplate it.

[*Myron T. Herrick served as Ambassador to France from February, 1912 to December, 1914. He was reappointed to that post in 1921. Herrick was Chairman of the Board of Union Carbide and Carbon Company and a director of the New York Life Insurance Company. He was a veteran G.O.P. politician from Ohio.*]

May 31, 1927

I haven't seen the Goldsmith open letter which is said to have been addressed to me and which has been published in Canada. Without criticising in any way the writing and publishing of letters of that kind in foreign countries—it is perfectly proper, our own citizens do it here and citizens of other countries can very properly do that in their own lands—I think some of you recall that Clemenceau wrote a letter of that kind either last summer or two years ago, but it isn't possible for the President to make public comment on letters of that kind. I assume that it has something to do about our Government. But we have official methods of communication with the governments of other countries and it is necessary for the President to keep within that bound, to carry on our diplomatic intercourse through duly appointed representatives, rather than to undertake to guide it through statements given to the press.

[*Georges Clemenceau was the Premier of France during part of World War I.*]

June 7, 1927

I have already extended half holidays for the Government employees to the very closely breaking point. It was done at their request. So that I am not expecting to have another addition to their half holidays because Captain Lindbergh is going to be in Washington on Saturday next. He isn't to arrive here until 12:00 o'clock. It is now planned to have the ceremony bestowing the Distinguished Flying decoration upon him something like an hour after his arrival. I am advising the Departments, however, that those of their people that are not needed to keep the departments running will be permitted to go out at 12:00 o'clock. That will give them plenty of time to attend the ceremonies which will be at 1:00.

Rapid City, S. D., July 29, 1927

If the conference will return at 12:00 I may have a further statement to make.

[*It was at this reconvened conference that Coolidge issued his famous statement, "I do not choose to run for President in 1928."*]

It is rather difficult for me to pick out one thing above another to designate what is called here the chief accomplishments of the four years of my administration. The country has been at peace during that time. It hasn't had any marked commercial or financial depression. Some parts of it naturally have been better off than other parts, some people better off than other people, but on the whole it has been a time of a fair degree of prosperity. Wages have been slightly increasing. There has been no time that there has been any marked lack of employment. There have been certain industries like the textile industry and the boot and shoe industry in certain localities like New England, which have not been running on full time. But generally speaking there has been employment for every one who wished employment. There has been a very marked time of peace in the industrial world. There have been some strikes. When I first came into office there was a strike in the hard coal fields and another strike I think in the same line a couple or three years later, but those differences have been adjusted without any great conflict or any great suffering on the part of the industries or the public, so that there has been rather a time of marked peace in industry as between employer and employees. There has been considerable legislation which you know about, and which I do not need to recount. There have been great accomplishments in the finances of the National Government, a large reduction in the national debt, considerable reductions in taxes.

MR. MICHAELS: Do you know the amount of the reduction in the national debt? About $4,000,000,000?

PRESIDENT: Well, it is close to that. It runs about $1,000,000,000 a year, some years less, between three or four.

August 5, 1927

I don't know of any amplification I could make to the statement that I gave out Tuesday. Mr. Sanders and Mr. Geisser knew that I was going to make a statement. Quite naturally I thought I would like to confide it to the newspapermen first, though it is necessary for Mr. Sanders and Mr. Geisser to know about it in order to have it prepared.

[*Erwin C. Geisser was Coolidge's personal stenographer.*]

August 9, 1927

I don't think the death of General Wood will make any difference about the administration of the insular affairs.

I didn't intend to indicate the other day that I had reached any settled conclusion as to where the Insular Bureau ought to be placed, if it is taken out of the War Department. I suggested that my offhand thought was that the Department of the Interior would seem to be the natural department for it to go to. I haven't felt, though, that there was much disposition on the part of Congress to make a change. General Wood suggested when he was here the setting up of an entirely new department in which all those things would be gathered. I haven't liked the idea of establishing a new department. As the conference knows, I have been rather more interested in the consolidation of departments already established than of establishing any new ones. Congress has set up and I have signed some bills for new commissions and so on, as there didn't seem to be any other way to do. I have done it regretfully and with the hope that it would be temporary. But after a commission is established you find that it always wants to enlarge itself, employ more people, is very busy with Senators and Congressmen to impress upon them the great value of the services of the commission, and even when I talk with people that I appoint to commissions and tell them that I would like to have them go on to the various boards with the idea that they may be abolished, they say they ought to be abolished, but when they have taken their position they very soon seem to change their mind.

[*Leonard Wood, Governor General of the Philippines, was a close friend of Theodore Roosevelt, a veteran of the Spanish-American War, and a one-time military governor of Cuba. His military ambi-*

tions were thwarted by President Wilson during World War I. He became a leading contender for the Republican presidential nomination in 1920. In 1921 President Harding appointed him to co-head a commission to investigate the possibility of independence for the Philippines. The commission's report was negative. Wood remained on as Governor General and was constantly at odds with Filipino leaders. See "Vexations of Imperial Power."]

November 22, 1927

I do not approve of the circulation of a petition, such as has been reported in the morning press, requesting me to run for President in 1928. I don't see that any good could come from it. I hope it will be discontinued.

December 16, 1927

Here is a question that recalls to me what I forgot the other day. I constantly have it brought to my attention, and I see statements in the press from time to time, indicating that I have undertaken to be engaged in one kind of employment or another after the termination of my office as President of the United States, and I was going to say that there is no foundation for any suggestion of that kind. I shouldn't give it a thought myself, if it had not been brought to my attention through the press and otherwise. I am very glad to suggest to you, and you can suggest to the public if you wish to, that all reports of that kind are without any foundation and will be unless they are officially announced by me, which is likely to be a very considerable time in the future. It is a matter, quite naturally, that I haven't given any attention. I think some one asked me out at Rapid City. I said there that I usually had brought to me plenty of work to do and had no doubt that would continue. But while I remain in the office of President I do not expect to make any arrangement whatever for any future kind of employment. Here is a suggestion inquiring whether I might go to the Senate or the House in the future. I haven't any present intention of going back on that end of Pennsylvania Avenue. There are going to be vacancies in the city government in Northampton. I do not know why the City Council of that town should be neglected in the press comments and reports.

December 20, 1927

President [Clarence Cook] Little of the University of Michigan came in yesterday—he is a member, I don't know but President, of what I understand is an association of Presidents of State Universities —to tell me of the interest that they have in the development of education and their desire to cooperate with the National Government along that line, and especially to be helpful in adopting the carrying out of a sound policy on the part of the United States Government in the expenditure of money that it appropriates for research and investigation and experimentation. We are making quite large appropriations of that kind which go to the agricultural colleges, I think almost exclusively. In many of the States those colleges are a part of the State University. In some of the States they are separate institutions. In Massachusetts, for instance, we have no university, because the field was very early covered by institutions that the state and local communities had contributed to in establishing, the first one being Harvard, and all our agricultural colleges are separate institutions.

PRESS: Was he the head of Massachusetts Agricultural College at one time?

PRESIDENT: No. President [Kenyon L.] Butterfield of the Agricultural College in Massachusetts was the President. So I told him I knew about the situation from my experience in Massachusetts, in part, and that I would do what I could to cooperate with him and see that the money that was appropriated by the United States Government was put into places where it could be best expended, but that I thought there would be a great deal of hesitancy on the part of Congress to make a division of the money and have part of it go to universities that had a State Agricultural College under them and part of it go to State Universities that did not have an Agricultural College under them. I thought the Congress would probably be very loath to divert any money that was going directly to agricultural colleges into the use of many of the state universities, even though there might be quite a strong reason for it by reason of state universities being better equipped in some instances to carry on experimentations and investigations that it is proposed to carry on under the money that Congress appropriates.

February 10, 1928

I think it has already been announced that I appointed Colonel Latrobe to be my Aide. He is a Baltimore man, who, as I understand, went down to Cuba and helped the Cubans in their contest with Spain before we went into the war and after that was in the service. I ran across him when I was out to South Dakota. Some of you probably remember seeing the detachment of cavalry go through Rapid City that he was taking from Fort D. A. Russell near Cheyenne to Fort Meade. I liked his appearance so much that I asked him to come on to Washington, and when he came here Colonel Winship seemed to be the most available man to go to the Philippines with Colonel Stimson, and so I am making that change.

[*Colonel Osmun Latrobe was commander of the Fourth Cavalry at Fort Meade. Colonel Blanton Winship became legal adviser to Henry L. Stimson, Governor General of the Philippines. See "Vexations of Imperial Power."*]

February 28, 1928

I understand that the Senate Committee is starting in to draft a flood control bill. I have talked with various members of the House and the Senate that are interested in this legislation with a view to seeing if I could not compose the differences that exist in the House and the Senate and some differences between what I would like to have and the desires of some members of the House and the Senate. My position, as I suggested the other day, was fully set out in my message, wherein I stated that I thought the property that was to be benefited ought to bear some portion of the expense. Now, it has been suggested to me that there are some localities that are unable to bear any expense, others that can bear some of it, others perhaps that could bear all of the proposal which I made of 20 per cent, which was 20 per cent of 180-odd million dollars, not of the 290-odd, because there was 110 million dollars of the Jadwin plan that applied especially to navigation and only 180-odd million that was specifically for flood relief. That, as I stated, would make the 20 per cent some $35,000,000, which would be payable over a term of years, probably running as high as 10 years in some localities, and make the contribution about $3,500,000 a year, which reduced to an acreage charge was about 3 cents per acre, per year, which made me think that it wouldn't be an onerous burden. But no survey has ever been made to determine just what the economic conditions are and just what communities can bear the burden and what communities can not. So I suggested to the three senior Senators from Arkansas, Mississippi and Louisiana, that that question might be determined by the appointment of a Commission that would make an economic survey and determine what each community could contribute, how it could be contributed, and how their costs would be financed—perhaps by the Treasury taking their bonds or something of that kind, and that is a proposal that I would like to see worked out. I don't know but there was some confusion the other day in my not making my statement entirely clear. Of course, the matter of $35,000,000 spread over 10 years is rather a negligible amount, so far as the United States Treasury is concerned, so that I said that if this Mississippi flood problem was the only thing that was to be considered that I wouldn't make very much argument about the contribution down there. It isn't the only thing that is to be considered, because there are now proposals for the United States Government to build levees and afford flood protection for practically all the rivers in the United States, which would be a very great cost, and for that reason I was quite anxious to maintain the principle of local contributions in the lower Mississippi. Some of the bills that have been drawn up have a section providing that the bearing of the entire cost by the United

States Government is not to be considered as a precedent. I suggested to one man that was in that if it could be done in this case anyone else that wanted flood control could also bring in a bill and put that clause in his bill that it was not to be considered as a precedent. It seems to me that the decision about that would be this—that this is something that the United States Government ought to do. If it was a good thing to do, to bear all the cost would be a precedent, and if it wasn't a good thing for the Government to do then it ought not to be done. But, as I stated before, I think the people interested are getting closer and closer together and will undoubtedly reach some conclusion that is fair. I wouldn't want the statement to go out too strongly that I had changed my position. The only addition that I have made to my position was the suggestion that this question might be determined by a commission that would go into the details and so take care of any communities that were not able to contribute. But of course the question comes in here of whether the land isn't already burdened with bonds and mortgages and obligations, that is all that it can bear, and if it is so burdened 3 cents an acre, which would in the course of years run into $35,000,000, might in some instances be more of a burden, it was argued to me, than could be borne. There is another angle to this—that if the United States Government is to pay all the costs the demands will be greatly enlarged. I should expect that under any commission that might be set up or any agency that might be used for the prosecution of this work, that it would be done in a business way. But it is very easy to get into something different and start out on the prosecution of a plan that as it progressed would reveal itself as one which was so ambitious that it might break down. There will be enlarged demands if the United States Government is to pay the cost. Some railroad men came in to see me yesterday that said that the cost to certain railroads down there, by putting these plans into operation, they estimated at about $70,000,000, and they wanted whoever was to bear the cost to reimburse them for such expenditures as they were required to make minus any benefits that might accrue to them. Of course, if their roads were put in a position where they will not suffer from floods, that would be a distinct benefit to them and might be set off against some of the cost. They have had flood charges for repairs and damages of an ascertainable amount running over a series of years, and if they were to be entirely relieved of those of course that would be a credit to be offset against the expense of putting them in a position where they wouldn't suffer any more from floods. I merely mention that as an example of one of the things that will constantly come up as the plans progress. I think it would be the best plan, so far as I can judge, to proceed to do this work in accordance with the present law;

that is, through the War Department, the Chief of the Bureau of Engineers, and the Mississippi Flood Commission. That is merely a matter of opinion. If someone can present a better method of carrying on the work, I should be glad to adopt that. But this method has worked out very well in the construction of levees and dikes. The work has been done in a businesslike way. I think I have suggested before that there is only one of the standard levees that gave way and all of the rest held during the last great flood. The plan of having a commission, of course, undertake to determine damages would not hold up the work at all. The work could go right on and the commission report to the next Congress, and on that report the next Congress would then legislate.

PRESS: How would that commission be selected?

PRESIDENT: Ordinarily it would be selected by the President and approved by the Senate.

April 10, 1928

The flood control legislation is getting into a very unfortunate situation. I was afraid it would, when it became apparent that there was great reluctance on the part of Congress to have any local contribution. Of course, as soon as that policy is adopted, then it becomes a bestowal of favors on certain localities and naturally if one locality is to be favored, all the other localities in the United States think that they ought to come in under the same plan and have their floods taken care of. The bill, of course, is an entire reversal of the policy that has been pursued up to the present time, which was that of helping the locality. This undertakes to have the United States go in and assume the entire burden. It is so drawn that the rule of damages is a new one. It seems to confer property on people and then in another part of the bill proposes to pay them for the property that has been conferred in the way of damages. There is grave danger too that it would leave the United States to be responsible for flood damage that might be hereafter incurred, if any levees should break, or the plan is inadequate, or anything of that kind, which would be a very serious situation, and the cost has mounted from around $300,000,000 to about $1,500,000,000.

PRESS: That was the Jones bill?

PRESIDENT: That is the bill as it has come out of the Committee in the House, the Jones bill with the House amendments. It leaves the United States Government also to pay all the major costs of maintenance, which it has never done before. It almost seems to me as though the protection of the people and the property in the lower Mississippi that need protection has been somewhat lost sight of and it has become a scramble to take care of the railroads and the banks and the individuals that may have invested in levee bonds, and the great lumber concerns that own many thousands of acres in that locality, with wonderful prospects for the contractors. Taking the management and the control and the letting of contracts out of the hands of the Board of Engineers, where it has been, and putting it into the hands of a new body that are to hold office forever would be, if not unresponsible, certainly unresponsive to anybody or anything. It seems to me we might have a flood control bill within reasonable limits that would take care of the situation adequately without the expectation of it costing five times as much as it ought to cost.

April 17, 1928

I have talked with some of the leaders of the House relative to the flood control bill. They are working on it with the interested parties. Of course, the plan as proposed by General [Edgar] Jadwin [Chief of Army Engineers] had $110,000,000 in it for navigation of the Mississippi. The other $190,000,000 was for flood control. The bill that passed the Senate is thought would run as high as $1,500,000,000. Now, taking the $110,000,000 out, it leaves $1,400,000,000. So that bill boosts flood control from less than $200,000,000 to nearly $1,400,000,-000, which is obviously a very large boost. That seems to be due in large part to the attitude of those that are interested in the lumber companies. That accounts for a good deal of the activity about here. And while I don't want to take any property that belongs to the lumber companies, or anybody else's—couldn't if I wanted to under the Constitution—without giving them just compensation for it, I don't think that in passing a bill of this kind the opportunity should be seized on to put the Government in a position where it would have to endow them with very large damages. That is the difficulty about the bill; the main difficulty about it. I don't know of any proposal that has been made, certainly since I have been President, and I doubt if any was ever made, of such an extortionate nature as that provided for in the bill passed by the Senate. I don't think the Senate understood it, what its implications were, or what is behind it. It went through there practically without discussion. It had been brought out of Committee very recently. I doubt if the Committee understood what the implications were. If the administration was attempting to boost a $200,000,000 proposition up to $1,400,000,000, I think there would be a wide discussion in the press and a good deal of criticism. I should think it would be a fruitful source of exploration for anybody that had the opportunity to look into it, investigate it, undertake to find out what is behind it, and what the motives are that are supporting it.

April 24, 1928

Some of the amendments which the House has incorporated in the flood bill improve the bill. The main feature of it is in relation to the method of adopting plans and letting the contracts. That I think is in fairly good shape. The other main feature is in relation to the payment of damages and securing rights of way. That has not yet been put into acceptable shape. I very much hope that it will be done. It is in that particular that the Government will stand a chance of having to pay a very great sum in damages, which I do not think are necessary. What I desire to have done is for the localities to furnish the rights of way on which the levees are to be built. That would be little or no expense to them and probably be a very considerable expense to the United States Government. I am willing that the United States Government should assume responsibility for damages that might accrue by reason of the water that would go down between the new levees in the spillways, and of course expect the Government to pay the expenses of the erection of the levees. That is, I want the United States Government to pay any damages that may accrue by reason of its taking any constitutional rights that the owners of property in that locality now have. I don't want to have it endowed with new rights in one section of the bill and then have the Government pay them for the rights in another section which we have just legislated upon them. I haven't any expectation of sending any special message to Congress dealing with flood control. Something might occur that would seem to make that desirable, but I don't know of anything now.

April 27, 1928

I haven't sent any memorandum to Senator [Wesley] Jones [Rep., Wash.] on the flood bill. General Jadwin and I made some notes on it and I think that the General was going to confer with the Senator relative to the notes which we made. As I said the other day, except for the administrative feature, the bill as it passed the House is no improvement over the bill that passed the Senate, and so far as the expense is concerned it is a more expensive measure. I have noted a tendency on the part of the dispatches that go out from Washington now to refer to this as the $325,000,000 Jones flood control bill. That is a very extreme euphemism. The bill as it is drawn would cost nearer $1,500,000,000 than $325,000,000, and all for the purpose of doing what the best engineering advice I can get indicates could be done for about $300,000,000.

I don't know whether the conferees can agree on a bill which I can approve or not. I hope they can. I want to have a reasonable flood control bill. I don't see any reason why one shouldn't be passed by the Congress and laid before me for my approval. I have very little difficulty with the people that live down in the region that is to be benefited. The main difficulty seems to come from those that do not live in the region, but who own property down there which they wish to sell to the Government. There are a good many features about the bill as it passed the House that I regard as very objectionable. I have tried to indicate those to Senator Jones with the hope that they may be amended.

May 1, 1928

I don't know of any particular analysis that General Jadwin has made of the flood control bill that went through the House. He and I looked over the bill together and made some marks on it, indicating some changes that we should like to have made in it. I presume that is the origin of any report that may have been made that he made an analysis. I don't know of anything that he has made relative to it that could be published. Anyone could take the bill and make an analysis of it. The financial features of it haven't been improved. Every time that changes have been made it has been to make the financial features more unacceptable. As it went through the House it had the Sacramento River, I think it is, hitched on to the end of it. I haven't much of any information about the Sacramento River. I know that the Government is helping out there. If it is a meritorious project, it ought to go through on its own steam, and not be hitched on to something else. That is the main trouble with this bill—too many interests, too many people want to ride on it, until it became loaded up with a great many objectionable features.

May 4, 1928

The report, I think of the conference committee on the flood bill, is in today's issue of the Congressional Record. It doesn't indicate that much has been done to meet my views. I expected to have an opportunity to confer with some members of the committee, but apparently they hurried the conference to an end and filed their report without giving me any opportunity to see what they were doing or to indicate whether their actions would meet with my approval. I notice that the press dispatches still refer to this as the $325,000,000 bill. I don't know why they do that.

I have recommended, I think in all my messages, that the building of the dam at Boulder Canyon be undertaken. I very much hope that some solution may be found at the present session of the Congress. I want the dam built for the purpose of flood control and for the purpose of giving Southern California a better domestic water supply. Incident to that would be some power development. I do not think that ought to stand in the way of a possible solution. A good deal of the power I judge would be used to pump the water over the hill to Southern California and some method ought to be devised that will meet the objections of those that do not wish the United States Government to go into the power business. This question has been before the House and Senate for a number of years. It has had mature consideration by the Department of Interior and they have provided a reasonable solution for it which I hope will be adopted.

May 8, 1928

I talked yesterday with the conferees and some others relative to the flood bill. I have been able to get that deflated some, so that I think it is a good deal better than it was when they started to work on it. It has some saving clauses in it. It isn't just such a bill as I would like, but the form in which I understand the conference is proposing to recommend its passage perhaps is as good as can be secured. The main difficulty has been over a possible payment of damages which is a new element in flood control, one that hasn't had to be met in any other efforts that have been made to control the waters of the Mississippi and its tributaries. But I think that has been put in very much better shape than it was at the outset.

May 15, 1928

I have the flood control bill here on my desk and I expect to approve it today.

Superior, Wis., July 3, 1928

I have no definite engagement to meet Mr. Hoover. I have no information of any kind or description as to whether he is coming here. I should assume, though, that if he was coming he would say something to me about it.

[*Herbert Hoover had just been nominated as the Republican candidate for President.*]

July 31, 1928

I haven't any plan for any particular activity during the campaign. I have been active during the interval that has accrued between the 2nd day of August, 1923, to the present time undertaking to so conduct the affairs of the Government that the record made by my party might commend itself to the voters of the nation. I am continuing in that hope and the conduct of the office at the present time.

December 4, 1928

This is perhaps as good a time as any to comment on what I think has grown into an abuse. Congress makes holidays and every time there is a holiday it is the practice for one department to telephone over to another department and say we are going to have an extra holiday in this department and what is your department going to do about it. Of course, the message is taken to the head of the department and we have usually been put into the position that it has been expected that in addition to the holiday that is furnished by law the President would furnish one or two more. If it comes on Saturday, they want a holiday on Friday, and, of course they couldn't come back and travel on Sunday and so they want another holiday on Monday to get back on, and while I like all the employees of the Government to receive such holidays as can be given, if that practice is to continue I think it ought to be established by law and let Congress say by law when there is to be a holiday giving Government employees additional leave of absence. I haven't any plan as to what may be done at Christmas and New Year and Washington's birthday. I don't know whether Lincoln's birthday is a holiday. I think it isn't. Those are the only three that are to come up during my administration. But it really ought to be taken up and regulated by law, in order to prevent the President and the departments being subjected to pressure every time there is a holiday for additional leave of absence, because those are holidays that are fixed by law and everybody knows they are to come. There are times that an emergency arises. Some great event is to be celebrated or some catastrophe arises, so that the President is justified in having the departments closed. That would be the case in the death of the President or the Vice-President, but in the case of events that everybody knows will occur it ought either to be provided by law or not provided for at all.

February 5, 1929

We have been making studies from time to time both in the War Department and the Navy Department to see if something could not be done relative to the promotion problem. No very good plan has ever been presented to me. There was a plan presented that provided for buying people off, virtually hiring them to resign I think, under which some men would get as much as $16,000 or $18,000. That didn't seem to be practical to me. If some method can be worked out, I should be glad to see it done. But I haven't seen any plan up to the present time that seemed to be feasible.

5 · The Role of Congress

IN HIS PRESS CONFERENCES the cautious Coolidge avoided any impression that he alone conducted the government of the United States. To Congress belonged the glory, or at least a fair share of it. He was not above flattering Congress and claimed that his relations with it were better than those of many of his predecessors. The President maintained his diplomatic contacts with Capitol Hill through individual congressional pilgrimages to his office and through group breakfasts at the White House.

Coolidge considered his "office" correlative with Congress. Each had its equal duties. He would respect Congress and in return Congress was not to poach on presidential prerogatives. He sometimes found Congress trying, as when the Senate turned down his politically unwise nomination of Charles Beecher Warren as Attorney General, the first time since Andrew Johnson's administration that a nominee for the cabinet had been rejected. Among other things, he complained to the press conference about the congressional requirement that commissioners for the District of Columbia be citizens of the District. Congress often tried to raid the budget, that bastion of Coolidge's presidency; usually anticipating such attempts, the eagle-eyed Vermonter successfully repelled them.

On a major domestic issue of the 1920's, immigration, Coolidge did not take a stand against Congress. The restrictive legislation of 1924 stopped a flood of immigration that had risen to approximately a million a year just before the outbreak of the World War. Included in the new national origins act, a thinly veiled excuse not merely to restrict immigration but to cut down the numbers of people from Southern and Eastern Europe, was an ill-tempered exclusion of Japanese. Had Congress limited the Japanese quota according to the formulas of national origin—which would have smoothed over what became a major diplomatic crisis—it would have allowed 109 Japanese to enter the country each year. Even if Coolidge had wanted to, he could not have stopped the demand for restriction. There is no reliable evidence that he tried. In any event, he signed the bill.

November 9, 1923

An inquiry also about the immigration law. I have no doubt that the incoming Congress will extend the law, which expires on June 30th next. Just what provisions will be adopted, of course, I can't tell. It is perfectly apparent I think, however, that we shall have very careful restriction of immigration.

November 13, 1923

An inquiry as to whether I shall deliver my message to Congress in person. I rather expect that I shall. For a great many years that was not the practice. I believe that Washington went up and delivered his message in person, and then after his administration it seems that practice fell into disuse clear up to the time that President Wilson came into office. Then he took up the ancient practice and it was continued for the most part by President Harding. I should be inclined to do what I thought the Congress liked about it. If they like to have the message delivered in person, well then I should want to try to do that. If they indicate that they very [much] preferred the message should be sent up in the way that was established between Washington and Lincoln, then very likely I should concur in their preference.

November 23, 1923

The Cabinet meeting was very short this morning, and about all that we took up was immigration questions. I am very glad you spoke to me about that because I was asked yesterday, or rather I inquired of a lawyer that was here, who told me that people came to America on boats with passports, and when they got the passports thought, of course, that gave them the right of entry. I said that was a matter that ought to be remedied if it were so. I inquired of the State Department this morning, and they say every individual that gets a passport signs a statement that he or she understands that it does not in any way entitle them to entrance into any port of our country. The passport is merely a statement by the State Department that, so far as the State Department is concerned, they have no objection to the entrance of that person. It doesn't have any jurisdiction over the Labor Department, nor, of course, over our immigration laws. They do sign, in every case where a passport is granted, a statement that they understand that, and know the significance of it. It is explained to them as carefully as it can be. But many times people come with passports that have been issued in South Africa, and so on, London or Paris, and it isn't possible for all of these different clients to keep in touch with each other and know just what the quota may be for any specific country at any specific time. So that some of the countries of Europe, who have nationals that are spread all over the world and come back to Europe with their passports, and sail from there to here, are subject to that condition without any blame attaching to the different consuls that issue the passports.

An inquiry as to whether aliens will be admitted at New York in excess of national quotas, and whether any arrangements have been made for such purpose. No general arrangements about it. A prominent lawyer came to see me yesterday about a boatload, I think, of some seven hundred that wanted to come in. Some are quite distressing cases. I took the matter up with the Labor Department and they tell me that in a case of that kind they try to take care of all cases of distress—those that you might call worthy cases; but when they are able-bodied men or people that don't appeal in any way to the sympathy or charitable instincts, why they have to be returned.

December 21, 1923

There is no action to be taken, so far as I know, with the Japanese Government on the immigration question. Whenever the question comes up of laws relative to immigration, it is quite natural that the different governments should be solicitous for the protection of the rights of their citizens, and it is not infrequent that they apply to the State Department to know about the conditions of the proposed legislation. There is nothing unusual in that.

PRESS: Would you permit a question about that subject, Mr. President? Have you or the Cabinet ever given any thought to translating the Gentlemen's Agreement into law?

PRESIDENT: No, I don't think so.

[*By the Gentlemen's Agreement of 1907-8, the Japanese government agreed not to allow laborers seeking to come to the continental United States to obtain visas.*]

January 4, 1924

I learned a great while ago that a proposal for legislation, or even the introduction of a bill that was not in accordance with sound policy wouldn't need any active opposition from the executive, in order to prevent its adoption. The legislatures with which I have had to deal

89

have usually been perfectly competent to take care of those questions themselves without outside interference. So that while there will be many bills introduced into the Congress that I shouldn't want to approve or to take any action about, or proposed amendments to legislation that is in and I wouldn't approve of, generally speaking I should not need to take action about that, because the Congress will look after it.

February 8, 1924

No official representations have been made to this country that I know of from Japan in relation to discussions looking towards a new Gentlemen's Agreement.

March 21, 1924

I have here a note of inquiry about legislation. It is always rather embarrassing for me to discuss legislation that is pending, about which there is a controversy in the Congress. As I have explained many times, I can't very well announce beforehand that I am going to veto a bill, or that I am going to sign it. I have to keep my mind open about those things until the proposal comes to me. Nobody knows what the bill may contain when it gets here, so that I have to wait and see. I have general policies about legislation which I have announced quite a good many times, and I think you won't make much of any mistake if you look and see what public announcements I have made about my policies, and until I announce otherwise you are probably warranted in supposing that is my attitude and mind.

April 4, 1924

I don't know as I can say there were any particular topics under discussion when the Senators were at breakfast this morning. I expressed to them a desire that they do what they could to expedite legislation. I received a report from Senator Smoot that they expected to be able to report the tax bill tomorrow or Monday. I think he said there was a suggestion that there be no session of the Senate tomorrow, in order to give the Finance Committee the entire day to consider the tax measure. The discussion didn't take up any particular bills or any particular topics. I wanted to find out what the prospect was of pushing legislation ahead, which everybody indicated they wanted to do and on which they thought the prospect was good. I don't know when I shall call in any more Senators or Representatives to break bread with me. I am liable to call them in any time. I am likewise liable not to call them in at all. I like to keep in touch, of course, with the members of the House and Senate. They are very busy men and unless I call them in in considerable numbers at one time, I don't have a chance to keep up that contact that I would like to keep. I can only see three or four or five men here in this office an hour, if they come in one at a time, usually for a period of about fifteen minutes, during only about three hours that I can devote to anything of that kind in the morning; so that unless I call them in in blocks, I don't have a chance to keep that intimate contact that otherwise I would like to have. Sometimes during the past season I have been able to do that Saturday afternoons on the *Mayflower,* but I have not been out on that for some time. Perhaps we can start up some trips on that in the near future.

[*Reed Smoot (Rep.) of Utah was elected to the Senate in 1903 and served continuously in that body until the advent of the New Deal. An arch conservative, Smoot was chairman of the G.O.P. National Committee from 1916 to 1920. The one piece of legislation usually associated with him is the Hawley-Smoot tariff of 1930, one of the most ill-advised acts of Congress during the last 60 years. It was adopted against the advice of over a thousand distinguished economists, bankers, and businessmen.*]

April 15, 1924

I don't think there is any comment that I can make in relation to the proposed legislation about the exclusion of Japanese and others, who are not entitled under our laws to take out naturalization papers and become citizens.

April 25, 1924

PRESS: May I ask if you can elaborate on what you have just said on the immigration bill?

PRESIDENT: I am attempting to see if there is any way that that question can be solved so as to satisfy those that want to have restriction and at the same time prevent giving any affront to the Japanese Government.

April 29, 1924

There isn't much of anything I can say about the immigration bill. That is before the Committee in Conference. They are undertaking to see if some arrangement cannot be made which will provide for exclusion and at the same time avoid wounding the sensibilities of a friendly nation. In that I am in entire sympathy. I think that statement covers quite a good deal. I don't know that I could add anything to it by undertaking to amplify it. There are two things, exclusion and the ordinary courtesy of conduct that ought to characterize all the actions of the Government of the United States of America.

May 6, 1924

There hasn't been any agreement reported to me on the immigration bill. Of course it needs to be kept in mind that we have exclusion now under the so-called Gentlemen's Agreement, so far as I know, and no one is suggesting that that be changed. That is what I mean when I say there is a general acceptance of the principle of exclusion.

May 24, 1924

I expect to pass on the Immigration Bill very soon. It has not yet come back from the Secretary of State and while I don't know what I shall do with it, it goes without saying that I shall sign it if I can. There are a good many things in this Bill. There are many things which are favorable to us and some things which I would have preferred not to have in it. But that is the case with almost every bill of any particular importance. . . . I don't think the State Department is taking any action in relation to the Immigration Bill with Japan. Nor would it be fair to suppose that Mr. Hughes has made anything like a personal issue of the immigration question. Of course the Secretary and myself are exactly in the same position about that. With my approval and with his approval, both he and I undertook to see if we could secure a satisfactory arrangement when the bill was being passed. We were not able to do this. We worked together on it and will work together on whatever there may be to do further about it. There is no reason for any suggestion that Mr. Hughes would resign, nor is there any reason for the suggestion that Mr. Mellon would resign, if either of them did not get exactly what they wanted from Congress; and I am not going to resign because I don't get what I want.

[*Secretary of State Charles Evans Hughes, former Supreme Court justice and Republican presidential nominee in 1916, was a holdover from the Harding cabinet. Andrew W. Mellon was Secretary of the Treasury. See "The Domestic Economy."*]

November 21, 1924

I don't expect to take any part in the organization of the House and Senate. I think that is a matter that the House and Senate particularly ought to decide for themselves. They can choose what person there is in the Senate they desire to follow very much better than I can tell them. They can choose such officers as they wish to have in the House to preside over them very much better than I can assist them in that matter. If it is a matter relating to legislation, why then of course I am a party in interest and one that has to act with them, and I am very glad to give my views on that. It seems to me that the Senators themselves can pick out the persons they desire to have for their leader and the other officers of the Senate, and the same is true in respect to the House. I am sure that there are a good many men in both parties capable of filling any position that there is there, and equally confident that anyone that the Senate and House wanted to choose for officers of their respective bodies would be persons entirely acceptable to me.

January 6, 1925

Here is a suggestion about a bill that has been introduced authorizing Cabinet members and other departmental heads to participate in debates on the floor of the House and Senate. I haven't any mature judgment about that. I should say it would depend mostly on whether the House and Senate wanted to have Cabinet members come on the floor, or department heads, and debate questions. It is a step, of course, toward the parliamentary form of government. That is a form of government that is well recognized and of course of great maturity on account of the policy of the English speaking people. Our own notion has been to keep somewhat separate the executive department and the legislative department. That can't be done in its entirety, but that is the policy that has been laid down in this country. There are a great many good points about it. Department heads and Cabinet members of course are constantly before the committees of the House and Senate, which gives them access to the members of the Congress and gives the Congress access to all the information that they have. Now, whether it would be expected that they would go on the floor and take positions in opposition to the reports of committees or not, I do not know. Many questions would come up, of course, in case the executive branch was of one party and Congress of another party, and there would be a very interesting situation. Whether, then, the Congress would want to invite the representatives of the opposition party to come on the floor, I can't tell. These are just offhand thoughts that come to me. It is an interesting subject, but I can't give an offhand opinion of it that is of any value. My attitude towards it is my general attitude toward all legislation. When a proposal of this kind is made it becomes the business of the committee to which it is referred to consider it and hear the evidence, and try to decide in accordance with the evidence and their own judgment about it. That is an opportunity that I don't have a chance to participate in much at this time. I am so constantly employed otherwise that I don't have a chance to call in people of various and divergent views and get the benefit of their information, so that I have to take a shot at these things somewhat on the wing. If the Congress wanted to do this, I don't see any reason why I should oppose it. On the other hand, if the Congress made up their mind that it was something in which they did not want to engage, I shouldn't have the slightest disposition to advocate it.

March 13, 1925

I have an inquiry here about Mr. Warren and his appointment as Attorney General. I chose him, as I have told you, after careful investigation and my own knowledge of him, and after an investigation made by the Department of Justice into that case that was tried in the Courts relative to the American Sugar Company and the beet sugar companies in Michigan; and it did not appear to us that there was anything there that constituted any blemish on his record. I thought that he was a man of high character, eminence at the bar, and great ability, and would make a fine Attorney General. He has given a great deal of time to public service and has been willing to accept this position at a good deal of personal sacrifice. The sacrifice he has already made would be represented by a very large sum. I thought that he had failed of confirmation by such a narrow margin, and the vote was taken at a time when it was not possible adequately to present to the Senate his qualifications. I think the judgment to take the vote at that time was correct. Those of you who know about the Senate know that a condition will develop where you can take a vote and then if someone gets up and says two words it may be two weeks before another vote may be taken. But a great deal could have been said about Mr. Warren as to his standing and as to the high opinion that the people of Michigan hold in relation to him, and it would have to be put on record, and so, on account of this sacrifice that he has made and he having been willing to accept the office because I sought him out and solicited him, I thought I ought to give him the benefit of another nomination, and so I have done that. Now, I do not know what the attitude of the Senate will be. They will have to determine that.

I have here an ingenious suggestion that shows perhaps the difficulty of living up to what the standards of some of the Senators seem to be in relation to appointees to public office. This suggestion is that I should ask the Senate to send me a list of a dozen men—ideal men. Now, I cannot find such men, but some Senators evidently think that there are some whom I ought to present for the office: "Irreproachable private character; proper legal standard; requisite executive ability; never in any way connected with any large corporate interest; never publicly discussed in a detrimental way."

Now, of course I have to appoint human beings to office. I want them to be honest and conscientious and desirous of performing public service, but I cannot find any men who quite come up to that standard and I doubt if there are any in existence. If I have to be held up to a standard as high as that, I shall not be able to make any appointments.

PRESS: Is the person who submitted those qualifications suggesting any names?

PRESIDENT: No. He says I ought to ask the Senate for a dozen men who could meet those requirements.

PRESS: Is he humorous?

PRESIDENT: No. It is a suggestion, so that I may put the Senate "in a hole," as they say. I suppose that is the meaning of it. Of course, that I do not care to engage in.

PRESS: Do you care to express any opinion as to whether Mr. Warren ought to have a chance of self-defense?

PRESIDENT: Well, I think that his qualifications ought to be presented to the Senate and go into the record, and that is one of the reasons why I have re-submitted his name. Telegrams have come in from people in Michigan, and I think that because of his character and eminence, it would be proper to have those go in the record.

I haven't thought much, if anything, about a recess appointment. I hope very much that the necessity for that will not arise. I cannot make any statement because I haven't reached any determination. I simply try to discharge my duties as President of the United States in a way that would seem to be best for the people. I haven't a private opinion about it. I presume there are a good many other good men who could be appointed, though I haven't been able to think of any-one that I could appoint who seemed to possess the qualifications as well as Mr. Warren does. There may be a good many others, and un-doubtedly there are. I do not know whether he would consent to a recess appointment. It is doubtful. I haven't considered that.

I think the Senate ought to realize that I have to have about me those in whom I have confidence; and unless they find a real blemish on a man, I do not think they ought to make partisan politics out of appointments to the Cabinet. I do not object to their criticizing any-thing I do or any nomination I may make—that is to be expected—but I do not think it ought to be made a partisan question as to whether the nomination should be rejected. Otherwise, I would be in position where I would not be able to function—I would not be able to fill up my Cabinet. I realize the responsibility that the Senate has. I want to discharge my responsibility with such candor as I can, and I think probably the Senate will do the same.

[*Charles Beecher Warren was selected by Coolidge to succeed Har-lan F. Stone as Attorney General after Stone had been appointed to the Supreme Court. Warren, a prominent Michigan Republican and chairman of the Platform Committee at the 1924 G.O.P. National Convention, was accused of having violated the antitrust laws as President and Counsel of the Michigan Sugar Company. In a close Senate vote Warren was rejected by a coalition of Republican Pro-gressives and Democrats. Had Vice-President Dawes been awake and present at the time of the vote instead of napping at his hotel, he could have turned the tide in Warren's favor. When Coolidge, indignant and insistent, again submitted Warren's nomination, the Senate re-jected it by a substantially greater majority.*]

March 17, 1925

I haven't reached any final decision about the Attorney General. I have several inquiries here. Senator Curtis and Senator Robinson are coming down as a committee to wait on the President—I suppose to inquire whether there is any more business to submit to the Senate, and if not, what arrangements can be made for adjournment. I want to talk with them about this situation. I do not think, from my talks with Mr. Warren, I am convinced that he does not desire to take a recess appointment. He would take one if I insisted on it, but that is not his desire. [Stenographer's note: At this point there was quite noticeable commotion.]

Well, now, if the members of the conference do not care to stay and hear what I have to say, I do not know whether I want to continue the conference. That is hardly courteous to the President, to come in and immediately when I make a statement, rush out. [Stenographer's note: A member of the conference stated to the President that he did not think any discourtesy was intended, and the President continued.]

I think it is due to me when I make a statement that they [the members of the conference] wait to see what the statement is before they rush out. I am not imputing anything. I am conscious of the great courtesy of the members of the conference to me always. So I say no final decision has been made. I want to confer with the two Senators who are coming down and see what plans can be worked out. I do not think Mr. Warren wants to take a recess appointment. Perhaps he would take one if I—I do not know just how to phrase it—insisted that he perform this additional public service. He has already responded very generously to our request. I do not know what to do about trying to get another appointee. I hesitate a good deal to subject anyone I might appoint to any such ordeal as confronted Mr. Warren. I do not know whether I can get other men who are willing to put themselves to such a hazard or not. I think perhaps I can, but, nevertheless, if they are willing to do it I hesitate to subject them to anything of this kind. So I will have to talk with the two Senators and see what I can find out about the situation.

[*Coolidge offered Warren a recess appointment, which he declined. Charles E. Curtis was a veteran Republican wheelhorse from Kansas. He was appointed to the Senate in 1907 to fill the unexpired term of J. R. Burton and subsequently was elected in his own right. He was Herbert Hoover's running mate in 1928 and was elected Vice-President. Joseph Robinson, Democrat from Arkansas, entered the Senate in 1913. He was Alfred Smith's running mate in the presidential election of 1928. Later, he became a stalwart supporter of Franklin D. Roosevelt. Robinson was a conservative Democrat but a strong party man.*]

February 26, 1926

I was especially gratified at the way the [revenue] bill went through Congress. I think the comment has already been made, but perhaps it won't do any harm if I reiterate that up to date this has been the most efficient Congress that we have had for a great many years. It has made its decisions, transacted its business and reached conclusions about the questions before it. I am very much pleased with the co-operation I have received from them. They have considerably more work to do. I mentioned three or four things the other day. Of course if anyone wants a complete list of things that I think Congress ought to do, they will find that by referring to the message I sent to Congress on the 1st of December, and what Congress wants to do for the remainder of the session of course is very largely for them to determine. I am willing to advise and cooperate and help in any way I can, but the Congress after all is the legislative body. It is moving so well and so efficiently that I don't think I can help it very much. I have my own idea about the desirability of letting Congress make its own decisions, so far as it can. There is a certain amount of help they can derive from the Executive which I try to extend. But the responsibility for legislation is theirs. They come in contact with a great many sources of information merely as a result of their large number that do not come to a single executive. Many questions have to be determined as a result of rather long and protracted hearings, which of course the Executive doesn't have a chance to participate in, and for that reason the Congress ought to be left with a pretty free hand to make its own determinations and reach its own decisions.

[*According to the 1926 revenue law, inspired by multimillionaire Treasury Secretary Mellon, taxes in general were lowered, though not evenly so. The most wealthy segment of the population was most benefited. The gift tax of the 1924 revenue act was repealed outright; surtaxes were reduced from 40% to a 20% maximum; estate taxes were slashed in half.*]

March 5, 1926

I don't think I can make any suggestion about the achievements of the administration during the past year, for the reason that I think perhaps it would be more appropriate for somebody else to dwell on that than it would be for myself. I would like to reiterate though that I have been exceedingly pleased with the cooperation I have had from the present Congress, and I think the country is reflecting the satisfaction that it has had with the businesslike way in which they have transacted the governmental affairs.

April 9, 1926

Here is an inquiry about the Brookhart election case. Of course the Constitution makes the Senate the sole judge of the election and qualification of its own membership and doesn't put any burden of the determination of that question on the Executive, and so I haven't any information about it that warrants my expressing any opinion on the intricate legal questions that I understand are involved in this problem. It is a question of what votes have been cast and what votes ought to be counted. A great many intricate and technical questions are involved and not having any information on which to base a judgment, I haven't formed any judgment, haven't expressed any, don't expect to make any investigation of the question or express any judgment in relation to it. You want to make that perfectly plain about what I have done and what I expect to do: I haven't made any investigation of the questions involved, formed any opinion of them, expressed or expect to express any opinion in relation to it.

[*Political opponents of Smith Wildman Brookhart, a Progressive Republican of Iowa, believed his middle name fitted him perfectly. Brookhart was a member of the small group of Middle Western radicals known as the "Sons of the Wild Jackass." Coolidge clearly looked on him and other Progressives with disfavor. In the senatorial election of November 4, 1924, Brookhart was certified by the Executive Council of the State of Iowa as duly elected, but the decision was challenged by his Democratic opponent Daniel Steck. The matter was given over to the Senate committee on privileges and elections, which finally voted on April 12, 1926, to seat Steck. During the controversy Coolidge declared his neutrality, holding that it was the Senate's responsibility to decide. However, the fact that Senator William Butler, Chairman of the Republican National Committee, had publicly announced for Steck was widely believed to be an indication of the President's wishes. Senate Progressives were furious. Brookhart immediately challenged Senator A. B. Cummins, a Coolidge supporter, in the Iowa G.O.P. senatorial primary of June 7, 1926, and defeated him by 71,527 votes. Brookhart was easily re-elected to the Senate on November 2, 1926.*]

July 6, 1926

I would like to say also that I am very much gratified with the work that the Congress did. There was a very large amount of constructive legislation. The principal thing that will affect the country is the reduction of taxation. I wasn't able to do a great lot with the reduction of expenditures, but we did keep expenditures down fairly well. There was no bill of general importance that passed that I did not approve. There were three or four small things. I sent up a couple of veto messages of personal and local significance and there were three or four bills that I decided not to sign. One of them I hadn't been able to make up my mind about it. That is the bill relative to taxation of lands in Oregon and Washington. That didn't come in until just as I was about to leave the office to go to lunch and from lunch to the Capitol, so I didn't have a chance to investigate it. I am investigating it now to see whether I ought to approve it or leave it disapproved. The tax measure I would say was the most important piece of legislation. The approval of the World Court and the manifest desire to place that on a basis where its independence would be made more secure than it is now, leaving the other nations to approve that policy, is a matter of importance in international relations. I think that there wasn't much of anything in the way of treaties. The Lausanne treaty and the treaty relative to the sale of arms and the use of gas didn't come up for final consideration. The Railroad Labor Bill will we hope develop into a very important policy, because of the significance of it of leaving the management of the railroads and the employees to agree among themselves with the very manifest disposition of a new desire on their part to harmonize difficulties that may arise and adjust them without the interference of the Government. And of course there is the building law which really represented a new policy of making a lump sum appropriation and leaving the administration of it and the disposition of it to the Secretary of the Treasury. I also believe the Postmaster General comes in on things that are of interest to the Post Office Department. Then the aviation bill was very important, which also is the adoption of a new policy of administration. With the great amount of discussion that had been going on through the summer months in relation to the aviation situation, the present bill is in a very wonderful way, I think, almost in entire harmony with the recommendations made by the Navy Air Board, a considerable step in advance. There are some things that remain to be done. We passed a bill that had been agreed upon in the fall as a result of conferences between the Secretary of Agriculture and the Cooperative Farm Associations that is of considerable importance for the betterment of the cooperative farm movement in the country. There are some things that have been left undone. Muscle Shoals hasn't been finally determined. I spoke of the two treaties. Coal legislation hasn't been finally passed upon. And legislation for the consolidation of railroads. Another matter of importance which awaits future action is legislation relative to the licensing of radio plants. I think those are the principal features of this Congress. But the fact remains that no legislation of general import was passed that didn't have my approval and in all the main features that I desired to have the Congress act upon I secured favorable action. I don't want to make the personal pronoun there too large. I happened to express it in that way. I think some of the success of the present Congress was due to the fact that they assumed very largely their own responsibility and undertook to function as an independent legislative body without too much interference on the part of the Executive or too much subservience to the wishes of the Executive. That is I mean, trying to determine questions on their merits. As a result of that policy there was very little of partisanship that was shown in the decision of any large questions. There is another item that I left out, which of course is of tremendous importance, and that is the settlement of our foreign debts. I would place that as one of the major accomplishments of the last Congress. I didn't make any memo, and I presume that after you are away several others will occur to me of important achievements. You have my consent to put those in, if any of you think of them.

[*In 1921 Secretary of War John W. Weeks asked for bids for the leasing of Muscle Shoals. Henry Ford submitted a bid and both the Senate and the House during the next two years approved bills to dispose of the Tennessee properties to the Michigan industrialist. But the bills, both amended, could not be reconciled by a Senate-House conference committee. In January, 1926 Senator George W. Norris introduced a resolution in the Senate for operation of Dam No. 2 at Muscle Shoals, for building other dams on the Tennessee River and its tributaries, and for establishment of a Federal Power Corporation. No action was taken. In December, 1927 Norris proposed another resolution providing for completion of Dam No. 2 at Muscle Shoals and a steam plant at Nitrate Plant No. 2. The Senate and House passed the resolution, but the bill received Coolidge's pocket veto in June, 1928.*

For Coolidge's more extensive comments on the World Court and the Lausanne Treaty, see "The Old World and the New."]

July 9, 1926

I think I will reiterate that I was especially pleased with the work that the Congress did and because I didn't want to take all the glory of it I hope that won't be misunderstood. I thought it was especially to the credit of the Congress that they had functioned as a legislative body in accordance with recommendations that I had made in my [message] without being constantly forced into some position by action on my part. I think Senator Curtis is entitled to great credit for his management in the Senate. It is a difficult position that he had. He possesses great tact and great experience, and has a wide knowledge of parliamentary law. I depended upon him when I was President of the Senate to advise with me about intricate questions of parliamentary law and found him very scholarly in that regard. And in the House the Speaker, Mr. Longworth, was equally successful—and Floor Leader Colonel Tilson. I saw more of Colonel Tilson than I did of the Speaker. That was because Colonel Tilson was directly in charge of things on the floor, though he always acted with the advice and concurrence of the Speaker, but it happened that I conferred with him oftener than I did with the Speaker on account of that arrangement that they had. I don't see how either body could have been conducted during the session better than they were, and it is very difficult to see how they could have produced more constructive legislation and spent less time in useless debate than was spent in the last session. I don't recall a time when there was greater harmony between the Executive Branch of the Government and the Legislative Branch than there has been

100

since I have been President. I have had the support of Congress in all major things that I have been interested in and some things that are not decided yet, but those that have been decided have almost all been decided in accordance with my recommendations.

[*Nicholas Longworth of Ohio entered Congress in 1903. He was married to Theodore Roosevelt's daughter, Alice, who made the often quoted remark that Coolidge looked as if he "had been weaned on a pickle." Colonel John Q. Tilson of New Haven, Conn. had been a Second Lieutenant in the Spanish-American War and a Lieutenant Colonel in the Mexican border campaign of 1916. He was first elected to Congress in 1909.*]

January 29, 1929

Mr. Sanders has compiled a report showing that during 1928 I made about 20 addresses and Messages to the Congress. I think that is 2 more than 1927, isn't it, Mr. Sanders?

MR. SANDERS: About the same.

PRESIDENT: It is too many, but it indicates something of the pressure that the President is under constantly to make efforts of that kind.

PRESS: Do you mind giving us an indication of how many invitations you have refused?

PRESIDENT: I wouldn't have any idea about that. A very great many.

6 · Frugal Government

IF CALVIN COOLIDGE prided himself on one single aspect of his execution of the presidency, it was his policy of fiscal economy. "I favor the policy of economy," he declared, "not because I wish to save money, but because I wish to save people." Coolidge balanced the budget and obtained a surplus. As day after day the President sat in his White House office, feet on the desk and cigar in mouth, looking over piles of reports, he read fiscal papers with an especially sharp eye. He considered government economy in terms of personal economy—a government debt was analogous to a private debt. In Coolidge's day there was none of the intricate calculation that would later grace government account-keeping, whereby the government debt became subject to management and in fact became a positive good, indeed a vital necessity for the nation's economic well-being. To Coolidge the debt was an unadulterated debit, an evil, something to be rid of as soon as possible. Retiring the debt, he said, was "the predominant necessity of the country." By economizing in government he could accumulate a surplus, throw it into the sinking fund, perhaps cut taxes. The President produced one of his most characteristic, if banal, epigrams in this regard: "Economy," he announced in his inaugural address, "is idealism in its most practical form."

January 27, 1925

I haven't any specific plan for the reduction of personnel in the clerical forces of the District of Columbia. I think in the last four years we have reduced personnel something like 100,000. Of course there is quite a large personnel now employed in the Adjutant General's Department on the work growing out of the law for the adjusted compensation or the bonus bill. As that work closes up a good many clerks there can probably be dispensed with. Some of them have been transferred to other places. And I wasn't referring last night particularly to the District of Columbia, nor was my suggestion last night one that was new. In practically every address I have made to the business organization of the Government I have suggested that the cost of personnel was one of the very largest items. A great many people came in, as you know, during the war—in the employment of the Government—and it is with a good deal of difficulty that they are discharged. It is a matter we don't like to do, but for that reason it is necessary for me constantly to call it to the attention of the heads of the departments and the managers of the business organization, so that they may make constant and careful surveys to see what is necessary in that respect.

PRESS: Mr. President, has any plan of dismissals been worked out yet to carry out the scheme?

PRESIDENT: No, that is for every department to work out itself.

PRESS: Have you any information from the heads of departments as to what plan would be the most feasible?

PRESIDENT: No. As I say, it is a general suggestion of what has to be met and an effort that the heads of the departments have to be constantly engaged in, otherwise the departments will be loaded up with a great many more people than is necessary for the conduct of its business. It seems to me that the Budget Bureau cut the appropriation for the White House, so that it would be expected that we might dispense with the services of one or two people there. That is the only specific instance that I have in mind. This, of course, didn't refer to the City of Washington particularly. It referred to personnel all over the United States.

PRESS: Mr. President, is it the intention that immediate action be taken by the departments to list the names of certain employees who are to be taken off the roll?

PRESIDENT: Well, I want constant effort in that direction, a constant checking up by the department to see whether they have any more employees than is necessary to carry on the work of the department. Whenever they find that is the case, well, they can drop them off. As I said at the outset, I think we have dropped off about 100,000, and I don't know, it may be more than that, in the last four years.

February 26, 1926

I don't think any further tax reduction will come for some time. Certainly not next year. And as I have indicated about 1927, I think we shall have to look very carefully for 1927 and 1928 to come within the present amount of revenue in making our appropriations. Ultimately we should of course have further tax reduction, as the debt is reduced, as the business of the country expands and revenue increases and expenses decrease. But there is the natural growth of business. I don't know what bills there are pending that call for additional expenditures. I think I had them checked up one time last year and found there were proposals seriously made and actively pressed that would have called for expenditures yearly of about $3,500,000,000 in addition to that which we already have, practically a doubling of the expenditures of the nation.

March 5, 1926

I saw a newspaper report that seemed to indicate that someone in the Treasury had undertaken to suggest that the statement I made about the coming deficiency wasn't correct. My statement was correct, and I think a careful reading of what the Treasury was said to have given out would have revealed that there was no conflict between what I said and what the Treasury said. I don't expect any deficiency for the present year. The indications now are, unless there are additional appropriations that do not now appear to be, that we should finish this year, the 30th of next June, with a small surplus. But for the year after that the indications are that there will be a deficit. I have suggested several times that if the Congress made a larger reduction in the tax bill than I thought was desirable, that I should expect them to take care of it by refraining from making appropriations that would cause a deficit. That is very important in relation to the business situation of the country. If Congress goes ahead and appropriates more money than there is in the Treasury, and makes it necessary to put in a bill increasing taxes, it won't encourage the business of the country. If Congress goes along as it is doing now, without increasing appropriations, I think the outlook for business would be very much more encouraging, and in that respect I want to commend the Congress for the prudent way in which it is making its appropriations. It is following the budget recommendations almost entirely. I don't think any bills that are coming along have had the recommendations that were made in the budget materially increased. There may be some trifling increases in some and some reductions in others, but the general result is just about what the budget recommended.

PRESS: If the Congress keeps within the budget recommendations next year, will there be a deficit?

PRESIDENT: No, because we should make the budget recommendations next year so that the budget will balance, of course. But I am talking now of the expenditures that would be required under the present budget and those that would naturally be expected under the budget of next year. It means that we shall have to prune somewhat.

March 30, 1926

I had a short conference with Colonel Tilson this morning in relation to legislation. I have already expressed several times to the conference my appreciation of the very fine work that the present Congress is doing. That work is apparently continuing. What I am especially solicitous about is the financial and economic condition of the Government. I indicated at the time of the consideration of the tax bill that the matter of what taxes should be raised was especially a matter that the Congress had under its jurisdiction and also indicated, and I want to stress that now, that after the Congress had passed a bill raising a certain amount of money, why of course it is obligatory on Congress not to encourage expenditures in excess of the money it has provided for raising by taxation. I think that is a very important consideration. I am not undertaking to shift the responsibility about that. Of course I am responsible for that as well as Congress, but I am attempting to emphasize it on all proper occasions. It is true that the Congress made a larger cut in taxes than I wanted to have made, because I knew that there would be great pressure for incurring some additional expenditures. I thought they ought to think carefully about it when they were passing the tax bill. I have no doubt they did. And having made the larger cut in taxation, I suppose they are prepared to resist the applications for increasing expenditures, especially in consideration of expenditures that call for permanent appropriations. We can make a capital expenditure for the erection of a building or something of that kind, and when that expenditure is made it is over with. But expenditures that call for increases that go on indefinitely, that is from year to year and which are increases of the annual expenditures of the Government, come in for different consideration and different treatment. It is in that direction especially that I want to avoid increases, so far as we can. Of course we have to take care of those people that are employed by the Government and those expenditures already provided for by law, but I want to avoid increases that are permanent so far as we can and it was in that direction especially that I was conferring with Colonel Tilson.

April 27, 1926

The budget is in this situation—the finances of the country. We shall come out at the end of this year with, nobody knows just how much, but there will be a comfortable margin. The figures for next year indicate a deficit at this time of $21,000,000, and any legislation that is passed that contemplates an expenditure of money in the next year's budget will have to take that into consideration. We can finance the requirements of this year all right. Continuing appropriations would be difficult to finance from the present outlook, on account of that situation. Of course if we should have a recession in business, so that our revenues should decrease, why the deficit would be increased.

June 1, 1926

It is expected, as I have said in the conference a number of times, that we can come through this year with a surplus. Nobody can tell what it will be because we don't know in the first place how much will be collected and in the second place because we don't know how much will be expended, so that nobody knows whether there will be a saving of between $22,000,000 and $30,000,000. There is not a great deal of difficulty in seeing what is coming into the Treasury, but there isn't any source from which you men of the press or anyone else can very accurately gauge what is going to be required to be paid out. So that all forecasts are more or less estimates. Our trouble is not with the present year, as I have said. Our difficulty, if it arises, is going to be with the coming year, and it is for that reason that we can make appropriations during this year that will be taken care of now and not continued along, but an appropriation that calls for continuing payments in the years to come, why those might be very troublesome. The condition of the Treasury, which now is being supplied so largely from income taxes, is very greatly dependent upon the general condition of business throughout the country. If the volume of business goes on increasing, why the condition of the Treasury will be easy to manage, but if we should get a recession in business, if profits were small and therefore income taxes greatly cut down, or our foreign trade diminishes so that our income from the tariff and customs diminish, it will be very easy to run into a deficit.

September 7, 1926

Not much change is being made in the personnel of the Government. In the Post Office, where the service is necessarily growing all the time, I suppose we have to employ more and more people. I think outside of that the last reports I had from General Lord showed that since June, 1923, there has been a reduction in personnel of 15,000 or 20,000 people. There isn't much that can be done in the matter of reducing the personnel, but I have to stress that question some all the time, otherwise there is a tendency to load up the service with unnecessary personnel. I was recently talking with a businessman that I came in contact with when I was Governor, who went into the management of a certain concern, and found at their headquarters between 250 and 260 people, as I recall it, which with their final methods of operation they were able to reduce to between 40 and 50. You can't do anything of that kind in the personnel of the Government. There are very few reductions that can be made. There may be some departments that can make slight reductions, but I am not looking for much of anything in the reduction of personnel. I am hoping to hold it about where it is. Perhaps we can make a little reduction here and there. I don't see much prospect of that.

[*General Herbert Mayhew Lord was Director of the Budget.*]

October 1, 1926

Here is a very interesting suggestion that I should discuss the administrative and political problems in the forthcoming two years. That I would hardly be able to do. There is one problem that I have to keep under constant emphasis, and that is economy and government expenditures. I think that in the past few weeks I have detected some evidences that in the coming session of Congress a good many efforts are going to be put forth to secure considerable expenditures of money. I think all problems requiring large expenditures of money ought to be very carefully considered before we embark on new enterprises. You will recall that we have provided a public building bill, which it is estimated will take about $25,000,000 a year. We are enlarging our river and harbor appropriation so that for the current year it carries $50,000,000—which is more I believe than at any time since the war. And I think, as I have said, that I detected in the air, as they say, the formation of plans to make a raid on the Treasury. Now, it is very important that this country keep down its expenditures. If it will do that, I think a great many other problems will solve themselves. But I have been over that so constantly in my addresses and in these newspaper conferences that I do not want to reiterate it now. In that connection, I learned this afternoon that one of those rather customary stories that start this time of the year and keep up until the Army and Navy appropriations have been made is about to be printed that the budget is going to require a large reduction in the Army. There is no foundation for that story.

November 19, 1926

I can see, as I stated some time ago, that there is going to be quite a good deal of pressure during the coming session for the expenditure of public funds. Quite a number of the members of the House and Senate that are coming back into town come into my office, a good many of them bringing some plan that requires an additional expenditure of public money. I am still very much in favor of conserving the resources of our country. I want to make all the expenditures that are reasonably required, but I think the country will be served best by making those expenditures as reasonable as they can be. That sometimes results in suggestions that the administration is resorting to cheese-paring. Well, we have a great many departments and a little saved in each one, each division, in the aggregate amounts to a very large sum. I don't know whether I ever indicated to the conference that the cost of lead pencils to the Government per year is about $125,000. Now, it would be thought to be rather insignificant to refer to saving a lead pencil, but even the use of lead pencils is a very considerable item. I have merely used that as an illustration. I don't think the lead pencils of the Government are wasted in any particular way, but that is an indication of the tremendous business that the Government does and the results that can be secured by a small saving in many different directions. I think the burdens of the taxpayer are greater than they ought to be. I would like to have them reduced as fast as possible. The only way we can secure that result is to refrain so far as we can from adding to the already great amount of our expenditures. That is what brings the surplus into the Treasury at the end of the year. Unless there is a surplus, why of course there is no opportunity for a reduction of the tax burden. I think I indicated some time ago that I can see in the process of formation a great many plans for further expenditure of public money. I hope that for the country's sake we can pretty generally avoid that.

September 16, 1927

I do not know of any needs in the War and Navy Departments that are likely to jeopardize the reduction of taxes. I am expecting some additional expenditure in those Departments, though I think that the Departments informed me that the additional expenditures would be rather for non-military purposes. The War and Navy Departments take a peculiar view of that. They always seem to think that if they can tell me that the expense is for non-military purposes it doesn't cost the taxpayer anything, and that, therefore, I ought to approve it. I am telling you that for your information—not for your publication.

October 4, 1927

I am having the usual experience with a good many members of the House and the Senate that are returning to Washington. They are all interested in some plan that calls for a very considerable expenditure of public money. Most of them are projects that have a great deal of merit, but a great many of them are projects that can't be taken up at the present time. I am exceedingly interested in reducing as fast as we can, and at the same time maintaining a reasonable rate of taxation, the national debt. That would constitute, if it could be retired, the very largest internal improvement that it would be possible to conceive. The benefits that would accrue from it to the nation would exceed those of any other project. In fact, it would be so large that the Government could afford to pay each year the entire damages that accrued from the flood and at the same time save money. I am not suggesting that that should be done. I am just giving you an illustration, as I understand that the outside estimate of the damages that accrued from the Mississippi flood this year are not so much as the annual charges at the present time of interest necessary to pay what is required on the national debt. I have spoken of it many times in

108

its military aspect. While I am in favor of very generous provisions for national defense, the weakest place in the line of national defense is at present the large debt of the country. So that I am trying to indicate that in my view the necessity of retiring that debt is the predominant necessity of the country, in an orderly way of course, and with a reasonable rate of taxation. But the burden that it entails and the menace that it constitutes are both large and grave. We made a wonderful beginning on it. Perhaps one of the greatest satisfactions of my administration lies in the very marked reduction of the national debt since I have been President.

October 7, 1927

I am very glad that this question has been asked about tax reduction and debt reduction. I intended at the last conference to be sufficiently specific and think twice I said I wanted a reasonable rate of taxation always, but I did speak of the great importance of paying off our national debt. Now the proper inference to have been drawn would be that I was opposed to extravagance, rather than that I was opposed to tax reduction. [Stenographer's note: quite loud.] I am opposed to extravagance, rather than to tax reduction. I thought some of the members of the press did not quite understand it. I want, of course, the payment of the national debt as quickly as possible together with any reasonable tax reduction that can be made. We have been pursuing that policy for several years successfully and I want to have it continued. So that while I am in favor of debt reduction and also in favor of tax reduction, I expect to accomplish both purposes by also being in favor of constructive economy and scrutinizing with great care all proposals to embark the Government in any new enterprises that are not absolutely necessary. We have to do such things as to take care of floods, whether they occur on the Mississippi Valley or are likely to come down through the White House roof.

PRESS: Has there been any such disaster, Mr. President?

PRESIDENT: I said likely to. Yes, we have sometimes had leaks in the White House roof since I have been there. But I think they have been taken care of now.

October 11, 1927

Except what I have seen in the press, nothing has come to me relative to the report that the United States Chamber of Commerce is interesting itself in the matter of tax reduction. I assume that practically everyone that pays taxes is interested in having their taxes reduced as fast as that can consistently be done. I do not mean that they are taking a selfish attitude about it. Most of them realize that we have not yet paid off the expenses of the war and the spirit among the taxpayers of this country is exceedingly fine and patriotic in their manifestation to do their part towards paying off the debt and bearing the burdens that were incident to the prosecution of the war. I have said a great deal about tax reduction, of course, since I have been President, but this always has to be borne in mind—that tax reduction is to be secured only as the result of economy. There are all kinds of organizations over the country that are promoting plans, most of them have a very great deal of merit, that involve the expenditure of large sums of money. Most of them are for things that ultimately will be done by our country. But the present debt of the United States is about $18,000,000,000, so that when anyone might think that because the war is over, therefore we ought not to have anything what might be designated as war taxes, of course entertaining such belief without giving any due consideration to the fact that so far as paying for the war is concerned it is only about half over. While I am exceedingly interested in having tax reduction, as I say, it can only be brought about as a result of economy, and therefore it seems to me that the Chamber of Commerce and all others that are interested in tax reduction ought to be first of all bending their energies to see that no unwise expenditures are authorized by the Government and that every possible effort is put forth to keep our expenditures down, and pay off our debt, so that we can have tax reduction. The suggestion here is that the Chamber thinks we might have a reduction of $350,000,000 or $400,000,000. I haven't received the figures from the Treasury, but it is my offhand opinion that any such reduction as that would be very certain to involve a deficit, and that it would not be wise to make a reduction that was anywhere near as large as that. But I wouldn't want to go on record as making any estimate now of the amount that taxes can be reduced. In order to find that out we shall have to have the estimates of the Treasury as to the income and the estimates of the Bureau of the Budget as to the probable expenditures. Since I have been President, of course, we have entered into a good many new expenditures. I think the largest annual item is probably represented in the cost of the adjusted compensation. The last Congress increased pensions and relief to go to all the veterans and their dependents some $68,000,000 a year. That is a large item, of course. And we have been able to meet these large increases by absorbing them through economies in other directions.

January 31, 1928

No evidence has come to me that the next Treasury surplus will be in excess of the $252,540,000 that has already been made public.

[*Coolidge was considerably off base. See his comment on July 3, 1928.*]

February 17, 1928

There is always danger that the Congress will be too liberal in the matter of appropriations. It doubled the appropriation that I proposed for the Shipping Board and I think added $6,000,000 or $8,000,-000 to the Army bill, and it is true that if it goes on at that rate there won't be any surplus with which to meet tax reduction. Of course, according to my best judgment, there should be added to the sums I have already mentioned $65,000,000 that has been put into the tax bill, which is in excess of what I believe tax reduction ought to include.

April 27, 1928

The tax reduction bill, as I understand it, to be reported to the Senate is fairly satisfactory as to the amount. I think it is a mistake from my point of view to repeal the automobile taxes. We had already repealed 40 per cent of them. We might reasonably look to that source of revenue for the expenses which the Federal Government is incurring in road construction. Road construction by the Federal Government, of course, is a new proposition. It is done especially for the benefit of the automobile owners. I think it would be ultimately for their benefit to have revenue accruing from that source, which would be applied for that purpose. I recognize, however, that the kind of taxes that are to be levied, and the sources that are to be looked to for revenue, are peculiar ones for the Congress to determine, so that my main concern is for a bill that doesn't deplete the revenue too far. Of course, that is one of the advantages of the automobile tax. It is a pretty certain source of revenue, which wouldn't be reduced very much if there should be a considerable reduction in taxes on incomes and corporation profits. But I think that the amount they have set is fairly satisfactory. It is a little too high, but if the Congress is discreet in the amount of appropriations it makes in other directions I should say that it was not so high that the Treasury couldn't meet it.

May 8, 1928

I am a good deal disturbed at the number of proposals that are being made for an expenditure of money. The number and the amount is becoming appalling. Practically none of those bills have reached me yet, and it may be that the Congress won't pass all of them. Of course, there is this flood bill. It is impossible to estimate what that will cost. If it is carried out as suggested, I think $500,000,000 would probably be the minimum. Nobody knows what the maximum might be. There is the farm bill calling for $400,000,000. The Boulder Dam bill. I think the lowest estimates on that are $125,000,000. Other estimates run to $250,000,000. There is a pension bill, running $15,000,000 or $20,000,000. The salary bill, the so-called Welch bill, of about $18,-000,000. The Muscle Shoals bill, which I think was reported to me would cost perhaps $75,000,000. I think that is rather excessive. That is only a part of them. I don't know just what will happen to the Treasury if we try to put all those proposals into effect. In addition to that there is the Post Office pay bill of I think $20,000,000, and the reduction of postage payments which has been reported in the Senate I think calls for—it seems as though it is $38,000,000. Those two together make a difference of $58,000,000 in the Post Office Department, which is already running a considerable deficit. There are $7,000,000 or $8,000,000 for the corn borer. There are $6,000,000 for vocational training. How many more bills there are, I don't know.

PRESS: Does this endanger tax reduction?

PRESIDENT: Well, there is a tax reduction bill of $203,000,000 reported to the Senate and $289,000,000 as it passed the House. If all these bills went through and became law I should think it would not only endanger tax reduction at the present time, but would make necessary the laying of additional taxes.

July 3, 1928

The surplus for the fiscal year of $398,000,000 was just about what we had figured it would be. Sometimes some money comes in that hasn't been expected and sometimes there is some that has been expected and it doesn't come until after the 30th of June. But the surplus was secured, of course, by very careful management of expenditures and will enable us to retire about $900,000,000 of the indebtedness for the fiscal year which would mean a reduction in interest of some over $35,000,000. You can see how important that is, if you recall that that is about the amount we expect to appropriate yearly for the purpose of taking care of the flood relief in the Mississippi Valley.

December 14, 1928

Of course, a good many proposals are made by people that have very excellent things that they would like to have the Government do, but they come from people that have no responsibility for providing ways and means by which their proposals can be carried out. I don't think in all my experience, which has been very large with people that come before me in and out of the Government with proposals for spending money, I have ever had any proposal from anyone as to what could be done to raise money, and very few suggestions of what could be done to save any money. Sometimes linked with the proposal for an immediate large expenditure is the suggestion that it ultimately will result in a saving. I think that is about the extent of the outside assistance I have had in that direction.

7 · The Domestic Economy

No accounting of Coolidge can avoid his most famous remark, "The business of America is business." In classroom lectures at American universities, this saying usually offers a platform from which facile professors of American history denounce Coolidge and all his works. Only, so runs the inevitable peroration, a Vermont philosopher, down in the basement of the White House counting apples sent to him by an admirer, could have failed to recognize that business in the 1920's rested on an insecure foundation and that government control over the speculative orgy in the United States was imperative.

In fairness one must say that almost no one in the twenties, neither the President nor anyone else, understood the rickety nature of America's postwar business structure. Perhaps Coolidge was even less able to sense the stupidities of American financial organization than were many other men. The President did not have the slightest inclination for stock market speculation. He observed with approval the increase in installment buying, but believed erroneously that it helped poor people budget their money. He read the magazine articles of Professor William Z. Ripley and agreed that it was wrong for corporations to issue nonvoting stock. Unfortunately he coupled this perception with an archaic constitutional interpretation, namely, that only the states, since they issued the charters of incorporation, could regulate corporations. Coolidge admired the great business figures of the day, recognizing, as indeed anyone recognized, that many of these men would have shown well in Coolidge's own field, politics, had they turned their energies in that direction. He especially respected his Secretary of the Treasury, Andrew W. Mellon, but not even that financial wizard completely grasped the intricacies of the new business finance. The economic frivolities of the day continued, and the Great Depression approached ever closer while the most frugal of recent American Presidents lived in the White House.

Coolidge was not, however, cheerfully oblivious to the plight of American farming. Farming was the sickest industry in the United States during the 1920's. An agricultural depression had begun early in the summer of 1920 and persisted with degrees of severity throughout the decade. Coolidge, of course, had grown up on a Vermont farm. He liked to pose (albeit in his business suit) leading a team of horses and could tell his press conference that he enjoyed going to the farm at Plymouth Notch once in a while to renew his feeling for the daily life of the average American. To the unsophisticated he seemed the right person to handle the farm problem. But the easy course was to voice concern for the farmer's plight rather than to do much about it. Coolidge, though sensing the malaise of American farming, shied away from treating it.

The farm problem arose because of overproduction and the inability of millions of small-scale farmers to organize for a hold on the market—as had, for example, the makers of steel. The farmers had expanded their acreage prodigally during the World War, and suffered with the postwar deflation of currency and demand. Moreover, in some agricultural regions, banks catering to the needs of farmers were frequently in a precarious condition. Coolidge favored a few palliatives, but the basic problem just rattled on despite efforts of the Farm Bloc, a nonpartisan pressure group in Congress, to commit the Federal government to an active role in the marketing of surplus agricultural staples, particularly wheat. Twice Coolidge vetoed the McNary-Haugen bill which would have set aside the exportable surplus and thereby preserved the domestic market from the limitations on prices imposed by the international market. Nonetheless, the Farm Bloc succeeded in committing the Federal Government to increased control of grain exchanges, packing houses and stockyards, assistance to farm cooperatives, and extension of liberal credit to farmers.

114

September 18, 1923

The Cabinet took up and discussed this morning, particularly, the agricultural situation, and it developed there that the cotton situation is fairly satisfactory. There is trouble in the South, of course, in certain sections, from the Boll Weevil, but, apparently, the general result of the cotton crop section for the present year will be to give them a larger money return than they had in pre-war times. The corn situation is also one that is fairly satisfactory. The price of corn is remarkably high and there isn't any real difficulty in that direction. The same is substantially true in relation to the animal industry, hogs and cattle. The encouraging thing about the raising of hogs is the very large number of them that there are on the farms. Of course, if the farmer has two hogs to sell instead of one, why he gets an additional income, even though the price isn't very much larger. The difficulty is particularly in the wheat belt and in that belt where there is oftentimes an insufficient rainfall. It makes the production of wheat cost more, and the production, per acre, of course, is not so large. There is a large production of wheat all over the world. Apparently, Europe will import about 200,000,000 bushels less of wheat this year than it has in preceding years.

We also discussed the effect that is produced by the prevailing rate of good liberal wages in the industries on the agricultural situation, and it was rather the opinion of those who were best informed that they had resulted in a very much larger increase in the consumption of meat products. That is where there is a hopeful situation for the hog industry and the cattle industry, but it does not have a corresponding good effect on the wheat industry, because as the standard of living begins to go up and they eat more meat, apparently they eat less wheat. So that they are getting the benefit in one direction, but not the benefit in another. We don't know yet just what is going to be proposed in the way of a remedy. The Secretary of Agriculture is making a particular study of the wheat situation and expects to be able to report on that to me by Thursday or Friday of this week. When that report comes in, it will undoubtedly set out the facts that will enable us to make some determination of what kind of a remedy can be proposed. There is great anxiety and great desire to do everything that we can for the relief of any of the farmers who are in distress, along sound economic lines, relieving a temporary situation perhaps, by trying to formulate a plan that will bring agriculture back on to a sound economic basis, so that we can have a balance of production. It may be that some of those that are raising wheat would do well to engage in the raising of some other kind of agricultural products. It may be that we ought to look about and see what it is that we are importing in the way of food products, and suggest that the wheat raisers, if they

115

can try to provide us here in America with some of those things that are being brought in. Sugar occurs to me right away as one of the things that we import to quite an extent, and probably shall for some years to come. It may be that those who are now raising wheat can profitably raise sugar beet or flax, and that we may be able to provide some remedy along that line. We also have in mind the possibility of some regional conferences. Some locality wants one thing done and another locality another thing, so that by regional conferences with the Secretary of Agriculture and perhaps by a representative of the Department of Commerce, for it is a commercial activity as well as an agricultural activity we must consider, that in that way we can furnish some needed relief.

September 25, 1923

Another inquiry about what the Cabinet did in relation to the farm situation. Secretary Wallace has made a careful study, especially of the wheat conditions, and the Cabinet took up and discussed several suggestions for assistance in that direction. One of them was a lowering of freight rates, especially on exports of wheat and exports of flour.

PRESS: Mr. President, has this report been made public?

PRESIDENT: I don't suppose it will be made public in its entirety, but I think you can get from Secretary Wallace an outline of some of the things he found. A proposal of that kind is already before the Interstate Commerce Commission to see what they can do. If rates are lowered for the transportation of wheat or flour, those roads in the United States that are not securing any more than is necessary for them to have to live on, will, of course, expect an increase of rates in some other direction. If all the roads of the United States were exactly alike, that, perhaps, might be easy to suggest. The main difficulty about that is that some of the roads make their living almost entirely from the transportation of agricultural products. They don't transport much of anything else and it would be very difficult to find anything that would compensate them for their loss of revenue, if there is a lowering of freight on agricultural products. But that is before the Interstate Commerce Commission and will be worked out, if possible.

Another suggestion of the possible change of the tariff on wheat. It is evident that the present tariff is working to the advantage of the American farmer on wheat. I think the spread between the price in America and the price in Canada is, or a few days ago was, something like 28 cents. That varies from one time to another. I don't know whether the suggestion of increasing the tariff would be a remedy. Of course we have a surplus of wheat here that we want to export and, where wheat is to be exported, the first thought would be to increase the tariff on it which wouldn't be of very much assistance. But that has been suggested to me by men who know something about how those things work. It is something that ought to be investigated and studied, and in their opinion it might be helpful. And for that reason that will be done. I don't want to put it out as a proposal on my part, or as something that certainly would be helpful, but, at least, it is worth considering.

January 18, 1924

PRESS: Did anything happen at the Cabinet meeting?

PRESIDENT: I was going to speak about that. We had considerable discussion about the difficulties that are arising in the northwest on account of the closing down of some banks up there, and we are making plans to see what we could possibly do to relieve that situation. The Federal Reserve Banks and the Federal Reserve Board are going to do what they can. I have been in conference with Comptroller Dawes about it, and the War Finance Corporation stands ready to be of any possible assistance. The situation is serious, though not desperately so. They have a great many banks in the northwest that are quite different from what we understand as a bank in the east, and with very small capital. I was astonished to find they had one bank for about every eight hundred people, which puts a good deal of a burden on eight hundred people to support a bank, but whether they have been wise in having that number, I don't know, and I am very anxious to relieve them by furnishing additional credits. Mr. Dawes has been in communication with banks in Chicago and with the Twin Cities. Mr. Meyer also is working in the same direction. I think they have a plan by which they can finance the troubles up there and get the matter straightened out as speedily as possible. I haven't any figures on the matter. There is a large bank in Sioux Falls, I think the Sioux Falls Savings Bank, that is the correspondent of quite a lot of other banks around there, and has their deposits and keeps for them their legal reserve. It is to relieve that situation and take care of the needs of those banks that had deposits there that Mr. Dawes and Mr. Meyer are especially solicitous.

[*Charles G. Dawes, a Chicago banker, was to be Coolidge's running mate in November, 1924. Investment banker Eugene Meyer, Jr. of New York was a member of the War Finance Corporation during World War I. President Harding appointed him director of the War Finance Corporation. Later Meyer was to head the Reconstruction Finance Corporation.*]

January 22, 1924

I haven't any recent information about the South Dakota bank situation. As I think you already know, Mr. Meyer and Mr. Dawes have started for that region, stopping yesterday I think in Chicago, in order to organize the banks there for the purpose of seeing what additional credit facilities could be secured and what help they could carry from that region to those banks that are now in distress in North and South Dakota. I haven't had any report from either one of them, so I haven't any information as to what they accomplished at Chicago. Of course the Government will do everything it can do to relieve that situation, and that is substantially all the declaration I can make about it. I don't want to have it said in the press that the Government can cure an incurable situation, or that where losses have been made through depreciation of property and loans have been found to be insecure and uncollectible it is possible for the Government to take action that will remedy all that. The Government can't do that, but it will assist in any way in which it can assist to furnish adequate credit facilities, or credit that may be needed at the present time, but of course nothing in the way of undertaking to replace losses that have already accrued; though its action might help very greatly to retrieve losses perhaps by an extension of credit to put the debtor in a position where ultimately he would meet his demands in full.

————————

Judge [Elbert] Gary of the [U. S.] Steel Corporation came in and I conferred with him about the abolition of the twelve hour day, which the Steel Corporation has put into operation. I asked him about the financial effect of it, and he said that it increased the cost of their production about ten per cent. They hope that through improvements and inventions and better operation they would gradually work that off, but that was the immediate effect of increasing the cost of their production by about that amount. Perhaps that is one of the things that might be remembered when we find we have to pay high costs for manufactured articles. We can't have good conditions for everybody without paying the price. If we are going to have an eight hour day and high wages, which of course we all want to have, we must remember that in order to have it we must be prepared to make something of a sacrifice for it. I think we ought to do it. But we ought to do it uncomplainingly, and we ought to do it without undertaking to assess the blame in some other direction where there is no fault.

January 29, 1924

Another inquiry as to whether the direct use of Federal funds is contemplated in the consideration of relief measures for the banks of the northwest. I am not quite certain what the question means, but according to my interpretation of it, I don't think the direct use of Federal funds is contemplated. There are two plans under consideration, or perhaps a combination of the two. One is for relief by the Federal Reserve Banking System, and the other is a relief measure by a combination of different moneyed interests to provide some capital and a local organization for administering relief, and they of course could be assisted financially by the War Finance Corporation. That is the plan that the War Finance Corporation has adopted right along, of lending money to the banks, or lending money through some local organization. Otherwise the War Finance Corporation would have to have such a large staff in the field itself, necessarily of men that were acquainted with local conditions, that before they could get an organization the acute need for relief would probably have passed and the opportunity for relief would be gone.

February 1, 1924

Here is an inquiry about stopping the sale of Treasury Savings Certificates in the northwest. Those certificates were put out in order that people themselves might deal directly with the Government, for the purpose of encouraging thrift, and with the expectation that ultimately such action would bring deposits in the banks. Reports came that people were drawing their money out of perfectly good banks and investing in savings certificates in a way that threatened to jeopardize the banks and make it very inconvenient for them by taking their deposits. I understand that the Treasury Department, which was acting in this instance through the Post Office Department—the sales being made through the Post Office Department—thought it was better temporarily to discontinue sales in some localities.

February 15, 1924

I have heard reports about the investigation of the Tariff Commission as to the cost of producing wheat in this country and abroad, and while I haven't any of the details of it, I knew in a general way that their investigation has seemed to be showing, so far as it has proceeded, a considerably higher cost of production in America than it is in Canada. Just what the difference will turn out to be, I don't know, but it is quite a material sum, and I think the indications were that it would be above the present tariff price of 30 cents a bushel. That affects I think especially the hard wheat, and a change in that tariff would be beneficial to the hard wheat region, which is the northern region of the United States, the Dakotas, Montana, Minnesota, and indirectly it might have some benefit on the soft region, but it would be especially beneficial in the hard wheat region, and that is the region in the most financial difficulty.

March 4, 1924

I have an inquiry here about the McNary-Haugen bill. I am in entire sympathy with the objects of this bill, which is to benefit the wheat raisers. That is a problem on which I have been constantly engaged ever since I landed in Washington last August. It is very pressing, and an important problem. I referred to it in my Message to the Congress, and I referred to that problem in my address in New York. I don't know that I can say anything further than what was presented in those two addresses. I have never been able to make up

119

my mind entirely about the benefits that this bill would secure to the farmers, and for that reason I have had it under investigation by experts. If it will be beneficial to the farmers, I think the country ought to adopt it, even though it might cost something out of the public treasury, though it is claimed that that would not be the case under the provisions of the bill. On the other hand, it is claimed it would simply be a delusion and not of any real benefit. But we have to know that before we undertake to put it into operation. It is a very intricate measure in its provisions. About all I can say about it is that my mind is open about it, as I have told people constantly. I understand that is exactly the position of the Secretary of Agriculture. He and I have discussed the measure and have never been quite certain about it. There are men in his Department that are very certain that this would be a very beneficial bill. If my investigation leads me to that conclusion, I shall favor it. If on the other hand my advice should lead to a different conclusion, and they seem to be conflicting at present, I should not want to favor it. That is the present state of my mind in relation to it.

March 18, 1924

The Cabinet spent considerable time this morning considering the agricultural situation, with which we are all pretty familiar. There is one phase of it, perhaps, that might be kept in mind, and that is the organization of that $10,000,000 Agricultural Credit Corporation. Now that there has been a failure to pass the diversification bill known as the Norbeck-Burtness bill, I am going to ask this Agricultural Credit Corporation to function in the same way that the provisions of that bill would have functioned: that is, to assist farmers in diversification. That organization was created as the result of a conference that I called here on the 4th of February, and the bankers and businessmen of the northwest, middlewest, and down as far as New York, at once joined and raised a $10,000,000 fund which of course can be supplemented by a loan from the War Finance Corporation, about $20,000-000 or $30,000,000 more, which ought to enable them to assist very materially in diversification. Dr. Coulter who formulated the plan that was embodied in the Norbeck-Burtness bill is the Vice-President of the new Agricultural Credit Corporation, and I am sure that he can be very helpful in transferring some of the activities of this corporation into the field that would have been taken up by the Government, had that other bill passed.

PRESS: Mr. President, is Agricultural Corporation the exact name?

PRESIDENT: The Agricultural Credit Corporation is the corporate name.

PRESS: Does this contemplate an increase in the capital of the organization?

PRESIDENT: No, the War Finance Corporation has been designated to help out the banks, and when this Agricultural Credit Corporation was formed it was expected that those farmers who needed assistance and advice and counsel would resort to this corporation for aid in that direction.

[*John Lee Coulter, Vice-President of the Agricultural Credit Corporation, was the author of the Norbeck-Burtness bill, which was defeated in the Senate by a 41-32 vote despite Coolidge's endorsement. The bill would have allocated $50,000,000 to farmers of spring wheat to finance a program of diversification, notably in poultry and livestock raising.*]

April 1, 1924

At today's Cabinet meeting I went over a very short and sketchy way the business situation. Some reports have been coming in to me that in certain lines there is a little slowing up. That is to be expected. So I was inquiring of Mr. Hoover whether from his observation and reports there is indicated a general slowing up of business. He says that it does not, that the steel industry which is a very good barometer is going ahead well, and that the building industry which I think reached its peak last year has a larger number of permits this year than it had last. Now that industry is basic. When the building industry is good, it includes iron, steel, hardware and wood, all kinds of materials, and all kinds of industries, and if that is good the basic industries are good, and we can expect to go along fairly well. I think the reason for the slowing up of business—as a whole business will undoubtedly go ahead well if it is assured that we are going to proceed as we have been doing with our policy of economy of Government expenditures, and in addition to that if there is going to be a reduction of taxes. My own theory is that if the tax bill had been passed as it was introduced by the administration within six weeks or two months after the coming in of Congress, the country would have seen a large increase in business, a stimulation in various activities. Just at the present time there is a good deal of money piling up in the banks, so that call money is very low. Now that is a very perfect example of the way the present tax laws work, because that means that the owners of that money are not willing to invest it in industry. They would rather let it lie on deposit at a very small rate of interest in the bank, or loan it out on call at something like three per cent, than invest it in industry as in ordinary times when the net return was 6 per cent or 8 per cent. With the present method of taxation that is not the case. It results of course in a slowing up of business.

July 25, 1924

I don't know as I can throw any new or fresh light on the effect or general reaction to the increases in prices of wheat and corn. I think it has been recognized that the prices of farm products for the past year or two have been below the price level of manufactured products. I think there has been a general recognition of the fact that it is desirable to have those price levels substantially the same. Sometimes one is higher than the other. I think in years gone by there has been a tendency of farm products to be somewhat higher than the level of manufactured products. That was so before the war, and I don't know what the relationship was before that, but for the last two or three years it has been the other way and farm products have been lower, although now there is a gradual coming together in the prices of farm and manufactured products. I think it would be better for the whole country if there was a substantial similarity in those prices, so that the purchasing price of what they call the farm dollar will be substantially the same as the purchasing price of the dollar that comes from industry. I know, of course, that there has been difficulty in meeting obligations in the agricultural section and some diminution in the buying power there. This I judge will give the agricultural sections a chance to liquidate their obligations, and the farmer a chance to pay off some of his debts, and will increase his buying power, and the general result of that ought to be better business conditions throughout the nation.

October 7, 1924

I haven't hastened about appointing the Committee to look into the agricultural situation because, as I indicated in my speech of acceptance, the agricultural situation has seemed to be to quite an extent taking care of itself, and this Committee or Commission I was proposing to appoint not so much for relieving the situation at the present time which has already been relieved by the rise in prices, as for taking advantage of the present condition which follows one of relief and seeing if we can take some action to prevent a recurrence of the conditions that confronted agriculture during the period of low prices. If there had been any emergency I would have acted on that. Then I have some people that I want to consult about it that I haven't been able to get hold of as quickly as I expected. My own thought was to find out what could be done while we have a breathing spell to prevent a recurrence of the decline and the period of the low prices of wheat, cattle, hogs and the larger staples of farm production at the present time when it is at a very fair level. I expect to appoint this Committee as soon as I can confer with two or three leaders in the farm movement, in order to see what we can do to prevent a recurrence of the bad situation that agriculture found itself in after the period of deflation.

November 11, 1924

The present increase in business activity I judge is what naturally might be expected after an election. Elections are always uncertain and people are inclined to wait and see how an election comes out before they commit themselves. I heard of one man before the election that said he had on his desk an order for $50,000,000 worth of merchandise, but that he wouldn't be able to place the order until he knew the result of the election. I think other orders have been given to be filled pending—or in accordance with the election result. Of course those orders now coming on the market are but the natural result of a business activity greater than that preceding the election. There were some suggestions, I think you will recall, prior to the election and during the summer that somebody that was interested in my election was putting up the price of wheat. I didn't know that anyone was doing that. I noticed that yesterday the price of wheat was $1.60 a bushel, and that it has gone up considerably since the election, which would probably indicate that either the rise in wheat was not due to the influence of the election, or else the people do not know yet that the election has been held. I judge that the result of the election, the decisive result, indicating an attachment of the people to their Constitution and the present method of transacting their business, a desire that enterprise and business activities be left in the hands of private individuals rather than a transfer of ownership to the control of the Government, has undoubtedly had an effect in stimulating private enterprise. It has given an evidence of stability on which people are willing to make investments, make commitments, plans for development, and plans for the buying and selling of merchandise, which results in an increase in production.

January 6, 1925

We have got so many regulatory laws already that in general I feel that we would be just as well off if we didn't have any more. I want to give people all the freedom of action that is possible for them to have, but when it is obvious that the freedom of action is abused, why of course someone is going to come along and take that freedom of action away. That follows inevitably and certainly, and can't be prevented. Oftentimes, as a result, many people that are entirely innocent of any wrongdoing or wrong intentions are injured as a result. It is probable that some of our railroads could have been better off, if we hadn't had so much railroad legislation. But the general condition warranted it, and apparently it was necessary to impose it. Now, it is probable that a large number of owners of real estate in the District that has been built for the purpose of rental are conducting their business in a perfectly legitimate way, and it will be a hardship to put them under regulation. But if there are abuses, there is no other way in which remedy can be applied, and we shall have to adopt something of that kind. I feel that a good deal can be done by real estate men and the banks and loan associations, if they will take hold of this situation themselves and apply the remedy to it that I think they can apply. That isn't always a pleasant operation, to go and tell someone he is doing something wrong and to stop, and it isn't a pleasant operation for the President to suggest to the Congress that people are engaged in wrong practices and it ought to be stopped by legislation. I am not making any criticism of the banks in general, or the real estate interests here, for not being able to apply that remedy. I think perhaps they can help, if they will, through their organization. It may be that something can be worked out that way. Now, I have only one desire here, which has been constant and uniform, and that is to find out what the real abuses are and apply any reasonable remedy. . . .

January 13, 1925

PRESS: Can you give us a "slant" on the Secretary of Agriculture?

PRESIDENT: No, I can't. I wish you would give me one. Of course the present Secretary will retire to become Governor of West Virginia on the 4th of March, and I shall have to get someone to take his place. The trouble with agriculture at the present time is in the marketing end. The Secretaries in the past have perhaps been roughly divided into two classes. There has been the practical farmer and the man from some agricultural institution, perhaps an economist or something of that kind. Those are the classes that have served as Secretaries in the past. What I would like to find is a man that can organize the business of agriculture. We are able to get along very well with our production. The agricultural college, of course, is putting its emphasis on production. That has been the teaching. It has not put so much emphasis on marketing. It is the marketing end that has to be organized at the present time and carried along and made effective, in order that the farmer may secure the results of his industry, and not have so much of it dissipated between the farmer and the consumer. That is a great economic problem. It is *the* great economic problem, to my mind, of the present time—how to secure for our farming population the rewards that they ought to have as a result of their industry.

[*Howard M. Gore, who had been Assistant Secretary of Agriculture under Henry C. Wallace, was appointed to the secretaryship on November 4, 1924, following Wallace's death. Gore, in turn, was replaced in March, 1925, by William M. Jardine, President of the Kansas State Agricultural College. Jardine opposed the McNary-Haugen bill.*]

February 3, 1925

I don't know as I can quite say that I have been assured of any Congressional action on agricultural legislation at this session. The report of the Conference has been laid before the Congress. They will have had at the end of the session about five weeks to act on it, and I think they ought to secure action within that time. The members of the House Committee and Senate Committee that I conferred with the other morning thought that they could secure some action at this session. The members of the Congress, and especially the members of the House and Senate Committees on Agriculture come from the agricultural regions. They are much better informed than I am as to the necessity for present action. If they think that there is an emergency that requires immediate action, why those two committees of course can draft legislation and present it for immediate action of the Congress and the representatives of the agricultural regions can make known to the Congress their position in relation to it and give the Congress information as to whether there is an exigency that requires immediate legislation. If there is an exigency, I am certain that the Congress will be able to pass legislation at this session.

February 10, 1925

No, I don't think the views of Mr. Hearst and Mr. Sykes, of Iowa, who came in this morning relative to the appointment of a new Secretary of Agriculture, caused any delay, because I found they were in practical harmony with my own views. I am trying to get a man who especially represents agriculture and who is sympathetic with the cooperative movement. I think it's the organization of Mr. (I don't know now which one it was, who is President of some producer's cooperative association) that handles a good deal of livestock—yes, Mr. Sykes. He showed that for the week ending February 6 their shipments of livestock totaled 444 cars. The highest that any other had was 255. Now that shows the development of a cooperative movement. I think that is a very promising field of development for the benefit of agriculture and any Secretary of Agriculture that I have I should expect to be sympathetic with that policy. Certainly he will be if he carries out my desires relative to the administration of the Department.

[*Charles E. Hearst was President of the Iowa Farm Bureau.*]

February 27, 1925

I don't know as I can make any particular comment about the rejection of the Conference agricultural bill. I don't know enough about the details of these bills to discuss the details with any intelligence. I have been going more particularly on my confidence in people that have made recommendations and not on my particular knowledge of the recommendations that have been made. Now here we have the heads of five great farm organizations and three or four experts from our agricultural institutions that are supposed to know something about farm economics. They made some recommendations about legislation. I don't think there would be anything in those recommendations that are likely to be harmful to the farmer. Now, you don't have to study the farm question but a very short time to find out that every time there is any effort made to help the farmer the people that live off the farmer or off the distribution of his products almost always come in and resist anything being done. I don't know what the reason for that is. They seem to think that if the farmer is going to be helped that means they are going to be injured. I don't agree with that view. The better off the farmer is the better off those will be that deal with him. But there does seem to be a very determined opposition on the part of those who act as distributors, not all of them, but quite a number of them, to any assistance being rendered the farmer. And they don't come in themselves and say, "I am dealing in farm produce." They reach over and get the farmer to come in and oppose it himself. Now that is a reaction that always occurs, so that we are not going to get any farm legislation without opposition, and the opposition will apparently come from the farmer when of course those with experience know very well that it originates with others. Then there are those who are determined that nothing shall be done for the farmer unless they do it. I have a good deal of sympathy with them and wish they would do more than they do. I am very glad to hand over to them the work of doing something for the farmer if they will do it, but they haven't been able to accomplish very much, and therefore I was hopeful that this farm conference recommendation would receive favorable action from the Congress. I am not entirely certain that it will not result that way now.

March 24, 1925

Not anything special came up this morning in the Cabinet meeting. I made some inquiries about the general business situation. Secretary Davis says there is some unemployment, apparently about the normal amount. What he is especially gratified at is the apparent inclination on the part of employers and employees to agree on wage scales whenever present contracts expire and to go on on substantially the present basis, and those agreements are being made without a great deal of difficulty. Mr. Mellon reports that insofar as he can observe there is a very general and healthy condition of good business. Those industries that are supposed to be barometers or indicators of what the general business condition is throughout the country all seem to indicate that it is fairly good. There has been some speculation in securities that seems to have been somewhat overdone that has caused a reaction in speculation, but it hasn't seemed to have any result in diminishing the general business activity.

[*Secretary of Labor James J. Davis had been born in Tredegar, South Wales. At the age of eleven he began working as a puddler in the iron and steel mills of Sharon, Pa. Andrew W. Mellon entered the banking business in Pittsburgh in the 1870's. Like Coolidge, he advocated low taxation, particularly on high incomes, and budget balancing. Appointed to the cabinet by Harding, he continued to serve as Secretary of the Treasury throughout Coolidge's presidency.*

To accept the cabinet post, Mellon had to resign, nominally at least, directorships in sixty corporations. Under Mellon, the Treasury Department made generous tax refunds to large corporations, which hardly needed tax relief. Several millions of dollars were refunded to Mellon interests, a fact which embarrassed the Secretary not at all. Mellon maintained, and Coolidge agreed, that low taxes would spur investment, which in turn would create more jobs and continue the nation's prosperity. Mellon was considered the Coolidge administration's chief oracle of prosperity, and when the economic crash came in 1929 his reputation as an economic soothsayer was destroyed.]

April 14, 1925

There was nothing particularly developed in the Cabinet meeting this morning, other than the report from Secretary Hoover, which I presume will be given to the press, relative to our exports and imports. The last month I think they were the largest of any during peace time, and if they were reduced to the same value in dollars and cents it would be—so as to have them the same as would be represented by prices before the war—they showed that our exports and imports are about 50 per cent larger than they were in 1914. Now, no other countries that were engaged in the Great War have been able to make any showing like that, and I think substantially all of them have exports and imports nowhere near what they were before the war; some of them very much less. But those of Great Britain, I think, are just about even. That is larger than what I thought their increase had been.

May 1, 1925

Now that Congress isn't in session I am rather aware of the paucity of news, though of course there are a lot of small things that are always developing in relation to our Government, and many times they have larger import and interest. I want to be helpful in any way I can to guide the press in their efforts for news items. My own thought about the situation at the present time is that I would like it if the country could think as little as possible about the Government and give their time and attention more undividedly about the conduct of the private business of our country. If that is a thought that you can develop in any way, I think it would be helpful. There are going to be a few months here when the Congress won't be in session, and when, so far as I can tell, there won't be any very large governmental matters projected by the Executive, and it is with that in view that the country may be relieved from having to look to Washington every day or two to see what is going to be done and given an opportunity to feel that things are as settled as they can be and the uncertainties removed as much as they can be, and that there is a foundation on which they can make commitments for the carrying on of their business without being in jeopardy of change of law or something of that kind that might change conditions in such a way that their investments would become uncertain.

On train en route from Minneapolis to Washington, June 9, 1925

Here is an inquiry about economic and political impressions. I haven't thought at all about political impressions until I got this inquiry. I don't know that I received any distinctly political impressions. The impression that struck me more than anything else was rather of a patriotic impression, an apparent general satisfaction with conditions in the country. Of course I didn't have any opportunity to confer with anyone about the economic condition of the northwest. I did learn that crop conditions through Wisconsin, Minnesota and North Dakota are good. I saw one man that had just been through North Dakota and he said that the crop conditions there were very promising. If you can base the economic condition of the people on their appearance, the way they are dressed, the general appearance of prosperity, I should say that it was very good. I don't know that that has any significance now, but I noticed most of the ladies had on silk dresses and I thought I saw a rather general display of silk stockings.

August 4, 1925

It would be possible to pass some laws that would be of benefit to transportation, but the main thing that it seems to me is needed in transportation is consolidations. There is one of those pending before the Interstate Commerce Commission, the Van Sweringens, and I imagine that some of the other transportation units are waiting to see how that comes out in order that they may get necessary information with which to proceed with consolidations. If we could get consolidations through, it would solve the problem, to quite an extent, of rates. We would then have sufficiently large units so that it would be possible to make a rate that would substantially take care of each unit and not give one railroad a very large income while another railroad under the same rate wouldn't get enough income to pay for its existence.

[*The Van Sweringen brothers, O. P. and M. J., were Cleveland railroad financiers who had built up a two-billion dollar "empire" of interrelated companies. At this time the Van Sweringens proposed to the ICC the merger of seven major lines representing a unified system of 9,000 miles of trackage. Coolidge rightly favored, though perhaps not always for the right reasons, railroad mergers.*]

January 12, 1926

Here is an inquiry about the purchase of commodities on the installment plan. I don't know as I can very well discuss that in a newspaper conference in a way that might not be misunderstood on one side or the other. The basis of installment buying is, I think, entirely sound. It is a provision of credit for those that otherwise wouldn't be able to secure credit. So far as the installment buying goes, I think it is a little better than the old way that was customary around my neighborhood when I was young—of going to the store, getting a bill and having no plan or purpose as to when it was to be paid. When a commodity is bought on installments, it means that there is then laid out a plan on which it is to be paid, and installment buying is really a plan of financing and extending credit to people who otherwise wouldn't be able to secure credit for the purposes to which it is extended. I recognize that it might be overdone like any kind of credit, but I think it is a step in advance of the old kind of credit that was given without any plan of repayment. So far as I can ascertain, it has not been overdone at the present time. If we should run into an era of depression where employment was not so abundant as it is now, some difficulties might arise. But the financial corporations that have been organized, and the whole credit system that has been organized for the purpose of extending credit on the installment plan, have those things in mind and are pretty well fortified to take care of any situation that might arise. So I really come back to the conclusion that while this might be extended too far, like any other credit, it doesn't seem that it has been done at the present, and I think on the whole it is a step in advance and a very helpful step to people that otherwise wouldn't get credit or wouldn't make a plan at the same time it is extended for its repayment.

January 19, 1926

Here is an inquiry about the MacFadden National Bank bill. I don't recall that I have seen that bill. I haven't seen it certainly this year. Perhaps it was brought specifically to my attention last year. I understand it is a bill to authorize branch banks. I rather think that something can be done in that direction. But it needs to be very carefully safeguarded, otherwise you will have just one great credit system built up here that will virtually control all the credits in the United States, and I wouldn't want to have that condition exist. We ought to have a reasonable competition in credits, and reasonable facilities for extending credits, so that borrowers can be accommodated. Oftentimes it happens that one kind of a bank is interested in doing one kind of business and another bank another kind of business. You will recall the names of banks that have been established in the past and their very names indicated that they were proposing to cater to a certain line of business—the Metals Bank, Commerce Bank and the Farmers' Bank, everything of that kind. A central bank, of course, with branches, tends to lend strength to the credit situation and provides opportunity to adjust resources, analogous to that which is done by the Federal Banking Board under the Reserve Act. But the main object to be attained here is to keep the avenues of credit open, so that no person can be denied credit in every quarter just because one quarter thinks it wouldn't want to extend credit to him.

February 12, 1926

It is rather difficult to comment on the feasibility of Federal arbitration boards in the major industries. The very first thing that we have to consider about arbitration is whether the parties agree to adopt it. If they don't agree to adopt it, of course it breaks down at the start. Where they do agree, it seems to me it is a feasible method. That is practically the method that has been agreed to between the employees and the managers of the railroads and I think holds out very great promise of success. But there it is not the first method that is used; it is the ultimate method. The first method which I think is correct, is negotiation between the parties, to see whether they can agree on the terms and conditions of service. Where in those activities which are necessary for the public welfare negotiation breaks down, then I think voluntary arbitration is the next method that ought to be applied. I am not in favor of compulsory arbitration.

February 16, 1926

I talked with Professor Ripley yesterday about the article that he had in the *Atlantic Monthly* (I think that was the magazine in which he published the article). I wanted to confer with him especially to see if he thought there was any abuse that ought to be remedied by Federal legislation. He didn't think that there was anything that Federal legislation could do in relation to the subjects that he discussed in the magazine. All of this is being done under the authority of state corporation laws. It isn't interstate commerce, and there is difficulty for that reason in reaching it by Federal legislation.

PRESS: What was the nature of the abuses?

PRESIDENT: That article you ought to read, if you haven't read it. It is a very interesting article in relation to the practice that is growing up of retaining control of large corporations in the hands of a very small amount of voting stock and then issuing to the public large amounts of nonvoting stock. He said that there were certain phases of that that might be considered sound and helpful but that it could be used for improper purposes.

[*William Z. Ripley was Professor of Economics at Harvard.*]

March 30, 1926

The reports in relation to business conditions in the country seem to be substantially as they have been for the past months. Employment apparently is plentiful. There are some strikes. That is always the case, but so far as the Department of Labor has information those who want to work at the prevailing rate of wages are enabled to secure employment. I think there have been some increases of wages, especially in the building trades, which are an indication that there is no lack of employment in that great industry, which is a very basic industry because it affects so many other things. A great many products go into building, and when that industry is flourishing it creates a demand for all kinds of supplies and has a beneficial influence on all kinds of production. There are some places where they are not working full time. I think that is the condition in some of the textile industries and has been so for quite a good many months.

White Pine Camp, Paul Smith's, N. Y., July 27, 1926

The business conditions in the country are more than meeting expectations. It had been thought at the opening of the year that there might be something of a slowing down in business. That hasn't seemed to materialize. The first six months of the current year showed good business conditions and since the first of July there has been something of an advance in general business conditions. I think that is attributable partly to the reduction of taxation. It takes some time to get the full effect of that, but it stimulates business by releasing money that otherwise would go into the public treasury which can go into enterprise. A very good example of that commented on in the press, which took place in the middle of June, was when the Secretary of the Treasury was able to meet out of the current funds all of the current expenditures. It had been expected in banking quarters that he would have to call on the country for a loan of some $300,000,000 and banks had accumulated funds for the purpose of making that loan to the Government. When the Government didn't call on them for that money it was at once available to go into business enterprise. As far as I can see myself and as far as I am advised by the members of my Cabinet, Mr. Hoover, who keeps very closely in touch with the business situation, and Mr. Mellon, who is in touch with the banking situation and the business situation, too, both advised me just before I left Washington that the business outlook for the coming period, immediate period, was good, and so far as there have been developments since I talked with them their expectations have been fully confirmed.

August 27, 1926

I haven't seen the article of Professor Ripley. I have seen some references to it in the press. So I don't know just what it is that he suggests that the Federal Trade Commission could do or should do or ought to be authorized to do by law. I am very keenly alive to the fact that we have in this country now about 20,000,000 security holders who have made investments in the business concerns of the country, and I want to have everything done that can be done adequately to safeguard their interests. That is a matter that I have had under consideration for a considerable length of time. I had a conference with Professor Ripley last winter relative to some subject that he had made suggestions about in a magazine article, about the issuance of stock that didn't have voting powers, and I understood that very largely I think because of the position that he had taken in his article in arousing public opinion that the listing committee of the New York Stock Exchange had indicated that they would look very carefully into the affairs of corporations that asked to list stock of that nature. Of course anyone that gives the matter a moment's thought would recognize the great difficulty of the Government in undertaking to say what securities are good or sound or some equivalent word and what are not. That has usually been left to the judgment and discretion of Commissions and various states have, I think, adopted what are known as Blue Sky laws. Of course there is a good deal of difference between saying that a security is good and sound and saying anything about the prospective price at which it may sell on the market. I think we all recall that Government bonds which were issued in time of war depreciated in market value quite a good deal. They have since regained their position and I think all of them now sell at par or better, some considerably better. That is perhaps an extreme example of the difficulty of making any future estimate as to what price a security may sell, even though it would have to be recognized as the best security in the world. So that I assume that what Professor Ripley is discussing is the question of corporate financing and the management of its business and the opportunity of the ordinary investor to get accurate information in relation to his investment. Any remedial legislation or action that might be taken to secure that result would have to be done keeping clearly in mind that these concerns are not national concerns, but that they are state concerns. They get their authority under the law and by charters that are granted to them by the various states. There is a little difference about that in relation to the railroads, but generally speaking all of our industrial concerns secure their rights and powers from a state charter and not at all from the laws of the United States. So that the United States doesn't have very complete jurisdiction over them. I should want to give some more thought and study than I have to the question to see where the line should be drawn and what action ought to be taken by the states and what might properly be done by the Federal Trade Commission. Broadly speaking, the Federal Trade Commission has jurisdiction over interstate commerce, that is jurisdiction over the commodity that an individual or a state corporation has created and which they propose to dispose of through the channels of interstate commerce, and having jurisdiction over the product of the corporation is quite a different thing than having jurisdiction over the finances and the corporate practices of the corporation. So that I should rather conclude that the best and most adequate protection that security holders would have through publicity of the financial affairs of corporations would have to be brought about by the passage of state laws, rather than by the passage of laws by Congress or the actions of any Federal agencies. Undoubtedly the Federal Trade Commission has some jurisdiction over the finances, but it must be incidental I assume to interstate commerce.

PRESS: He says in his article that there is a case stated before the Supreme Court to test whether the Federal Trade Commission has that power over finances.

PRESIDENT: Well that rather confirms what I say, that it is a question that would need considerable study and investigation in order to determine it, but I should think it would be plain that whatever powers, as I stated the Federal Trade Commission has, would be incidental in some way or other to interstate commerce. I think it has been decided that the securities that are issued by a corporation are not interstate commerce. I suppose it is possible that they may be made such when they are sold from one state to another. There again you come to the product and not to the action itself. The more I think of it, the more I come to the conclusion—I have been giving a little thought along that line until I began to discuss it here—that any real remedy to secure publicity or give the shareholder the right to know what is being done with his money, how the business of his concern is being conducted, would have to come almost entirely from state action rather than from national action. Professor Ripley is a man of large experience and recognized ability, and he is an expert on matters of this kind, and any suggestions that he might make would be entitled to very careful consideration before they could be dismissed, and any theory that he might propound as to the powers of the National Government would likewise be entitled to very careful consideration before it could be dismissed as unfounded.

PRESS: The Professor also seems to indicate that one of the difficulties now is that there are such a large number of forms of reports. Would that be remedied in any way if they had similar statements?

PRESIDENT: Well, those forms are all forms that are required by the state laws. I came in contact with that in my law practice and my experience in Massachusetts. The Commissioner of Corporations there makes up the legal forms on which corporations that are incorporated under the laws of Massachusetts and those which are incorporated under the laws of other states that come into Massachusetts to do business have to make reports.

PRESS: Did you have a hand in the passage of the Massachusetts Blue Sky law?

PRESIDENT: I don't recall that I did. I am not sure about that one way or the other. I know that there were some bills of that kind while I was in the General Court and I think there were some brought up while I was Governor. We had some regulations and restrictions there, but we didn't have that need so much in Massachusetts, because in order to come in there and do business corporations had for a long time been required to file certificates with the Commissioner of Corporations and make a complete disclosure, and those were made public, so Massachusetts wasn't a very fertile field under the law for the sale of securities that didn't have a firm foundation to warrant the assumption that they were proper investments.

PRESS: He points out an example in his article that corporations ought to be required to file a balance sheet as well as an income sheet, and he said the Massachusetts law requires them to show the balance and he thinks the reports ought to be more adequate, to show depreciation and so on.

PRESIDENT: That rather carries out what I have been saying, that where the state law is adequate and proper you get the result that Professor Ripley wishes to have and where they aren't adequate and proper I have considerable doubt as to whether the National Government can interpose to make it so. Whatever power it has would be under the Interstate Commerce laws to the Constitution. That is a broad power, but that relates generally to a commodity after it has been produced. I think the Court has decided that the mining of coal in and of itself was not interstate commerce, but after the coal is brought up on top of the ground and started to be shipped away then it becomes interstate commerce and the Federal Government has jurisdiction over it. But those are law questions and it is a well-recognized principle of legal practice that advice is not to be given without first reading the document that the advice is to be given about and secondly, without the consulting authority carefully investigating what the statutes may be, so what I have said would have to be taken with that qualification.

October 19, 1926

I had a very agreeable call from Charles M. Schwab yesterday. I could not help but think as he came in and went out how well he represented the result of America. Beginning, as he did, with no property and with meager opportunities he has developed a great manufacturing plant for the service of the people of America and is doing considerable business abroad. He told me that he started the Bethlehem Steel works with $12,000,000 capital and now it represents $800,-000,000 capital. I have forgotten how many employees he said, they run into the scores of thousands.

[*Charles M. Schwab was Chairman of the Board of Directors of the Bethlehem Steel Company. After his interview with Coolidge, which*

*Schwab refused to discuss, he predicted continuing prosperity and de-
clared a long-term depression impossible.*]

August 12, 1927

The business of the country is in very fair condition. Labor conditions are extremely satisfactory. Wages are on a very liberal basis.
There is some unemployment in certain lines, not anything more than
what is usual. That is always the case, that there are some lines lag-
ging behind.

[*Coolidge probably premised his remark on a report he had received
from Labor Secretary Davis asserting that unemployment was no worse
than in 1926. However, reports from New York and Chicago at this
time noted that unemployment was on the increase. The Chicago report forecast the worst winter unemployment since 1921.*]

August 19, 1927

I have stated my position relative to our merchant marine several
times in my messages to the Congress. I haven't changed my views on
it. I am not in favor of the United States Government embarking on
another program of building ships. We have just had an experience in
building $3,500,000,000 worth of ships on which we lost over $3,000,-
000,000. We have a large number of ships on hand that are not in use.
Nearly all the ships we are operating are operating at a loss. I think
I might with a great deal of safety say that no ship the United States
Government is operating is now operated at a profit if you take into
account the capital outlay. What I desire especially to do is to get our
merchant fleet into private operation, with sufficient guarantees to
have it kept in operation.

September 13, 1927

I haven't any information about the action of the Federal Reserve
Board in lowering the re-discount rate in Chicago. I think I have indicated to the conference a great many times that that is a board that
does function and ought to function entirely apart from the Executive,
acting almost entirely in the nature of a judicial position. I have sometimes made some comment on what they have done and the beneficial
effect that I thought had accrued from it, but I do not recall that I
have ever made any suggestion to the Board as to any action that it
ought to take. I think the question involved here is one of the interpretation of the statute under which they are acting. A good many
times if members of the press want to comment on a matter of that
kind it would be very helpful to them if they would get the statute
and read it. I find in making my decisions it is often very much sim-
plified if I find out what the law requires and then go ahead and do it.
It answers a great many questions that might otherwise arise. A great
many times a question seems to be very complicated and almost in-
soluble. If I take that course I find it is a very simple matter.

October 28, 1927

I don't recall any communications from representatives of the chemical industry favoring legislation to revise the Sherman Anti-Trust Law. It is very possible, though, that such communications have been addressed to me. Do you recall any such communications of recent date?

MR. CLARK: Nothing of recent date.

PRESIDENT: Mr. Clark says he doesn't recall any. I think it is more likely that some effort in that direction might be made by the producers of petroleum than by the chemical industry, on the ground, I assume, that it is a very limited natural product and that there ought to be an opportunity for the producers of it to make some kind of an arrangement for its conservation, which I think they claim they can not do now without running counter to the provisions of the anti-trust law. It is desirable, of course, to conserve our petroleum. I should want to make a very careful exploration of every other avenue, before resorting to any change in the anti-trust law. We might give them a different status from that held by other industries.

[*Edward Tracy Clark, a graduate of Amherst College, had been secretary to Senator Henry Cabot Lodge from 1900 to 1916. He was recommended by Frank W. Stearns and served as Coolidge's personal secretary both when he was Vice-President and President.*]

November 15, 1927

From such studies as I have made, I have never thought that there was much of a chance to help agriculture by a reduction of the tariff. Some 47 per cent of our exports, I think, are agricultural products. The main market for agriculture, of course, is in this country. I have worked rather on the theory that it would be more beneficial to agriculture and the country as a whole to do what I could to stimulate the market for agricultural products in this country, which means the general policy that I have pursued of encouraging legitimate business, reducing the tax burdens on it, and to produce a condition of confidence under which business would go forward. Of course, we have a very large amount of imports, running up to some four billion dollars a year, and those necessarily must continue if we are to have exports. I don't know how it would be expected to benefit agriculture by a reduction of the tariff, except on the theory that if we could get the manufacturing of this country done abroad then the people that do it abroad would buy more of our agricultural products. If our manufacturing is done abroad, of course it can not be done here, and it would seem to me that we would lose a correspondingly large home market. That is why I say I shall be interested in seeing what facts are set out to support their [National Industrial Conference on Agriculture] conclusions.

December 9, 1927

Such comment as I care to make at this time relative to rivers and harbors and inland waterways improvement and navigation of inland waterways is in my message. There is one comment that I might add—that it is quite discouraging for the United States Government to undertake to help people and find that it only lands itself in a very disagreeable controversy. That has happened on some of our irrigation projects, where the Federal Government has expended a great deal of money and was under a good deal of expense in order to irrigate land and redeem it for cultivation, and sometimes the results have been that the Secretary of the Interior was hung in effigy for his pains. We have gone to a great deal of trouble and a perfectly enormous expense in relation to shipping, and our being in that business is something that also lands us in a good deal of controversy. There is some controversy, I don't know what it is, about the Mississippi barge lines. I thought we had gone a considerable distance, and been quite generous in providing for it. Now, these are not reasons why the United States Government should not go ahead and do whatever is required to be done, but they are difficulties that it seems might be eliminated to a considerable extent, if those for whom these things are done would try and have a reasonable appreciation of the efforts that are being made in their behalf. Of course, the principle that I am trying to elucidate is the very extreme difficulty of the Federal Government engaging in the transaction of business that isn't strictly a government business. As soon as it undertakes to do that the people that are helped or harmed immediately begin a political agitation about it. It results in controversies that it would be much better to keep out of and is one of the main reasons why the United States Government ought to keep from undertaking to transact business that the people themselves ought to transact. It can't function along that line. As soon as the Government tries to transact such business, the people with whom it is being transacted don't regard it as the Government's business. They regard it as their business. They think it ought not to be done for the benefit of the Government in a way that would be for the benefit of the Treasury or all the people, but that it ought to be done for their benefit. And that always creates a situation that it is extremely difficult to contend with and one which is practically impossible. So that it is my policy, in so far as I can, to keep the Government out of business, withdraw from that business that it is engaged in temporarily, and not to be in favor of its embarking on new enterprises.

January 6, 1928

I am not familiar enough with the exact workings and practice of the Federal Reserve System so that comments that I might make relative to the amount of brokers' loans and so on would be of very much value. I do know in a general way that the amount of securities in this country has increased very largely in recent years. The number of different securities that are dealt in on the stock exchange are very much larger than they were previously. The deposits in banks also are larger. And those two things together would necessarily be a reason for doing more business of that kind that is transacted by brokers and would naturally result in a larger sum of money being used for that purpose. Now, whether the amount at the present time is disproportionate to the resources of the country I am not in a position to judge accurately, but so far as indicated by an inquiry that I have made of the Treasury Department and so on I haven't had any indications that the amount was large enough to cause particularly unfavorable comment.

January 10, 1928

I don't know what kind of a proposal, if any, has been made, according to a question that has been presented to me, to sell some of our merchant ships or all of them to the Brown Boveri group. My policy relative to the sale of ships is well known. I discussed it a great many times in my messages and addresses. I have had quite a good many investigations made by members of the Cabinet and I think you will recall that I had Mr. Dalton of Cleveland make an investigation of our shipping situation two or three years ago. All of them have advised the sale of ships. The present law under which the Shipping Board operates directs the sale of ships. It has always been difficult to secure action of that kind. There is one member of the Board that I think has a perfect record of opposing every sale of ships that has been made or proposed. Not knowing what the terms of the offer may be of this group I wouldn't be in any position to judge as to its adequacy, but I should think that would be the main question to investigate, as to whether the offer was adequate and what the offer might demand of the Government. From all the studies that I have made and all the investigations I have had made, I am convinced it would be greatly to the advantage of the country and greatly to the promotion of the merchant marine interests if we could get our shipping into private hands.

[*The American Brown Boveri Electric Corporation applied to the United States Shipping Board for a $120,000,000 loan to help underwrite its proposed Blue Ribbon Steamship Line, which would establish a 4-day transatlantic run between the United States and Europe. The Corporation, which planned the construction of several 20,000 ton liners, estimated the cost of its project at $200,000,000. The $120,000,000 requested fell within the 66⅔ per cent maximum loan provision according to existing law.*]

I have just spoken about the matter of the merchant marine. I knew that some bill had been reported out of the Senate Committee. I should doubt if it was expedient, for the reason that I have just stated, to have the unanimous agreement of the Shipping Board for the sale of ships. That would mean that one member of the Shipping Board was a majority, and I don't think the sale of a ship necessarily requires the meticulous care that we think is necessary in undertaking to convict one of our inhabitants of crime. In that case we require the unanimous agreement of 12 jurors. I don't think the sale of a ship is so important a function as that. I don't see any reason why it should require the unanimous consent of the Shipping Board. One of the reasons that I think our ships ought to be sold is the difficulty of the United States Government to transact business. Business is carried on for purposes of profit. The United States Government isn't carried on for that purpose at all, and if anything is to be done about a merchant marine the place to begin is to secure an adequate administration of it. I do not think that can be secured through putting operation and control into the hands of a Board of 7 men. I don't know of any private business of any consequence that could be undertaken through that method and our shipping business suffers from the effort to administer it by that clumsy method. I am not in favor of having the United States Government build any ships at the present time. I think that an investigation would show that we have sufficient tonnage to more than carry all the freight that is offered and as I indicated at a previous conference what our shipping interests need is not more ships, but more use of the ships that we have, by people in this country that have merchandise and freight that is to be transported by water. Once in a while there is a temporary and local shortage of shipping, due to a seasonal movement of corn, or more especially cotton and wheat. That was because two years ago there was an unexpected movement through the Gulf ports and there was a slight shortage there for a very short period, because at that time there was the coal strike in Europe, especially in England, and the tramp steamers that are usually available for temporary work of that kind were all engaged in carrying coal and that made a slight shortage. Last year there was no shortage. I don't know of any shortage of ships at the present time. Certainly, we can't be expected to build any ships for profit. I think I am well within the mark when I say that the next day after a ship is launched it could not be sold in the market for 25 per cent of what it cost. Now, I am very much in favor of maintaining an American merchant marine. It is very important to the interests of the country, but I think it can be best maintained and best carried on through the avenue of private ownership. But I realize that it will be necessary to give it some support from the Government, as other countries give their merchant marine support, through mail contracts or through some arrangement about the masters and crews of ships who are regarded, of course, as an auxiliary of our Navy, and who might well be taken into consideration in the matter of some payments or assistance of that nature for the maintaining of an adequate merchant marine.

February 28, 1928

Business conditions seem to keep along about the same. There has been some increase in some lines. I think the different steel companies report increases in their business. There was a report published by the Federal Reserve Board a day or two ago that reported increases in certain lines of merchandise, some increase in movements of freight. I think the department store business was reported as not quite so good.

March 16, 1928

I am quite anxious to get some railroad consolidation legislation. I have referred to that several times in my messages, but I think it would be especially helpful at the present time, because there are a number of roads that if they could make their consolidation arrangements are ready to put in additions and improvements in the way of building and construction that would furnish quite a large market for materials and quite an opportunity for increased employment. The railroads have been waiting for several years for legislation of that kind and meantime their plans have been held up and their improvements and their extensions haven't gone forward, and with the increase in business that has come to the railroads they are feeling more and more the necessity of expansions of that kind. I am advised that there is a very good prospect of securing favorable action from the House and the Senate at the present session. It would be exceedingly helpful to the situation if that could be secured.

March 20, 1928

I saw some headline relative to a proposal that was made by Governor Fisher for a conference for the purpose of trying to arrange some adjustment of the coal industry. If it is true that he is suggesting that representatives of the states and of the operators and of the miners and the National Government should all come together, my offhand opinion would be that such a conference would be so large that any practical and affirmative result would be very doubtful. You will probably recall that the Secretary of Labor, with my approval, called a conference of miners and operators just at the opening of the Congress, which did not result in any affirmative action. Some of the operators did not appear in person, but sent messages. If this was a mere question of wages, something of that kind might hold out more promise of effective success, but it is a question of reorganizing the coal industry. I don't want to indicate that if Governor Fisher wishes to have a conference of that kind that I should in any way oppose it or fail to have representatives of the Labor Department there. Now, it may be that he has something in mind that will be very practical and helpful. He is, of course, quite conversant with the coal industry and the coal situation and any suggestion he made ought to be given very careful consideration. Of course, if he meant to have a small conference, that would remove some of the objections that at present appear to me, but I assume he intends to have representatives from quite a large number of states, and if there are going to be representatives from all the operators, and from those who are engaged as employees, it would make it quite a large gathering. The operators perhaps might send one or two operators, perhaps the employees might send one or two representatives, and in that way keep the conference from being too large.

[*In a speech at the University of Pennsylvania, Governor John S. Fisher, a Republican, praised Coolidge for his decision to retire and compared him to George Washington in his refusal to seek another term in the White House. Actually, of course, Coolidge was elected only once to the presidency; he served out Harding's term after the latter's death.*]

April 10, 1928

I haven't had any suggestion that the farm bill might be modified. There are some things in there that I think I suggested in my message, but not more than 6 or 8 of them I think, though the bill has been changed somewhat, perhaps, since that change was made, and there are a large number of things still contained in the bill that it was necessary to criticize in my veto message of last year. The equalization fee is still there. While the Attorney General held last year that it was unconstitutional, I don't know of anything that has been done to render it constitutional this year. I should like very much to have a measure for helping the farmer in accordance with my various messages to the Congress. It seems as though such a measure might be worked out by the various committees and adopted.

[*The McNary-Haugen bill provided that an Agricultural Export Corporation would purchase on the domestic market at a designated ratio price the surpluses of such basic farm products as wheat, flour, corn, cotton, wool, cattle, sheep and swine as could not be absorbed by the domestic market. The surplus, in turn, would be dumped on the world market for whatever price it would bring. To compensate in part the Government for the loss it would suffer from the transaction (since the world price would be substantially lower than the domestic ratio price), the farmer would be charged an equalization fee on those products which the Agricultural Export Corporation sold abroad. Thus, the farmer would receive the tariff-protected domestic price less the amount of the equalization fee.*]

141

April 24, 1928

No information has come to me concerning the increase in rediscount rates, except that which I have seen in the press. That is a matter entirely for the Federal Reserve Board, a matter that I wouldn't happen to know anything about.

[*Coolidge, of course, has been the subject of sharp criticism because of his failure to familiarize himself with the policies of the Federal Reserve Board. The above statement hardly reflects well on his presidential leadership in economic affairs.*]

I was informed this morning that our exports are about what they were last year and especially our exports of manufactured goods. One of the main reasons for that is the increasing prosperity of the rest of the world and the stabilization that has come from their getting their finances into better order and securing reforms in their currency, getting back onto a gold basis and stabilizing their currency. This increase in exports is going to almost all of the countries of the world.

April 27, 1928

The farm bill meets 3 or 4 of the objections that I raised to the bill of last year in my veto message. There are a great many other objections that I raised that the present bill doesn't meet. I am advised that the claim is being made that all the objections that I raised have been met, with the exception of the constitutional objection to the equalization fee. That doesn't appear to me to be the case. I hope that none of the members of the Congress will be misled by any rumors of that kind. I hope they may pass some reasonable farm legislation, but I am afraid that the present bill will not meet what I held to be the requirements.

May 1, 1928

I have no information relative to proposed legislation about loans on securities. I saw by the press there was a bill pending in the House or the Senate. I don't know what it is or what the provisions of it are, or what the discussion about it has been.

May 18, 1928

I have very little information about the investigation going on before the Federal Trade Commission relative to the electric power companies. I had some talks something more than a year ago with a Harvard professor, who had two or three articles in magazines relative to the organization of electric power concerns—

PRESS: Professor Ripley, Mr. President?

PRESIDENT: Yes, and from such thought as I gave the subject at that time it seemed that the matter was almost entirely one for state action as distinguished from action by the United States. This investigation by the Trade Commission may perhaps reveal facts that will be helpful to state commissions in administering the powers that have been conferred upon them for the regulation and control of electric companies and the Commission may develop some facts that would call for national legislation, though the facts that they have developed so far that have come to my attention seemed to me pretty much matters for the states, rather than for the Federal Government.

[*The investigation revealed that Republican Senator Irvine L. Lenroot of Wisconsin had received $20,000 to oppose Senator Thomas Walsh's resolution for an investigation of power companies by the Senate Commerce Committee. Former Ambassador to Italy Richard W. Child, an admirer of Mussolini, was given $7,500 for a book condemning the proposed Boulder Dam project. The power companies were highly successful in obtaining removal from public schools and libraries of books supporting government ownership of public utilities.*]

May 25, 1928

I haven't seen the Muscle Shoals bill and know but very little about it. I will take it and look at it when it comes and try and decide it on its merits. I have discussed that problem several times in my messages. If you want my views more in detail you will find them there. I have of course been trying to get Muscle Shoals out of the hands of the Government and into private operation. I hope that this wouldn't put us any further into Government operation than we are now.

January 8, 1929

I haven't a great amount of information concerning the business situation, but I was advised this morning by the Department of Commerce that the last six months, according to their reports, was better than the first six months of the year 1928 and was up to the standard of 1927. So far as they can determine present conditions in business throughout the country are good and the prospect for the immediate future seems to be as good as usual.

January 25, 1929

So far as I know it is a very good idea of the Interstate Commerce Commission to direct Commissioner [Claude R.] Porter to prepare a plan for the unification of railroads. The law required that of the Commission ever since I have been President. I suppose they have done something about it, but they have also recommended nearly each year that that part of the law be repealed. One of the troubles with the Interstate Commerce Commission is to my mind the difficulty of getting any action out of it. The United States Government had a very sorry experience in that respect. There was pending before the board a case to fix the amount which would be paid for the transportation of the United States mails. It took three years to determine it and when it was finally determined we were told that we owed the railroads $45,000,000 for previous services. Of course, I have refused to recognize the validity of a decision of that kind and have refused to make payment. I suppose it will go to the Court of Claims to be decided whether the Commission has the right to make a retroactive finding. The question wouldn't have arisen if there had been a decision made within what seems to me is a reasonable time. While I think on the whole we have a good Commission and they function very well, I think their position would be greatly strengthened and their services would be of much greater value if they could make a decision promptly and expeditiously.

PRESS: We never had the valuation of railroads yet, have we?

PRESIDENT: Well, they never can have that. They might just as well hunt for a will-o-the-wisp. I think that is said to have cost about $100,000,000, and of course it can never be completed because as soon as one phase of it is completed, why it is necessary to go back and complete some other phase. I think the Commission has done as well as they could on that. Then as soon as it began to turn out that the proponents of valuation had been wrong, of course the proponents didn't press for it, and nobody else was greatly interested in it. Now, I suppose the Commission will say in answer to all these things that they couldn't make their decisions faster because they didn't have a larger force to spend more money. That is the standard reply of any department. If I ask them to buy paper or pins they always send back word that they have known for a long period of years they have been in need of paper and pins, but the budget has prevented their having them.

· III ·

THE UNITED STATES
ABROAD

8 · The Defense Establishment

IN THE 1920's the defense establishment—the war establishment, as it was then called—was comprised of the Army and the Navy. The air force was a part of the Army. Little popular interest was taken in the Army, which was a fairly small organization (less than 119,000 men after 1927) with relatively inexpensive equipment. Indeed, even in terms of the primitive military hardware of the twenties, the Army was badly off. The new advocates of military airpower, led by General Billy Mitchell, pushed for an independent air force that would match that of any other power. But the President found the rambunctious Mitchell irritating and completely thwarted him.

In contrast to the Army, the Navy was a strain on the national resources, and for this reason much discussion centered on naval affairs. Considering the small size of the total federal budget, a few billion dollars, expenses of the Navy loomed large. Moreover, public sentiment following the Great War was antimilitaristic. Americans dreamed of peace through arms limitation or disarmament. In such an atmosphere the Navy did not thrive. It had aspired to become perhaps "second to none" by achieving the building program announced in 1916, but the State Department dashed these hopes at the Washington Naval Conference of 1921-22.

When Coolidge was attempting to achieve his primary objective as Chief Executive—a budget surplus—the Navy appropriation was a natural subject of his scrutiny. But Coolidge knew that if he trimmed the military, particularly the Navy, unduly, he would lessen his country's influence in foreign affairs, on the old principle of Frederick the Great that "diplomacy without armaments is like music without instruments." The President had not ventured outside the continental United States, except for a honeymoon trip to Montreal in 1905 and a two-day visit to Cuba in 1928, but he understood power politics. The native of Plymouth, Vermont, was no extremist—although he believed strongly in economy and mildly in disarmament—and he was unwilling to sacrifice the Navy in the interests of either.

August 24, 1923

An inquiry about naval expenditures objected to by the Japanese Press. I wouldn't pay too much attention to an objection by a foreign newspaper. I haven't seen this and am just throwing out that hint as a general suggestion. If an objection should come to our State Department from the responsible authorities of Japan, of course, any such objection would be taken up, the matter discussed with their appropriate representatives, and an amicable conclusion would be reached. They have their papers over there that want to print things that, perhaps, may seem helpful to the interests of Japan, the same as we have papers here that, of course, print things that they consider will be helpful to the people of America. Sometimes they are on sound foundation and sometimes not. I haven't known of any objection on the part of Japanese papers or on the part of the Japanese Government. But, of course, the details of anything of that kind, you can get at the State Department. I am merely speaking on a few general observances.

November 16, 1923

An inquiry also about a constitutional amendment making property as well as persons and lives of citizens subject to conscription for the defense of the nation and that necessary legislation be enacted by Congress to that effect. I thought that that principle laid down by President Harding in one of his messages covered this very completely and answered a question of this kind very satisfactorily. I should say about that, that in time of war authority to take every resource of the nation, in persons and property, at reasonable pre-war rates of compensation without any profiteering would be a fair policy of operation and a fair principle. Now that is very difficult of practical application. When war arises necessarily it is followed by a tremendous force behind it to stimulate production and stimulate all kinds of activity, and the method that has been used for that purpose has been to increase prices. If you want to get more work done, more production, you pay a larger price. Wages rise, and prices of all kinds of commodities rise.

So that whether that exact principle would be one that could ever practically be put into operation, I think is a question. But in theory I think it is perfectly correct, and if it could be done it would make the question of national defense one much easier than it is at the present time.

March 25, 1924

I have one or two inquiries about the amendment to the Naval Appropriations Bill for calling another Disarmament Conference to complete the work of the Washington Conference. Our Government has made no inquiries about that of foreign governments, so far as I know. I think I have stated once or twice my position about it. There were some things that our Government would have been glad to do at the Washington Conference which we were unable to accomplish. It may be that there is an opportunity arising in the near future, though I don't think it appears to be here at present, for taking up some of those questions and getting a solution to them. If that should appear to be the case, why it would be in order to consider it. My general opinion has been that in the present condition of Europe, it would not be of any use to approach them with any general suggestion about a disarmament conference, or a further disarmament conference, though I suppose everyone knows what the American position was and what the agenda proposed by the American Government required, and that some of those positions were not met. The American Government at the present time I feel certain would be glad to have those positions met that were proposed at that time. I should think that the first thing to do would be to consider what would be the agenda at a conference of that kind. A general disarmament conference, I think, would be hopeless of accomplishing very much at its very outset. Then there are other matters of consideration that might be taken up—undertaking to see what could be done about international laws, which our country had in mind for such a long time but on which it could not get any action.

[*Coolidge was afraid that disarmament agitation might go in a general, rather than a specific, direction; he wished to continue the effort toward naval limitation begun at the Washington Conference. The latter meeting had stipulated limitation only of battleships and aircraft carriers. The President wanted limits on lesser naval craft: destroyers, submarines, and especially cruisers, in which category a race was developing among Britain, Japan, and the United States. The American Government was holding back for budget reasons; in the absence of a conference the United States might have to compete more vigorously. There were also broad questions of international law— neutral rights, in particular rules for submarines in wartime—which the Coolidge Administration wished to take to an international meeting.*]

149

April 11, 1924

The Cabinet didn't discuss the Government's rights under the disarmament treaty to convert its coal burning ships to oil burning. The matter was merely mentioned there by Secretary [of the Navy] Wilbur as one that was under consideration between him and the Secretary of State. But there was no discussion of it, and no conclusions. Of course we have in mind a general policy of not wanting to do anything that would cause an increase in the outlay of naval armaments of the United States or any other country. That is somewhat regardless of the treaty. Very likely our country in this particular wouldn't be especially solicitous to put in oil burning apparatus and convert ships from coal burning to oil, if that of itself would make other nations who are parties to the treaty think that they must go to a corresponding outlay. One of the very basic foundations of the disarmament treaty was to get away from competitive armaments, so that as a practical question our country wouldn't want to embark on the rebuilding or reconditioning of its ships if we know it would cause a large outlay on the part of other countries.

[*The Navy sought to modernize the American battleship fleet by installing oil burning apparatus and by elevating the big guns to obtain longer range. The President resisted any interpretation that the Navy could not modernize the battleships under the Five-Power Naval Treaty of 1922.*]

May 9, 1924

I haven't any plan other than that which was outlined in my address before the Associated Press at New York, relative to another conference of the powers for the purpose of disarmament or the consideration of the codification of international law. I don't know whether both of these questions could be considered in the same conference. The question of disarmament is one that affects certain large powers. The question of international law is one that affects all the nations of the world. I should think from what information I have now that it would not be practical to call one during the summer. There is a political campaign that will be going on during that time, and I don't know now what the condition in Europe will be. I indicated in my New York address that before there would be much hope of a successful conference it is necessary to have European questions settled, so far as they can be, and a more composed state of mind there than there apparently exists at the present time. There are very hopeful indications that a settlement will be made in Europe, but when, no one can tell. They have had elections in Germany. Elections I think are to be held this month in France. Those elections may have something to do in determining what the attitude of France may be, and after the elections I suppose it will be some time before the coming in of those

who are chosen, and naturally it will take some time after that to arrive at a settlement on the part of the governments concerned. With
all those things in mind, I don't see how it could be possible to think
that there was a practical hope of success for having a conference during the summer here.

August 22, 1924

Everybody in? I have several inquiries here about a conference for
further limitation of armaments. I spoke of that in detail, first in the
address that I gave at the Associated Press meeting in New York in
April, and I spoke of it also in my address of acceptance. Now that lies
in my mind this way; that when the situation in Europe is settled
down so that they have the matter of their reparations out of the way
and they appear to have reached a stable condition so that they are
not disturbed lest they be attacked by each other, such a time would
be an appropriate occasion for calling another conference for limitation of armaments. I suppose that means that there will have to be
first an approach to find out whether such an invitation would be
acceptable, and so on, and so forth. But I mention that as indicating
my desire to call one at the earliest possible moment that it would
seem to be practicable. I don't think it would be practicable until
they reach a somewhat stable condition in Europe.

[*Coolidge had just accepted the Republican nomination for the
presidency; Europe was dealing with the Dawes Plan (see "Debts and
Reparations"); it was a happy combination of activity.*]

August 29, 1924

I haven't seen the British protest against increasing the range of our
guns on American battleships. I am not certain whether any formal
protest has been received. My position about that would be to maintain whatever right the American Government has under the treaties,
as a matter of right. Now, in addition to that is the matter of policy.
Our Government, in conjunction with others, is trying to discourage
competitive armaments. It entered into treaties for that purpose. It is
also known that the governments in Europe are struggling along
under a heavy burden of debt. I don't want to do anything here that
would make it necessary for them to start increasing their naval
armament expenses for the purpose of building new ships, or changing
over those ships that they already have. I should be very loath to start
in on a policy of that kind. But that is entirely apart from what right
the American Government may have under the treaties. As I say, whatever right we have I shall assert at all times. I don't want to surrender
the right. That is somewhat different from what we might consider a
practical policy to pursue. I think the practical policy to pursue at this
time is not to enter into a competitive method of arming ourselves. As
I have already indicated, they have staggering expenses abroad. I don't

151

like to refer to it too often—they owe us money over there. I should very much prefer that they should take their money and pay us, than on account of any action we took over here feel that they should take their money and build battleships. I think it would be very much better for all concerned to adopt a policy of that kind. I never knew of just how much importance the British protest was, whether it was a natural form they took for the purpose of filing a protest in order to save any right they might have and to indicate they might not want to start in on any competitive armament at this time, or whether they thought it was a distinct injury to them or a violation of the spirit of the treaty. I haven't seen the protest. The time for action on it wouldn't arrive until we made an appropriation by the Congress, and then undertook to determine whether we wanted to spend the appropriation that had been made. I think I have made myself clear—that is, to assert all the rights we have and surrender none of them. But so far as the policy is concerned, I am very loath to take any action that would cause the governments abroad to think they must spend great sums of money on their naval armaments.

[*Coolidge's irritation was understandable. If the Europeans built warships the American budget might be doubly hit: war debts probably would not be paid and the United States would itself have to spend money constructing ships.*]

September 2, 1924

There was nothing of importance discussed at the Cabinet this morning, other than the statement made by Mr. Hughes, which has been on paper and which will be given to the press if it has not already been given out, in relation to our participation in an effort to control the sale of arms. That is a different thing, as you see, from disarmament. This is a matter of selling it. We participated in a discussion of it and we have agreed on certain proposals. Then there came a proposal that we should sit in with the League of Nations for discussion, and our reply was that our position had already been made known and we would be glad to participate in an international conference, where of course we can sit in on an equality with everybody else, and enter into any kind of an arrangement that might seem practical and on which we thought we would be able to secure legislation to carry it into effect.

September 5, 1924

I didn't know that there was any difference between the Navy Department and the Bureau of the Budget over naval estimates. There is a general difference, practically speaking, that way between all the departments and the Bureau of the Budget, but that is in the way of a preliminary examination of each department's estimate, and they have an opportunity to come to me when the budget is finally made. It is my budget. I have to take the responsibility for it when I submit it to the Congress, and I am here if the departments want to talk to me about any parts of the budget.

[*Coolidge was an efficient administrator. He delegated tasks to "my Secretary of State" or "my Secretary of the Navy," expecting them to do the job. In contrast to his successors, Herbert Hoover and Franklin D. Roosevelt, he refused to get bogged down in details.*]

September 16, 1924

Here is another inquiry about the guns on the American battleships —elevation. Nothing new developed in relation to that. I think I made my position quite clear the other day. We want to maintain all the rights we have under the treaty, but as a matter of policy I doubt whether at the present time I would want to advocate any expenses that aren't absolutely necessary on battleships. An additional reason has developed in relation to that within the last week, by reason of the return of the American fliers from around the world. I have read a great many times in the course of a short life that battleships are to become extinct. They never have. And I should hesitate some to put a lot of reliance on that kind of a statement now and to adopt that policy. But it was reported to me that one result of this world flight has been a demonstration of future ability to carry on warfare through the air and that it made the position of the large battleships very much different than it has been in the past. The statement was that we couldn't go to Europe now as we went in 1917 and 1918, and that it would be impossible to pursue the policy that we had adopted of transporting troops and munitions on account of the development of aerial navigation. Now, I should have to take that into consideration before I want to authorize much of an expenditure on large battleships. Also it is to be considered that we have 6 or 8 battleships under the treaty that will come up to be scrapped in the course of a not very long time in the future, 6, 8 or 10 years. It is a question of whether we want to expend a lot of money on those battleships that will be scrapped in that time. Those are the only differences that have occurred to me in the situation between now and what it was the other day.

PRESS: Mr. President, doesn't that make your position in relation to the next disarmament conference stronger by not bringing our forces up to the stipulation in the treaty?

PRESIDENT: I have seen considerable discussion to the effect that our Navy was way below the treaty limit. I should want to have quite a careful inventory and analysis made of our Navy before I subscribed strongly to that. You gentlemen are all familiar with the military policy. It seems to be the classic one of securing an appropriation for either the Army or the Navy. That policy doesn't have very much effect around this office, nor I assume on the Congress, suggesting that our Army is running down in materials and personnel, and that the Navy is just ready to drop into the sea. I couldn't go into details, but my belief is that the Navy at the present time is in perfect condition, pretty efficiently manned, entirely well equipped, and that it is able to shoot a little better than it was ever before. Now, I don't want anything said that will deter the Congress from making an adequate appropriation. I want to see the policy of the budget maintained. I want to maintain it and the only way that it can be broken down is through the action of the Congress. I want to try to have the Executive Department maintain that policy, and just at the present time before I should want to approve of a very enlarged appropriation for any department I should want to make a very careful survey of the department to see that every possible efficiency is being secured out of the present appropriation.

PRESS: Mr. President, are we to understand that this is the reason for Mr. Wilbur's coming back to Washington so hastily?

PRESIDENT: I wouldn't say that. Some of the press, I thought, rather overemphasized that. I want to see him about matters in the Navy and so I sent him a telegram asking him to return. It didn't portend any crisis, or anything of that kind.

PRESS: Mr. President, could you give us any information about the estimates?

PRESIDENT: For my own information I asked the Bureau of the Budget to find out how much we were spending for aviation, and the figures are $32,174,000 total; for the Army $12,435,000; the Navy $16,-150,000; then the Advisory Board has $450,000; and the Post Office Department $2,750,000. [Stenographers's note: The President left out a figure.] That doesn't, of course, in the Army and Navy, represent the pay of the personnel.

PRESS: Those are figures for the current fiscal year?

PRESIDENT: Last year, I believe. I think the salary of the officers and men is all in addition. I think that is the largest amount that is expended by any government, with the possible exception of France. I rather doubt if they are making as large an expenditure as that. I wouldn't want to be too certain of that. Their expenditures on account of differences in prices and so on are somewhat different from ours.

PRESS: Mr. President, do you have the figures showing the increase?

PRESIDENT: I don't know. I don't imagine there is an increase over the preceding year. The total is $32,174,000, which is a fairly large sum to expend on aviation. It is not so very long ago that the appropriation for the Navy didn't exceed that amount.

PRESS: Mr. President, what is the basis of these figures—to see whether it shall be increased or decreased for the next year?

154

PRESIDENT: No, but I have seen some newspaper comment about the amounts that we were proposing to expend on aviation, and for my own information I sent out to find out what the amount was. It may be that we ought to expend more than that. It may be that that is adequate. I merely mentioned that as the only element that I thought of that would come into consideration at the present time in relation to expending a lot more money on battleships. The round-the-world flight to some minds has demonstrated that the position of the battleship has become one that is obsolete. I rather think that there would be a little lack of logic in spending a lot of money on battleships and at the same time spending a lot of money on aviation. I am not quite sure about this, but if the battleship has become obsolete because aviation has become powerful, it seems to me that we had better stop spending very much money on battleships and more on aviation.

PRESS: Mr. President, will that idea be carried out in the budget?

PRESIDENT: I don't know that the idea has developed far enough yet. I wouldn't want to pass judgment on it. Of course that is a matter for the experts of the Army and the Navy. They haven't made any formal report to me, but I am just speaking about this as to what seems to me rather an inevitable result. If battleships become obsolete we wouldn't want to spend a lot of money on them, and if aviation becomes more efficient perhaps it is reasonable to spend more money on aviation.

[*During the decade preceding World War I, large battleships were the symbols of naval power. When the British Navy launched the* Dreadnought *in 1906, all the major naval powers rushed to build comparable vessels. But the great sea Battle of Jutland, something of a draw between Britain and Germany, and the subsequent role of the high seas fleets convinced many observers that the gargantuan ships were overrated. The success of postwar experiments in sinking vessels from the air provided further evidence for such opinion.*]

September 23, 1924

I don't know of any plan to increase the scope of the proposed aviation board to include not only the Navy but the Army, or a civilian membership. What I am particularly interested in here is the relative value between aviation, surface vessels and submarines. That is pretty purely a naval question. I haven't had a chance to talk or discuss it with the Secretary of War [Weeks]. I shall want to do that. My own impression is that perhaps this could be handled by the general Navy board by their taking advantage of any testimony that they could secure from the Army. It may be that it would be desirable to join the Army as a member of the board. But my first impression is that that wouldn't be necessary; that they could get all the information that the Army might have through testimony from the Army, and keep the two services separate as they are now. But I shall want to talk with the Secretary of War about that before making a decision. The aviation situation was not discussed at the Cabinet meeting this morning. None of the members of the Cabinet had anything to bring before the meeting, so it was very short.

[*The proponents of what Coolidge quaintly called "aerial navigation" were convinced that only a special presidential board could settle the controversy over air power. Such a board, headed by Dwight W. Morrow, then a partner of J. P. Morgan and Company, recommended, and the Army appointed, a special Assistant Secretary for Air.*]

December 16, 1924

Here is a question into which I am not going to enter for the purpose of making any detailed discussion, but it relates to a comparison of our Navy with that of other countries. Now, I have tried to indicate that I don't want to proceed on that theory. I don't see any hope in the future for competitive armaments. Of course the minute that you begin to say this country is building so many, and therefore we must build so many, you are right back on the old competitive theory of armaments, and I want to keep off that. I am in favor of an adequate defense for our own country. I stated my position in my first message to the Congress. If any of you care to read that, you will see what it is.

[*Whenever a naval appropriation bill was before Congress, the Navy's procedure was to compare the American Fleet with foreign fleets, especially that of Great Britain. It was not difficult to produce technical comparisons which showed the American Navy to be far inferior. The President heartily disliked this tactic. British admirals made their budget points in precisely the same manner. Some wits suggested that the best solution was to exchange fleets.*]

December 30, 1924

I do not know just what budget estimates will be made for beginning work on the additional cruisers or for work that is contemplated on our battleships. My general directions to the Bureau of the Budget were to investigate the needs that arise on account of the passage of the legislation, which include a number of things, and to recommend appropriations that will put them into effect. I did not imagine that it would be thought best to lay down all of the eight cruisers during the present fiscal year—which is the one that ends June 30th—but whether or not all of the eight cruisers ought to be provided for sometime during the next fiscal year after this, I would not be in a position to state at the present time.

[*In the years preceding the Five-Power Naval Treaty of 1922, ships ranging from little more than destroyer to virtual battleship class were categorized as cruisers. Their tonnage and guns depended on the mis-*

sion: to protect commerce, guard other vessels of the fleet, scout for the battleship force, fight off large enemy ships. The problem concerned the new "heavy cruisers," vessels of approximately 10,000 tons displacement equipped with 8-inch guns. They became of interest to navies essentially because the Treaty of 1922 had set 10,000 tons and 8-inch guns as the points beyond which a vessel automatically was classified as a battleship. The Navy found the distinction between heavy cruisers and battleships highly useful; American cruisers, constructed mostly before the war, were light, usually 6,000 or 7,000 tons, and few in number. The British Navy, with many cruisers, almost all of them light, hardly wanted the American Navy to add heavily armored vessels which could outgun its own cruiser fleet. When Congress passed an eight-cruiser bill in 1924, the President delayed construction as long as possible, preferring to hold it as a threat against the British and, to a lesser extent, the Japanese. When the latter embarked on a naval race in the mid-30's, the lid came off cruiser tonnage and guns.]

January 6, 1925

There is nothing I can say in relation to a new arms conference. It has no relationship, so far as I can see, to any discussion about our debts. It is held up at the present time, as I have already indicated, on account of the proposal that is pending to have a conference on that subject under the patronage of the League of Nations.

[European nations, understanding the connection between debts and disarmament, were not above contending that if they limited their navies the United States ought to reduce their war debts. A disarmament conference was being considered; as a result of the Locarno Agreements of 1925 and the admission of Germany to the League, in 1926 the nations called together a Preparatory Commission which met sporadically until the World Disarmament Conference opened in 1932.]

January 9, 1925

I am opposed to raising the elevation of the guns on United States battleships for reasons I have already given. I don't know why there is constant agitation about that, unless it be the result of an attempt to try and break down our system of limitation of armaments and resort to the old policy of competition. Now, I don't think it is a question of whether by a technical construction of the treaty we have a right to elevate these guns. Suppose we have; suppose we haven't. If we are going to have the policy here of limitation of armaments, we shall never have it by reason of that treaty we have made, but by reason of a public sentiment that exists in the country in favor of that policy. If you break down the public sentiment you will begin to dig down under the treaties that are in existence at the present time, and when you get far enough under them they will explode something and destroy them. That is the main reason why I am opposed to the elevation of the guns. $8,000,000 is not a large sum to expend for the elevation of guns, but the work will extend over some years. Then these ships, as I have already explained, will become obsolete in a short time, and our naval treaty lasts ten years and is drawing to a close. I think it is much more important to do what we can to promote sentiment here as in favor of limitation of armaments and against competition than in that direction. Otherwise, we will be right back in the place that civilization has found itself ever since it began and an inability to rely on anything except the number of guns that it has for the protection of its interests. I am desirous of promoting the other policy, so I am opposed to elevating the guns at this time. I think it would be hailed as the beginning of the breaking down of that policy. I am sending up to the Senate in response to their resolution, a copy of the letter which Secretary Hughes, after consulting with me, had already sent to the Committee on Naval Affairs in the House, which gives all the information and some other information that the Senate has requested. Japan as I understand it doesn't think it is contrary to the terms of the treaty, but the British have raised that question.

February 10, 1925

I don't know that I have any mature views about the proposal to create a unified and independent Air Service. I haven't been inclined to favor it. One of the reasons is that they are putting through a reorganization bill, or are going to, and one of the first proposals there was that we should have an entirely unified Army and Navy, to put that all under one term, "National Defense" or something of that kind, with sub-heads of those who are to look after the Army and those who are to look after the Navy. This runs counter to the general policy. I think the general policy of Government administration at the present time is unification, rather than the establishment of new and independent services. Then the Air Service is a new arm of the service and has not yet been developed. We don't know what its value is. It is evidently a service that holds great promise, and I consider it as a very important adjunct of our national defense. I want to see it developed to the fullest extent. That can be done by discussion, exchange of views, and experimentation. I have noticed several suggestions that we have spent some $400,000,000 on the air service and don't seem to have secured any very great results. I think one of the reasons is in the word I have just used. It is still in its experimental stage. If you have had any experience at all with government experimentation you know it requires a good deal of money to carry on. My first experience came when I was in the legislature, I think I was in the Senate and was Chairman of the Committee on Agriculture. The experimental station at the Agricultural College pursued a great many experiments that didn't turn out to be of any great value, other than to demonstrate that results could not be secured by that line of procedure. Now, it is the same in our Air Service. We have to make experiments with planes of different makes, patterns, engines, and everything of that kind, and oftentimes the experiment only demonstrates that if you want to secure a result you have to proceed in another direction. That costs money. So I don't think it is a real criticism that although we have spent a great deal of money we have not accomplished altogether results on the practical side.

March 13, 1925

I want to see a further limitation of naval armament. I would delight to see something relative to a limitation of land armament, but we have made our reduction of land armament and we haven't anything we could offer in that respect. Several of the European nations have made their reduction, so that they have nothing to offer. And I would not want to put the United States and other nations in a position of attempting to coerce any of the nations that might have considerable land armaments into a reduction against their will, as such action would not be helpful—it would not be productive of that harmony and peaceful intercourse that we want to maintain with all other armed countries. But if it appears that the European proposal has been definitely abandoned, why then I am going to take up with Secretary Kellogg seriously the question of whether the time has come when we can take some steps.

[*Frank B. Kellogg had succeeded Charles Evans Hughes as Secretary of State on March 4, 1925.*]

July 21, 1925

Senator Hale talked with me yesterday about the Navy and I have asked him to make an intensive study of the Navy to see if we are maintaining any useless activities in it, so that there might be a possibility of saving money to the taxpayers by discontinuing them. You will recall that last year we made an authorization for some new cruisers, submarines and so on to the extent of a great many million dollars. That work will have to begin in the near future. I would like to find a place in the Navy where we can make sufficient savings to go some way towards taking up this new work. I should be very glad to consult General Mitchell about any subject that he is familiar with on which he can be helpful. I have consulted him a number of times in the past and expect to in the future.

PRESS: Mr. President, do you recall about how much that outlay was?

PRESIDENT: I can't give the figures. I think there was an authorization for a number of new cruisers and they cost—I think a new cruiser costs fully as much as $11,000,000.

[*Senator Frederick Hale (Rep., Maine) was chairman of the Naval Affairs Committee. General William Mitchell was about to be court-martialed (October 28-December 17).*]

July 28, 1925

There isn't any change in the status of the proposed disarmament conference. One thing or another has developed in Europe that hasn't made it seem quite opportune to propose it. Just at present the matter of the security agreement is pending. Of course if that can be arranged, why it will lay a very broad foundation for further disarmament. With that undecided the question of how far disarmament could be carried would not be one that they could make an accurate decision about. Now, I am quite aware that there is never going to be any perfect condition under which disarmament conferences can be called. First, I didn't want to insert that question into an international discussion during the work that was going on on the Dawes plan when the question arose about putting the Dawes plan into operation. Then the question came up at the Geneva conference. Now it is the question of the security pact. What I have been waiting for was a time when Europe had seemed to arrive at as stable a condition as we can hope to have there, with all pending difficulties over there, so that there will be a situation that would make it seem that a disarmament conference would have the largest possible promise of being successful.

[*The European powers, seeking some sort of security pact, had rejected the Geneva Protocol, but in 1925 concluded important interlocking agreements at Locarno.*]

August 25, 1925

I have got two or three questions here about the Army. I don't think I would take too seriously the dispatches from Washington that purport to emanate from the General Staff. It is one of the characteristics of the reports that purport to emanate from that source that they always represent the Army as just on the point of dissolution. We are spending I think about $300,000,000 on the Army. Before the War it is my recollection that we spent $120,000,000. I don't want to be held too closely to those figures, and I suppose as long as we continue to spend $300,000,000 that the General Staff would be able to provide the nation with a fair degree of defense. I am quite sure they are competent to do that, so that any dispatches that seem to indicate that that result won't be accomplished would appear to me to be so much a reflection on the ability of the General Staff that I don't place any great credit in them.

September 8, 1925

I don't know enough about the suggestion that the Premier of France [Paul Painlevé] has made that the League of Nations call a Disarmament Conference. I can't make any comment about it. I should have to be careful about making comment on a matter of that kind, because of course our country doesn't want to put anything in the way of any action that the Europeans might take which they thought would minister to their general security.

I have forgotten whether I said anything the other day about the proposal that I have made to have the conference in Washington. I had that in mind for some time, hoping that events would shape themselves by the settlement of the reparations question over there, and perhaps by a security pact in Europe, so that we could have another conference with a practical hope of success in Washington. Of course the main thing is not where the conference is held, but the main thing is to have a conference that holds promise of securing practical results. I think there is now a proposal before the League, or some of the nations of Europe, for holding some Disarmament or Arbitration Conference in Geneva, and while that was pending was another reason why I thought it might not be quite proper for me to undertake to hold a conference here.

[*The matter at issue was whether to hold a general disarmament conference under League sponsorship or a naval conference perhaps under American sponsorship. Excessive American initiative might give Europeans opportunity to bargain away debts for disarmament.*]

September 22, 1925

I don't want to make any definite statement about the attitude of this Government towards a Disarmament Conference by the League of Nations. Before we could undertake to participate in a Disarmament Conference of that kind I should think we ought to have the authority of Congress. I have been basing my recommendations for a Disarmament Conference on the clause that is annually put into the appropriation bill, I think for the Navy. I think it goes into the Army bill. I know it is in the Navy Bill, and that gives Congressional authority. I don't want to say anything on the other hand that would discourage the calling of a European Conference because I realize that they have delicate questions over there which touch their conditions particularly and in which we are not so much interested. If they can solve those problems themselves, nothing would be more agreeable to our people I believe, and I am sure nothing would be more agreeable to our Government, so that I don't want to have anything that I might say taken in any way as undertaking to discourage their attempt to solve their own problems in Europe. Of course in the general question of disarmament we are interested. The Government as at present constituted is committed to it, believes in it, and I think the country believes in it, and we ought to do everything we can to encourage it.

[*As Coolidge pointed out, it was easier for the United States than for European nations to be interested in the general question of dis-*

armament. The American Army was so small and poorly equipped that disarmament, practically speaking, applied only to the American Navy, which the Coolidge Administration was quite willing to do in conjunction with similar naval limitations by Britain, Japan, and perhaps France and Italy.]

November 17, 1925

I don't know of any change in the attitude of the United States Government in relation to submarines from the position that was taken at the time of the Washington Conference. I don't want to say that the United States Government wouldn't be willing to change the policy that it announced at that time, but the policy then announced is the policy that we have at the present time, a limitation of submarines, with an open mind to hear and consider any other suggestions that might be made in relation to the use or abolition of submarines.

[*At the Washington Conference of 1921-22 the United States and Great Britain had discussed limiting and possibly abolishing the submarines, a threat to their merchant fleets. Smaller naval powers, with low merchant tonnage, were less interested. Submarines were relatively inexpensive to build; large, ocean-going submarines were not needed by the Continental nations.*]

February 23, 1926

. . . there is of course the report of the Aircraft Board. I am anxious to have legislation that carries that out. I am almost equally desirous of not having legislation that goes beyond the report and recommendations of that Board. I feel quite confident that when the various committees come to study the subject they will come to the same conclusion that the Air Board reached. You will remember that there was a great deal of confusion about our Air Service last summer. That was my state of mind. I presume that if you will hark back to it you will find it was your own state of mind. It was very well cleared up, I thought, by the report of the Air Board. The central thought of that was that our country was not in immediate jeopardy by reason of any lack of our Air Service or of any attack that could be made on us by any other country. Now, I want to have a good Air Service here, the same as I want to have a good Army and Navy, but I don't want to run to extremes about it. There is some pressure in the country, perhaps from people that haven't made a careful study of the subject and a careful perusal of the report of the Air Board, to build a very large air fleet. I don't think that is necessary. I am opposed to it because it would be an unnecessary expenditure of money and because the theory of it would be to go back to the theory of competitive defense. Of course if we arm ourselves with a great air fleet, the necessary reaction will be that other countries think they must do the same and then we are off again competing in armaments. There has been one development in relation to this which I think has been helpful, and that was to bring to the attention of men in the service that it is especially their business to be Army and Naval and military men and function in that direction, and not undertake to function in other directions. In our service there is the Army and Navy, the Reserve Officers Corps, the National Guard, altogether making I think about 550,000 men. Now it is quite obvious that if everybody in that service should start out to bring to bear great pressure on Congress for everything that they might think they wanted at any time, the result wouldn't be good, and if as the result of our actions we should make a great Air Force there is a good deal of question as to whether after we did create it the same forces wouldn't be demanding that it be used in some direction or other, and we would have established here almost before we knew it a great military nation, which nobody that I think gives the subject careful consideration would want to have done. So we have had to bring it rather sharply to the attention of men in the service that they ought to obey that injunction of the service rules which requires that they shouldn't volunteer to influence legislation—give their opinions when they are asked of course; but to form any organization of a military nature for the purpose of influencing Congress would in the end be productive of embarrassing results.

March 5, 1926

I can't set any amount that would be said to be a practical amount for an Air Service appropriation. I think our present Air Service appropriation is about $70,000,000 a year. The present budget carries somewhat more than that. The total appropriations in the present budget for the Army and Navy would be $674,000,000. That is $11,-000,000 more than last year. There are some bills pending in relation to the Air Service, one for the Naval Air Service, and there is a bill being drafted, I think, for the Army Air Service. With these large appropriations that are now being made, it seems to me that we ought to get along without enlarging appropriations. If more men are to be taken into the Air Service, why then I should think an arrangement should be made so that more men could be dispensed with in some of the other branches of the service. We have a force in this country, I think I have stated it, of about 558,000 men that could be put into the service almost overnight, which would appear to be ample for any needs we may have. The Army has 118,000 enlisted men, the Navy I think 82,000. Now, if it is desirable to have more men in the Air Service and more officers, why I think some provision ought to be made to meet that expenditure by a reduction of expenditures in some other direction, especially so on account of the present condition of the Treasury.

March 1, 1927

To recur for a moment to the matter of limitation of arms. I don't know whether it would be feasible to secure any agreement with Japan and Great Britain. It might be that some progress could be made by a three-power agreement. But I should think that would be doubtful. The position of Great Britain, as I recall it, at the Washington conference was that unless some arrangement could be made with France for limitation on submarines and so on, that of course they couldn't make any limitation on those vessels that are used as a defense against submarine attacks.

[*Coolidge was considering a five-power conference on naval arms— United States, Britain, Japan, France and Italy.*]

June 7, 1927

Of course, I can't speak as an expert regarding the appearance of the fleet at the review which I attended last Saturday. I was naturally very much impressed with the fine appearance that was made by the fleet, both in the large number of vessels that passed by and in their generally efficient appearance. We had but a few of our destroyers there. We have a great many of them. We have a good many battleships and cruisers and an airplane carrier and a hospital ship, which is the only hospital ship in the world which was built exclusively for that purpose in serving a national navy. I don't think that anyone could have viewed the parade of the ships that went by with the knowledge that it was only a part of our fleet, without realizing that we have, as everyone knows, one of the most powerful navies in the world.

[*The President enjoyed sailing up and down the Potomac in the* Mayflower, *but probably did not take pleasure in reviewing the fleet beyond a breakwater. Photographs which caught Coolidge watching the parade of ships revealed him sporting a naval cap, but showing signs of boredom and* mal de mer.]

June 24, 1927

I thought the Naval Conference at Geneva started off very well and of the proposals that were made by the three governments each of them indicated very clearly that they were very sincere in their desire for further naval limitations. I don't care to discuss the details of them while the conference is going on, because it often happens that in the somewhat informal methods of discussion here in the conference when the reports are carried abroad they are given quite a different impression from what I had intended to give to the conference. So while the conference is in session I shall not undertake to discuss in detail the questions that it has before it.

[*The Geneva Naval Conference opened on June 20, 1927. The United States, Britain, and Japan sent representatives; France and*

164

Italy, observers. Coolidge and Secretary of State Kellogg hoped to obtain an agreement limiting construction of cruisers.]

June 28, 1927

PRESS: Is it fair to assume that they [the Geneva Conference delegates] might get new instructions that they didn't have before they left as regards Japan, or perhaps Great Britain?

PRESIDENT: I don't know about that. I don't want to make any comment about that. Anything that the delegates, our delegates, ask instructions about, instructions will be given.

[*Coolidge was extremely reticent about the Geneva Naval Conference. Chief American delegates at the conference were Hugh Gibson and Rear Admiral Hilary Jones.*]

July 19, 1927

I think all the information that I have has already been reported in the press relative to the Naval Limitation conference at Geneva. They are evidently having some difficulty in reaching a final agreement about cruisers. As I am sure that each of us went there with a desire for an agreement that would afford limitation, I have every hope and expectation that some agreement will be reached, not probably just an agreement that any one of the nations would wish, but some point on which all can agree.

[*The conference was already in rough water; the British Government refused to cut its cruiser fleet down to the size desired by the Americans. Great Britain had a great many light cruisers in commission and had learned from the World War that they were very effective vessels. The British began by speaking casually of maintaining a large cruiser tonnage of 750,000 tons. Eventually they came down to 562,000 tons. The Americans, with a virtually obsolete cruiser fleet, wanted no more than 400,000 or 300,000, or even 250,000 tons, and a total of twenty-five heavy cruisers. If tonnage went over 250,000, the United States would build the balance in light cruisers armed with 8-inch guns. The British were incensed that the Americans would seek to impose on them a navy which was completely inadequate for a country engaged in global affairs.*]

July 29, 1927

I think the press has all the information that has come to me relative to the Naval Conference at Geneva. The proposals that have been made by the representatives of Great Britain seem to us to call for the building of a much larger navy than we think is necessary, so that we haven't been able to agree. Now, whether those proposals may be modified as the result of conference and discussion, I don't know. The proposals that have been presented, as I understand them, call for the building of a larger navy than we should wish to agree to. I think that is the main obstacle. There are some other collateral questions about the tonnage of ships and the caliber of the guns, but I think the main difference is in the size of the navy. We called this conference, thinking that it might result in placing a limitation on armaments which would perhaps help the countries interested to reduce some as years went by the size of their navies, which would result in making economies, and secondly, what I thought was of even more importance, the promotion of a spirit of peace and good will and better understanding. I have placed that, of course, as the main object in view. The matter of the removal of the burden of taxation and the economic benefits would be the natural consequences of peace and good will among the nations. But up to the present time the expressed desire on the part of representatives of the British Government is for so large a navy that our representatives and our Government haven't been able to agree. As I said before, I want to emphasize that discussion may modify it to such an extent that we can agree.

MR. MICHAELS: Would you care to go beyond that point, in case we don't agree?

PRESIDENT: Well, in case we don't agree we are right where we are now.

MR. MICHAELS: Well, I mean as to what we will do with our Navy in the way of building?

PRESIDENT: Right where we are now. We have no agreement now and will be in the same position we are in now.

MR. MICHAELS: I meant as to a navy program. Do you think we ought to build as to where Great Britain is?

PRESIDENT: Well, that is a matter to be taken up in the future and on which at the present time I would express absolutely no opinion. And when you have questions, Mr. Michaels, you ought to submit them in accordance with the custom of the conference.

August 5, 1927

It is too early to tell just what will be the effect of the conference we held. Careful statements were made by Mr. Gibson and a statement was made and given out by Secretary Kellogg that cover the position of our Government, to which I do not see that I could add anything.

I do not expect that the failure to reach an agreement at Geneva will have any serious effect upon the peace of the world. I use the words that are in the question here. It leaves us, as I said the other day, where we are now with the utmost of friendly feeling and cordial understanding between the three governments that were represented there and just because they were not able to agree on a naval building program doesn't interfere at all with the peaceful relations that exist between the three countries. When you write that out you had better say "among the three countries." It is better English.

[The conference had adjourned the day before, a failure.]

September 23, 1927

I noticed that the American Legion passed a modified resolution in favor of a unified department of national defense. I have forgotten just what language they put it in—whether it was as soon as expedient or as soon as it could be done or something of that kind, or a modified suggestion. That question was taken up and discussed to a considerable extent at the time President Harding had a commission working on the reorganization of the different departments. I think the commission rather favored it, and a bill was prepared with that in view. When I came to canvass the situation after I became President I was quite convinced that a provision of that kind in the bill would probably jeopardize its passage, so I think I recommended to the Congress the passage or the adoption of the recommendations of the commission with that exception. Of course, national defense is unified in the President, who is Commander-in-Chief of the Army and Navy. I do not know of any other way to unify it except by having a secretary of national defense, and then I think under him it would be necessary to have a secretary for the Army and a secretary for the Navy. I do not mean necessarily a member of the Cabinet but an assistant secretary. That would be necessary to work it out that way. The result in the Army and Navy I think would not be very much different than what it is now. There would be an assistant secretary to run the Army and an assistant secretary to run the Navy. My own opinion is that the suggestion for a unified department is going to prove more or less academic. It is probably theoretically correct. It is the system we have in this country under the President and the system that goes into operation right away when we go into a state of war, because then the President takes immediate control and gives his attention to national defense. I think it is more or less academic to discuss it because I am quite certain that Congress would not look with favor on the adoption of a policy of that kind. As far as I can see there is very little difference one way or the other. One method works out in practice about the same as any other, but I think there would be a good deal of opposition to a change of that kind both in the Army and in the Navy.

No definite program has been decided on relative to the Navy. I suppose it is generally understood that it will be felt desirable to build some more cruisers. I do not know just what may be necessary in the way of submarines. There has been something of an authorization of submarines since I have been President, and that program I think is being carried out as it was intended. We have recognized all along that more cruisers were to be built. Eight have been provided for since I was President, and undoubtedly the coming Congress will provide for some more. That has been expected all the while. If our recommendations had been adopted at Geneva that is what we should have done— we should have built more cruisers—but as they were not adopted we shall naturally go on proceeding in the usual course of business of keeping our Navy thoroughly equipped. It is my own feeling that the results at Geneva will probably make little difference one way or the other with the number of cruisers that are likely to be authorized at the coming session of Congress.

[*The Navy's ideal number of 25 cruisers never had importance to civilian members of the American Government; at the London Naval Conference in 1930 the Hoover Administration compromised drastically, going down to 15.*]

December 2, 1927

I didn't notice whether the Soviet proposal for the abandonment of all armaments was to apply to all the world or whether it was a European proposal. We do not maintain much of anything in the way of an army in active service. It is reduced to the proportions of a police force. I am speaking now of what we would call the Regular Army. Of course, when it is supplemented by the National Guard and other forces that could be called out it is a considerable force. So I suppose that if that proposal was to apply to all the world, so far as it would affect us would be the Navy. I do not imagine it would be for the welfare of the world entirely to abandon navies.

December 23, 1927

This is the season of the year when the press begins to have stories about the destitute condition of the Navy and the deplorable plight of the Army. I think I have had occasion before to comment on the fact that we never get the Army and Navy appropriation bills through without stories of that kind. I don't know just why they are put out. Perhaps it is a continuation of the days gone by when it was difficult to get appropriations as large as the War Department and the Navy Department wanted for national defense. That isn't the case now. Congress is disposed to be very liberal in providing for national defense. Of course, the budget estimates are always liberal. My budget estimates for the present year are creeping up towards $100,000,000 more for national defense for the War Department and the Navy Department than they were for the appropriations two or three years ago, and I think the country can rest fairly easy under the knowledge that the Bureau of Operations of the Navy and the General Staff of the Army are composed of very competent men and that if they are expending the $700,000,000 or $800,000,000 that are expended for national defense purposes the Army and Navy are in pretty good shape. They are never as large or as well equipped as some people would like to have them, but I think it is safe to say that both the Army and the Navy are in better shape than they ever were before in time of peace. Some of our naval ships are getting into condition where it is necessary to have renewals and that is the reason for part of our building program. Some of our war material will have to be renewed. Perhaps it is some indication to you of the amount of war material we have on hand when you recall that the freight bill for moving part of it that is located up near Baltimore and in New Jersey is going to be over $2,000,000. It takes quite a considerable amount of war material, which it will be necessary to move to keep those places in absolute safety, when the cost of the freight for such a move is . . . over $2,000,000. And that is only a part of the ammunition that we have on hand. I referred to all these things in my message. We have need from time to time to renew our ammunition. It deteriorates somewhat after it has been kept on hand for a number of years, and that is the case with some of our ammunition now.

January 24, 1928

My position relative to the Navy was all set out in my message to the Congress. I don't know of anything I can add to what I said there. I have commented so many times about the statements that always appear at this season from quarters that are interested in national defense, that I don't know that there is anything I can add. I don't know why it is, when other appropriations go through without any effort to alarm the country—the Post Office Department has an appropriation of some over $700,000,000, I think, and it isn't considered necessary to resort to inflammatory statements to secure the passage of that bill—that it is supposed that the passage of the appropriation bills for the Army and the Navy won't go through unless somebody asserts that the country is about to be engaged in war. There doesn't seem to be much of anything the President can do about that. I suppose the press likes to have it done. [Stenographer's note: laughter.] Well, I say that in all seriousness. There is every indication that that is what they like, because you know the very alarming criticism that the press would make if anybody suggested to men in the Army and the Navy that they ought not to say things of that kind. It would be asserted on all sides that they were muzzled, and that someone was attempting to cut down their privilege of free speech, and so on. I do suppose that when persons go into the Army and the Navy they go in on the understanding that they will conduct themselves in such a way as may be best for the country which they serve. I find in my own case that my privileges of free speech are a good deal curtailed, because I am President. I think that rule might well be taken to heart by the military men of the country. I don't think there is any reason for taking seriously any suggestion that the country at the present time is in danger of being attacked. I know very well that we do not harbor any

169

intention of attacking anyone else. But I suppose that those who have on them the burden of national defense naturally dwell on it, amplify it, enlarge it, and emphasize it. I don't know that they would be of very much value to the country if that wasn't the case. But I do not agree with the methods that they sometimes employ. I don't see why the press should take them very seriously. I haven't any way to make any change in it.

February 14, 1928

I am not, of course, an expert at all on what is the type of ship that we need most, but I am advised by the Navy that it is in the matter of cruisers that we are most deficient. I have understood that there was something of a propaganda under way against any Navy building program. That, I think, always happens whenever the Congress starts in on building additional naval vessels. There are opinions about that, of course, on both sides. There are some letters being received here at my office against the building program and some communications are being received in favor of it. But I think if it is understood that this is a plan toward which the Navy is to work in the future as funds become available, and that so far as the cruisers are concerned it is to quite a large extent a matter of replacement, that a good deal of the opposition on account of the financial aspects and so on, that has been expressed, would probably be withdrawn. If this program were carried out, it would leave the Navy ultimately with about 43 cruisers, it having at the present time 40. No, I have given you the wrong number. We have at the present time of finished cruisers 32, and 8 building. That is, we have 18 cruisers built and building, besides the 22, so that when we get through would have 43 instead of the present number of 40.

February 28, 1928

Several representatives of church organizations came in yesterday to present to me some views that they brought in their representative capacity relative to the building program of the Navy. I assume that they gave to the press the statements that they made. I told them, of course, that they would be taken into consideration. I judge, though, that the views that they presented to me were in relation to the program that had been proposed by the Navy and not in relation to the bill that has been reported by the House Naval Affairs Committee. Whether that would make any difference in their position, I am not able to state. I think perhaps it might modify it some. I did suggest to them that the bill as now reported by the Committee was for the purpose of a building program that was not in excess of the minimum that we had suggested at the Geneva Conference. Our suggestion there was 300,000 tons. If this program were carried out, it would leave us with a little under 300,000 tons, and on that I suggested to them that instead of alarming any other country as to its size it would probably be regarded by other countries as very moderate, because when we presented to the Geneva Conference the suggestion that the limit be 300,000 tons it was suggested to us that that was altogether too small. I think the British at that time stated that their requirements were for 595,000 tons. So that if we were engaged in a moderate building program of this nature that I did not see that it could possibly alarm any other country.

August 3, 1928

I am glad that the French and British have made an agreement relative to the limitation of auxiliary warships, if that is true. I have no information concerning the terms of the agreement, so I could not express any opinion as to whether it would interest us in any way or not.

[*The tentative agreement between the two nations seemed innocent enough, merely a plan to limit the building of capital ships, that is, ships of over 10,000 tons or with guns of more than 8-inch caliber; aircraft carriers of over 10,000 tons; surface vessels of or below 10,000 tons armed with guns of more than 6-inch and up to 8-inch caliber; ocean-going submarines over 600 tons. Actually, France and England were limiting precisely those naval vessels—heavy cruisers and large submarines—which were unimportant to them but important to the United States.*]

August 17, 1928

I have no additional information as to the Anglo-French agreement about limitation of naval armaments. I understand it is more in the nature of a proposal than an agreement. I am not contemplating at present taking any further steps about the limitation of armaments. There is a preliminary conference going on that has been going on for some years, which we have been attending. There isn't anything outside of that that I know of which is contemplated at the present time with a view to securing further limitations.

October 9, 1928

So far as I am advised, we have no official information relative to the action which the French Government is reported to have taken relative to an American newspaperman for publishing some articles relative to the English and French naval agreement. That may be entirely a domestic matter and as such this Government would not be warranted in interfering in it. Of course, we do undertake to protect the legal rights of our citizens when we find on representation that they have been infringed.

[*Perhaps by dubious means, William Randolph Hearst had obtained news of the Anglo-French naval compromise. His correspondent in Paris, Harold J. T. Horan, was accused of obtaining the information from two minor French officials. Horan was seized and given the choice of imprisonment or leaving the country. He left. Two years later Hearst was expelled from France because of the affair. He declared that he had obtained the information in 1928 by "good, direct, 'Go-and-get-it' American methods."*]

October 23, 1928

It isn't possible to say whether, now that the English and French naval suggestions have been published, it would be probable that any further naval limitation agreements can be reached before 1931. I think it is fair to say that so far as we have been advised concerning the agreement made between France and England it didn't seem to advance the probability of further agreements about naval armaments. The only advance it could be said to have made was a certain change of attitude on the part of the French and English relative to limitation, but it was a change of attitude with which we were unable to agree. I do not understand that either Italy or Japan agreed to it. But they did not set out their position with the fullness of detail that we did. I think their attitude in relation to it, so far as it has been disclosed, is very similar to our attitude. Not exactly like it, but along the same lines. That means two countries have indicated that they might agree to something, if others would agree, but it is apparent that other countries do not agree to it, and so there hasn't been much of any progress made. The encouraging part of it is that France, which didn't attend the naval conference I called in 1927, and the English have indicated that they were willing to change their attitude and they might be willing to change it further.

[*Coolidge was not planning to do anything further about arms limitation until the Five-Power Treaty of Washington ran out in 1931. He was vexed by failure to reach a cruiser agreement with England as well as by the attempt of France and England to limit naval vessels.*]

November 16, 1928

I haven't seen any report of a suggestion that it is said here was made in the House of Lords yesterday proposing an English-American mutual arms limitation. It doesn't occur to me offhand that that would be feasible. Of course, our country would consider any suggestion that the responsible authorities of the British Government wanted to submit to us.

January 22, 1929

. . . it is never possible to make much of a determination in advance of what the action of the Senate will be relative to the time of securing a vote on any question that is pending there. Oftentimes it looks as though there would be a long debate and it is determined within an hour. Sometimes it is apparent that a vote will be reached very soon and something comes up that makes the question drag along for weeks. But the Senate has a way of reaching a vote when it wants to and I have no doubt that that will be the result on the cruiser bill. It looked at one time, you will recall, as though there might be a very extended debate on the peace treaty, but all at once the Senate agreed and were able to take a vote on it. Very likely, the same result will occur in relation to the cruiser bill.

[*The simultaneous appearance before Congress of two measures— the Kellogg-Briand Pact (see "The Old World and the New") and the Fifteen-Cruiser Bill was incongruous. The Pact received advice and consent on January 15. The Cruiser Bill was passed shortly thereafter.*]

February 15, 1929

I have a telegram from Mayor [Malcolm E.] Nichols of Boston urging construction of one of the new cruisers at the Navy Yard at Boston. I think every time there is any naval construction work to be done that each of the navy yards in the United States sends word to the Department and the President, and oftentimes their delegation waits on the Department, and urges that the work be done in their yard. All that I can say to any of those is that we will try and have the work done where it seems to be most advantageous to the country and the Navy, and also do anything we can to assist any locality. Navy yards, you know, really ought to be for the benefit of the Navy and the country. Yet, they are generally considered to be for the benefit of the locality in which they are located.

9 · Debts and Reparations

Dᴇʙᴛs ᴀɴᴅ ʀᴇᴘᴀʀᴀᴛɪᴏɴs were a major concern in Coolidge's day. The erstwhile Allies of the World War owed large debts to the United States; raising the money through the Liberty and Victory Loan drives, the American Government had extended credits, both during and after the war. According to the peace settlement of 1919, reparations were to be paid by the defeated nations, in effect Germany, to the Allies.

Negotiating these accounts after the war took an inordinate amount of time. If Europeans and Americans had spent an equal effort in seeking political solutions to their major national rivalries and in supporting the League of Nations, the international anarchy of the 1930's might not have occurred. In retrospect nothing would have been lost had the interested nations forgotten debts and reparation; in the 1930's they forgot them anyway.

Admittedly, transferring the funds between the Germans and the Allies and the Allies and the United States involved complicated arrangements. In view of the inadequate economic knowledge of the time it may have been too much to have expected payment of debts and reparations. Unquestionably the nations could have paid them. But part of the difficulty was that the Germans did not want to pay reparations. Somehow or other in the next decade they found money for rearmament, spending a sum greater than their reparations account. Allied payments to the United States also were possible theoretically, but the Allies had too many other uses for their money. Gold covers of their currencies were thin, and national income hovered perilously close to outgo. It

174

seemed prudent to avoid the American account as long as possible and then to repay as slowly as possible. The people of the former Allied nations strongly supported their governments on this policy. French opinion rechristened Uncle Sam *l'Oncle Shylock.*

The Coolidge Administration insisted on repayment of the war debts as if national existence depended on it. There was no precedent for waiving international debts. While small Latin American countries might thumb their noses at creditors, such behavior was not expected from self-respecting nations. Moreover, Coolidge's preoccupation with balancing the budget and reducing the national debt made him sensitive to war debt payments. The budget balanced closely and such payments could make the difference between a sizable surplus and a deficit. Coolidge, indeed, may be forgiven for remembering that the debt had reached a figure of about $22,000,000,000 in 1923 partly because of the World War loans to the Allies.

During the 1920's the flimsy structure of international payments to debtors and creditors preserved an appearance of stability. As holes appeared they were filled—first by the Dawes Plan of 1924, which put German reparations on a plan of payment, and then by the Young Plan (named after the American financier Owen D. Young) which reduced the original estimate of reparations, set in 1921 at roughly $33,000,000,000, to $8,000,000,000 payable over $58\frac{1}{2}$ years at an interest rate of $5\frac{1}{2}$ per cent. The total reparations bill under the Young Plan, including principal and interest, would have been about $26,000,000,000.

Before the Armistice of November 11, 1918 the United States Government lent the Allies a total of $7,077,144,750 in cash, nine-tenths of which was spent in the United States for war supplies. After the Armistice the United States lent the Allies an additional $3,273,364,324.70; European succession states, even Austria and Hungary, received some of these funds. Initially the interest rate on the debts was five per cent per annum, because the United States had raised the money by bonds which paid $4\frac{1}{4}$ per cent, and it seemed eminently sensible to add an extra $\frac{3}{4}$ per cent for service charges.

In the 1920's the Government, renegotiating the interest charges of the principal debtors, determined the rates roughly on ability to pay. Congress in 1922 created the World War Foreign Debt Commission, which between 1923 and 1930 renegotiated the debts to an average interest rate of 2.135 per cent. It also made obligations payable over a sixty-two year period. Principal plus interest would have totaled more than twenty-two billion dollars. The British Government in 1923 received a reduction of interest to 3.3 per cent, France (1926) obtained a new rate of 1.6 per cent, and Italy (1925) 0.4 per cent.

It is difficult to know, incidentally, whether Coolidge said, "They hired the money, didn't they?" His biographer Claude Fuess could not discover a source for this remark. Mrs. Coolidge did not remember it, although she said it sounded like her husband. Lyle Wilson, a member of Coolidge's presidential press conference, believes the President made the remark to the reporters, although it appears nowhere in the transcripts.

October 5, 1923

An inquiry about the cancellation of debts, stating that the new President of the American Bankers Association says that he is going to start an immediate campaign for cancellation, and wanting me to state my views on the question. I gave you the views that I held at one of our very early conferences, which was opposed to the cancellation of debts. That doesn't mean that it isn't open to negotiation as to terms and conditions and so on. We made very liberal terms with Great Britain in the matter of interest, and all that which, if figured up, I presume would show, as a matter of arithmetical determination, that we would be more than cancelling the original debt, considering the reduction that we made in interest. Something of that kind, perhaps, would be considered. Some of the countries are not paying us any interest at the present time. But the matter, of course, is in the hands of the Commission that was appointed, as the result of an act of Congress, with power to negotiate, and the terms are laid down in that Act, and those are the terms on which the American Government stands until they are modified.

PRESS: Any indications, Mr. President, that any other powers are ready to negotiate now?

PRESIDENT: Not that I know of.

October 26 1923

An inquiry as to what will be the next step toward the disentangling of Europe's affairs. That depends, of course, upon what results from the action now being taken. If the proposal is accepted, I should say the next step would be the securing of the representatives of the different governments, and their meeting in conference. Whether the American experts will be nominated by the Administration, or whether the choice will rest with the Reparations Commission as its own initiative, depends, of course, upon what answer may be made by the various governments that are concerned.

Whether France will accept a scaling down of reparations. Of course, that is a matter that has not been considered. That will be for France to determine herself. As I understand the proposal, it is to secure information in an advisory capacity. The reparations commission would use this conference in order to secure the opinion of experts, and then to advise their governments as to what could be done.

[*On December 15, 1923 Coolidge appointed the financiers Charles G. Dawes, Henry M. Robinson, and Owen D. Young as experts on a commission to investigate German finances. The committee, taking the name of the well-known Chicago banker Dawes, reported on April 9, 1924.*]

October 30, 1923

An inquiry about my understanding of the function of the conference of expert financiers—whether the report of the conference will be made to the Reparations Commission, or will the report of their findings be made to the respective governments concerned. I have here several inquiries about reparations. I wouldn't be able to answer that question in advance, or give any suggestion or opinion about it that would be worth while. As I understand the situation, it is this. A proposal has been made for experts to undertake to assess what they think Germany can pay. That plan has been accepted, apparently, in principle, by the interested governments. I understand that Poincaré has indicated that it was acceptable to him, in a communication. Now the question comes of working out the details. That is under consideration by the interested parties, and no decision about that has been made, as to the scope, or just how the thing could be done, either as to how the appointments are to be made, or what is to be considered in detail, after the appointments have been made. Nor has it been determined where the Commission would meet, or anything of that kind. But there is, apparently, a hopeful avenue before us, that plans have been accepted in principle, and that the details are being sympathetically worked out.

An inquiry here about the conditions laid down by Poincaré that there be no reduction in the German debt. That, I think, would be answered by a careful reading of the note of the Secretary of State. There wasn't any suggestion in that, of course, of any reduction of anybody's debt. It is a simple and plain suggestion that a committee of experts be appointed to try to assess the amount that Germany is able to pay. The rights of France are fixed by her treaty. There can't be any reduction except by the consent of France.

177

[*The exact amount of the German reparations debt had deliberately not been fixed at the Paris Peace Conference.*]

November 2, 1923

I have another question about the reparations question, which, perhaps, I have already covered. Are the financial experts empowered to inquire into Germany's present capacity, but without authority to recommend any change in the amount of 132,000,000,000 gold marks? Of course, it goes without saying, from a reading of the note, that it isn't proposed to make any change in the treaties that Germany and France, and the other powers have made with each other, nor is it proposed that the findings of this Commission are to be binding on anyone. It is simply an inquiry into the capacity of Germany to pay; not a proposal to make any recommendation whether the reparations shall be diminished or increased. It couldn't be done without the concurrence of the French Government.

[*Under terms of the Treaty of Versailles, an Allied Reparations Commission in 1921 put German indebtedness at 132,000,000,000 gold marks, roughly $33,000,000,000. This figure, however, was only tentative—in effect a wild guess as to how much Germany would eventually pay.*]

No steps have been taken towards the appointment of an American member, and anyone that is designated, doesn't go, insofar as I have in mind any plan now, representing the American Government. That, too, is carefully stated in the note. He goes as an American, to assist—not at all to represent our Government. Nor do I know whether our Government would take any steps towards making an appointment. It is suggested that Americans could undoubtedly be secured who would participate in such an investigation. Now, they might be chosen by the Reparations Commission, or chosen in any other fashion. But it was carefully stated that they are not to represent the American Government.

[*Coolidge wisely preferred that any American on the forthcoming committee be an unofficial representative, for if the Government sent an avowed delegate it would amount to admitting a connection between war debts and reparations. The British Government was trying to establish such a connection to put the United States in an ungracious light—a grasping creditor seeking to impoverish Europe. According to the note of Foreign Secretary Balfour, dated August 1, 1922, Britain was not going to be unduly difficult with Germany and other creditors: "In no circumstances," he said, "do we propose to ask more from our debtors than is necessary to pay our creditors. . . ."*]

November 6, 1923

Whether the position of the United States is changed in regard to entering into European embroilments. I don't know of any change in that respect. Our position has been carefully and definitely stated a great many times, both in speech and in writing, and it has been stated, also, by our actions. I think you know of the events that led up to the present situation—the suggestion that was made here as a result of some inquiry that we still had a desire to be helpful in Europe whenever the opportunity offered itself, and the note that came from the British Government, and the reply that was made to that note, which is known as the Hughes note. Now, I think almost every possible inquiry that you can devise will be answered by a reading of the note. I think you will find the answer to the inquiry there. It states the position of our Government definitely and fully, and that it is the desire to be helpful. We haven't any other motive. We have no direct interest to serve, no expectation of reaping any reward. We are undertaking to discharge our obligations—of lending our counsel, if we can, in order to settle a long standing difficulty. Now, there isn't any occasion for being disturbed or discouraged, because we aren't able to step in and settle, in twenty-four hours, a difficulty that has engaged the attention of Europe for hundreds of years. We have got to be patient about it, and try to do the best we can. We observed that the French have taken possession of the Ruhr, and as a result of that there was that passive resistance on the part of the Germans. That finally came to an end, and it seemed to us that that might furnish an opportune moment for a suggestion that we lend our counsel, and that we would be helpful, if our help was wanted. We aren't trying to do anything more than discharge what we think is our duty. We hope that we can be helpful. But that depends on the state of mind that exists over there. If it is one that wants to be helped, then I think we would be warranted in looking at it very hopefully. If it turns out that the state of mind is not one that wants help, why, then there is nothing that we can do. But of course, our people here, we hope people generally throughout civilization, will understand that we tried to do our part. That answers, I think, quite a good many questions.

[*Apparently the President was referring to the "Hughes note" of October 15, 1923, an* aide-mémoire. *The communication declared that "present conditions" made it imperative that the nations find a suitable financial plan in order to prevent economic disaster in Europe. Secretary of State Hughes expressed hope that the German Government, by abandoning resistance to the French and Belgian occupation of the Ruhr, would "present a freer opportunity and an immediate necessity for establishing an economic program."*]

November 9, 1923

A statement that there is emanating from Paris today a report to the effect that Premier Poincaré will insist upon reparations from Germany to the full capacity of Germany to pay, and wanting to know if I have any sort of statement to make relative to the American position. No, our position is stated fully in the note. If it meant our position relative to the restrictions, and more especially that restriction which provides that the experts be limited to an inquiry into the present capacity—actual I think is the word that is used by the French in that connection —I think that I am safe in saying that if it is to be limited to merely present capacity of Germany to pay, that that would be such a limitation as would make an inquiry useless and futile. There wouldn't be any use for calling together the experts of four or five nations of the earth. That would be something almost that could be done by any ordinary auditor. A limitation of that kind would seem to make the inquiry useless, and I don't see any reason why we could expect to be of any help by participating in it.

PRESS: There is a report that the French propose the inquiry to take in the capacity of Germany to pay for six years—up to 1930. Have you heard of that, Mr. President?

PRESIDENT: Yes, I had heard of such a report, and up to 1930 would include what I have had to say. It would be such a short time that I don't see any reason to expect that in that short time Germany could re-establish its industrial organization and its production to such an extent that payments could be made which would amount to very much. They could hardly begin, in so short a time, to meet the reparations.

December 11, 1923

This Government has been informed that the Reparations Commission is considering the establishment of two expert Committees. One to consider the means of balancing the budget of Germany and the measures to be taken to stabilize her currency. The other to take up the question of the capital which has been removed from Germany. That is the property of Germany that is said to have been removed and which is now located in other countries. The inquiry of the first Committee would comprehend all the conditions to be realized and the measures to be taken to accomplish the results desired. All the representatives of the governments' members of the Commission, have expressed a desire to have American experts on the two Committees. It is understood that the Government of the United States is not in a position to be represented on these Committees, and that the invitation to the American experts will be extended directly by the Reparations Commission. That wants to be made plain—that the Government of the United States does not participate, but that experts, economic experts, to participate by the direct invitation of the Reparations Commission. This Government believes that the proposed inquiry will be of great value and in view of its direct interest as a creditor, you may recall that I developed that somewhat in my message, speaking of the European debt that is due us and also the debt that is due us from Germany. The German debt in and of itself will amount to about three-quarters of a billion dollars—about $750,000,-000. We can't tell yet just what the Mixed Claims Commission may find is the amount due, but it is of such a sum as joined to the bill of $255,000,000 that is due for the Army of Occupation will amount to about $750,000,000. So that we have an interest there as a direct creditor and an indirect interest as a creditor of the other nations there, and of the importance of the economic recuperation of Europe, it would view with favor the acceptance by American experts of such an invitation. We have the interest of our debt and our interest in the economic recovery of Europe. The immediate proposal before the Reparations Commission has been made by the French delegate and President of the Commission, and has the support, it is understood, of all the allied governments. The French delegate is the President of the Commission, and he is the one who has made the immediate proposal. The British Government has informed this Government of its desire that American experts should participate in the inquiry. That takes care of all the allied governments.

Now, this is a very important addition. The German Government has also brought the matter to the attention of this Government, stating that it would be much appreciated if an American expert were to participate in the work of the first Committee, as above proposed, as it is believed that in this way important progress could be made toward the solution of the problems underlying economic recovery.

You see, that makes the entire approval of the allied governments and joined to that is the request that comes from the German Government. I think that is very important, of course, and a very significant development. There has been abroad many times some criticism of our Government, of our people, and our ways, but that has demonstrated, I think, that when they are in real trouble and real difficulty over there, they turn to us as a nation that will be fair with them—one in whose judgment and in whose character they can rely; and notwithstanding differences that have seemed to exist, they are willing to abide by the faith that they have in us, and I think it is a very substantial accomplishment.

PRESS: Mr. President, is this the carrying out of the New Haven speech?

PRESIDENT: Not exactly, but it is along that line. This little statement I will have set up on the typewriter and it will be ready for distribution for you in fifteen or twenty minutes.

PRESS: Mr. President, would it be proper to ask, in view of our interest in the $750,000,000, why we do not participate officially and directly?

PRESIDENT: Well, that is a matter that hasn't yet been adjusted. The Mixed Claims Commission is working on that, the mixed claims part. Then we have some adjustment of the bill for the Army of Occupation. I am speaking of that for the purpose of indicating our direct interest in the situation.

[*The Mixed Claims Commission was a German-American group set up under the Treaty of Berlin of 1921, a peace agreement entered into independently by the United States and Germany. The American reparations bill was modest. The United States demanded only funds certified by this commission and recompense for troop maintenance in the Allied Army of Occupation. In the New Haven speech Secretary of State Hughes proposed that German reparations should be settled by eminent financiers, not politicians. His recommendation eventuated in the Dawes Committee.*]

January 15, 1924

Another inquiry about the possibility of a loan to Germany by the War Finance Corporation for the purchase of food. I think I have commented on that two or three times. The last I knew there was a proposal being entertained by the Reparations Commission to permit a loan to be made to Germany, part of which I understood was to be expended in this country and part somewhere else, and part was to be taken up in this country, and part somewhere else. I never knew what decision was reached. It was necessary for them to give their approval of it, otherwise the loan would be on top of the German reparations, and payment would be very far in the future—very likely it wouldn't be much more than mere paper. So that an attempt was made to get in under that, and I don't know what decision has been made. Then after that I think there were some foreign banks that were proposing to make a loan, which looked more practicable and encouraging, and more immediately available. The last time I had any talk with Mr. [Eugene] Meyer he spoke about that and I never heard what decision had been made. It looked quite encouraging at that time.

As I have said before, Mr. Dawes and his associates you know, and the public I think knows, went over there at the invitation of the Reparations Commission, and the other members of the board are there by the representation of their respective governments.

PRESS: Mr. President, can you say whether the Reparations Commission pays their expenses?

PRESIDENT: I understand it does, or else they pay their own. I don't know about that. I should expect that they were paid by the Reparations Commission. Usually the party calling in an expert, I found, has to pay his expenses.

March 14, 1924

The administration hasn't any new attitude about the loans of private American financial interests to foreign governments. Technically, I suppose that in time of peace in a way any American has a right to lend his money wherever he thinks it will secure him the largest return, taking everything into consideration. I think large loans are not usually made to foreign governments by private interests unless it is known that the United States Government has no objection. Not that the Government takes any responsibility about it, but simply that it indicates it has no objection to it. This recent loan that was made came to my attention first through press information. Very likely there was inquiry made at the State Department about it, though about that I have no information.

As I understand the attitude of the American Government about things of that kind, loans to foreign governments, it goes right along that line. It recognizes the privilege of American financial interests to place their money where they think it will be of the greatest service to those to whom the money belongs. Sometimes it is necessary to take a rather broad view, to consider not merely the immediate financial return, but the general result. That is especially true under present conditions, when large sums of money are owed to us by European countries, so that on that account we have what we might say is a direct financial interest in the economic reconstruction of Europe and in those countries becoming financially able to repay us. We are collecting very large sums from Great Britain and naturally would not want anything to occur that might jeopardize those payments, and we should be glad to have any reasonable action taken that might put other countries in Europe in a financial condition to consider repayment to us of money due us. That has relation merely to our debt. I don't want to bring that up at this time as indicating a determination to press it or anything of that kind. I simply speak of it as a present condition. Then of course there are always the trade relations. I think it has been for many years the policy of the British financial interests to make investments abroad for the purpose of the commercial advantage of the people of Great Britain. Sometimes that takes one form and sometimes another, but as those investments are made abroad they result in credits there and financial obligations which it is supposed have been a very dominant influence in increasing the trade of Great Britain. So that our country would be glad to have surplus capital of our nation invested in that way. Then of course we always have to look at our domestic conditions. There are times when credit in this country is scarce and money is high and dear, and when there are conditions of that kind our Government would probably not want to encourage the investment of money abroad. They would rather have it retained at home where, in taking a general and broad view, it would be of more advantage to the American people. Now all of this comes down to one thing. It ought to be the attitude of the American Government so to encourage the use of American capital as best to administer to the welfare of the American people. Sometimes that is done by suggesting that we make no investments abroad. At other times it would be done by encouraging investments abroad. I suppose that the recent loan took all of those conditions into consideration. No doubt they thought it would be best for the welfare of the nation and for the welfare of those who hold the money to make, or to stand ready to make, a large investment abroad for the purpose of protecting American interests. Of course there is a little broader view than that to take—of assistance to those that are in distress. That is a duty that always falls on us, as well as merely taking care of our own material needs. It is a real duty, one that we can't escape, and one that we always have to consider in determining questions of this kind.

[*Because of the confused structure of public and private loans in Europe and the possible diplomatic repercussions of loans to Latin American and Far Eastern countries, during the twenties the State Department attempted to supervise, unofficially, the flotation of foreign loans. The policy was an uneasy one. In the 1930's, when many of the private loans which had been approved by the State Department turned sour, some investors believed that the Government had deceived them.*]

April 15, 1924

There is very little that I can say about the Dawes report. I haven't examined it minutely. About the only expression I can make about it is the hope that it will result in a settlement. There is an inquiry here as to whether that would have any effect on the payment to the United States of the amount that is due it as the cost of the Army of Occupation. I don't understand that it has any effect on that, though as I say I haven't read it carefully enough to be certain. If it had affected it in any way, I am rather certain that I should have been informed about it through the usual diplomatic channels. Mr. [James A.] Logan [Jr.] who represents the Government over there would have informed the State Department and the State Department would have kept me informed of anything of that nature that might affect any claims that were due to the United States.

June 24, 1924

I don't think any invitations have been received to participate in the allied conference on reparations, though I notice some suggestions in the press about it. I suppose that the attitude of our Government would be the same about that as it has been constantly about European affairs of that nature. We wouldn't want to take a part in their political discussions over there, and on the other hand we want to do everything we possibly can to assist in any way we can without getting into their political difficulties. Their political difficulties they can determine and decide themselves. Such assistance as we can give we are of course willing and anxious to give.

PRESS: Mr. President, do you think we are likely to be represented by an unofficial observer?

PRESIDENT: I don't think there will be any representation by our Government. It is very likely that what we should do would be to keep someone there who would keep us informed of what course affairs were taking. Of course it is recognized always that we have some interest in Europe direct and indirect about which we need to have information in order to protect our Government and protect our citizens. I shouldn't suppose that General Dawes would attend the conference on account of his participation in the campaign. Secretary Hughes would not reach London anyway until after July 16, and as our Government would not be a participant in it, I do not think he would attend a conference of that kind even if he were there.

[*General Dawes was currently Republican nominee for Vice-President. Hughes was going to London to attend a meeting of the American Bar Association. The London conference to which the President refers was a formal meeting of government representatives to accept recommendations of the Dawes Committee. James A. Logan, Jr. and Frank B. Kellogg (then Ambassador to Great Britain) were official delegates of the United States. The Dawes committee eventually led to a third formal session: a meeting of representatives in Paris to decide upon the division of reparations payments agreed upon in the protocol of the London Conference.*]

July 18, 1924

I don't know enough about the progress of the London Conference to express any opinion on it really satisfactory to myself, for you and your readers. I haven't any information on it other than what I have seen in the press. I judge that that is entirely accurate, and I don't say that in any way of depreciation. Of course you know and I know that it is difficult to get foreign news in the press that you can always rely on, but I think the reports that have come relative to the London Conference have every appearance of being authoritative and especially reliable, and judging from that I think it is making satisfactory progress, though judging from the personnel of the conference and what I know of its objects and its plans, I felt quite sure that that would be the result. And also judging from the rather optimistic note that Ambassador Kellogg sounded just before the Conference met, we might expect a great deal from it. He is a cautious man, and doesn't make statements unless he has a pretty secure foundation on which to base them.

[*Coolidge's estimate of Kellogg, whom he was soon to nominate as*

Secretary of State, is revealing. Kellogg proved an able Secretary.]

I haven't any information other than what I have seen in the press of a report that the post of Reparations Agent General had been offered to Owen D. Young. I don't know whether it would it be proper for me to make any comment on that in advance. I suppose it would. This appointment is made entirely by the European authorities. It isn't an appointment that has anything to do with directing the Government of the United States. It is as though they wanted an engineer, or that they wanted a high class surgeon . . . or something of that kind, and decided that they had found the man with the right kind of equipment in America. They asked him to come and serve, undoubtedly, in this case. No one would accept an appointment of that kind without inquiring if such action would embarrass the United States Government, or whether it would be satisfactory to them. I do not know of any reason now why Mr. Young wouldn't be entirely satisfactory to our Government, and I don't see any reason why we shouldn't be very much pleased if he is willing to accept such a position, if it were offered to him. I think I have seen the statement from him that no such post had been offered and didn't know it was going to be. So I can't make any direct statement about it. I suppose it would go without saying that he served over there in the capacity of an expert acceptably in a way that was very satisfactory to our Government, and that we would have every confidence in him to meet any kind of situation that he might undertake.

[*Another American, S. Parker Gilbert, received this post.*]

August 5, 1924

Here is another pertinent question that I should have referred to in relation to the developments at London. I should judge that the probable effects there would be exceedingly good on American business conditions. I should expect that it would stimulate business, I don't mean export business, but a general feeling that at last we are reaching a stage where we can see stable conditions in Europe, and that would mean a stabilizing of conditions here, and a minimizing of the present uncertainty, so that people would feel that they could go ahead with their business enterprises.

August 8, 1924

I haven't received any information from London other than what is in the press about the French and German compromise on the Ruhr situation. I don't know whether it is expected that the French will evacuate the Ruhr soon or not, though I had the impression that it was expected and that an agreement would be reached under which there would be an early evacuation.

I think there is to be a conference in Paris on the allocation of German reparations, and if that is the case we shall be represented there, because that is a matter that affects us. There are quite considerable claims against Germany, and the outcome will depend on the result of the findings of the [Mixed Claims] Commission, which is now at work on that. We have a claim for the Army of Occupation, which is roughly $255,000,000, and then there are the other claims arising out of damages that accrued just prior or after our going into the war. Those, when they were presented, were quite a large amount, but my understanding is that the findings of the Commission have reduced them very materially, so that I don't think it will run over half a billion and may be quite a considerable amount less than that.

PRESS: Represented officially or unofficially, Mr. President?

PRESIDENT: Of course we shall be officially represented. It is a matter to determine how the German reparations are to be allocated, which will mean that it will be determined there by what method, what time, and in what amounts we are to receive compensation to meet these claims that we have.

PRESS: Has a decision been reached as to who will represent the United States?

PRESIDENT: I think Mr. Kellogg would be sent over, if Mr. Herrick is not there. Perhaps Mr. Kellogg will assist Mr. Herrick. And of course Colonel Logan, who is very familiar with all these questions.

I haven't had any information at all about any suggestion about refunding the allied debts. Nothing has come to me about that.

August 22, 1924

I don't know as I can define what would be the chief issue in the foreign field. I have an inquiry here as to whether the World Court would be one of the chief issues. That is a project which I desire to see carried out. I shouldn't think it would be so important as the results that might be obtained and which I hope shall be obtained from a conference for disarmament, though it is a very important matter. The codification of international law I regard as important. Of course, the matter of chief importance in the foreign field is the settlement of reparations, because on that hangs almost everything else.

I am not certain that I can give you any exact and detailed information about the next step in the reparations. I understand that the next step is the acceptance or ratification by the German Parliament and the French Parliament. I can't give any new idea about the way it will affect American trade or prosperity or export trade. I think there is a general agreement that it would be greatly for the benefit of American trade, as well as European trade, if they could have a definite determination of what Germany is to pay and what France and the other countries are to receive. It would undoubtedly enable France to turn her attention more vigorously to commercial affairs. It certainly would have that effect on Germany and probably on Great Britain. And anything that would stimulate production over there I should judge would be of benefit to us here, as it would result in an exchange of commodities and give us a chance to manufacture and sell to them and give them a chance to manufacture more and sell to us, which would be to our benefit as long as such goods came in on a basis that would enable our manufacturers and our laborers to maintain their present American standards—I mean such a tariff basis to be kept in effect.

September 16, 1924

I haven't any plan or policy about the settlement of the French debt at present. That is all provided for by statute law, and I suppose that the only representation I would be entitled to make about it is that which I am ordered to make by law. That states in what way it may be settled, the rate of interest, and length of time the matter is to run. Of course, in addition to that we have a Commission. Mr. [Edward N.] Hurley is a member of the Commission and a very efficient member. If the Commission, after conference with representatives of another country, should recommend to me that we should go to Congress and ask to make a settlement with a country on terms different from that provided by law, very likely I should undertake to secure consent from Congress. That was what was done with the British debt. It wasn't settled exactly in conformity with the terms of the law. The law had to be varied to meet the conditions. I couldn't pass any judgment before the event on anything that they might want to oppose. I should give great weight to the opinion of the Commission and undoubtedly would adopt any suggestion or recommendations that they might make to me, and make it my own recommendation, so far as it might be necessary, to present to the Congress.

PRESS: If there were a modification of the terms now enjoyed by Great Britain we would have to modify their terms at the same time, wouldn't we?

PRESIDENT: I don't see why.

PRESS: Mr. President, you couldn't expect them to pay in harsher terms than Italy, for instance, if you should make the rate of interest lower?

PRESIDENT: Well, Great Britain now is paying, and one or two other nations are paying. Some nations are not paying any. There is a difference in conditions now, and those conditions might continue.

PRESS: Isn't there something in the statute which provides that settlement must be made with all countries on the same basis?

PRESIDENT: Well, you may be right about that. I didn't have it in mind that the statute did provide that there must be the same terms between the nations. Perhaps it does. My recollection was that there was an original statute passed creating this Commission and directing them under what terms and conditions they should make settlement. When they came to make their settlement with the British they found the British couldn't comply with those terms, and therefore submitted a new proposal to the Congress who passed a special law. Now it may be that in that special law it is provided to apply the same terms to all countries.

PRESS: If it didn't, Mr. President, you couldn't expect Great Britain to pay harsher terms than others.

PRESIDENT: Of course, the British are paying now. The others are not paying anything. It doesn't at all follow that because France or Italy or some other country can't pay but $50,000,000 a year and we have to extend their payments over 75 years, that the British are not abundantly able to pay their amount in 62 years. It is a question of the ability of each country. There is great force, though, in what you say about treating everybody alike. I should like to do that. I doubt very much if the British would make any complaint about any settlement that we might make with any others. They have made their settlement on what they thought they could do. What we have constantly kept in mind in that policy is that the debt that is due to us from one country hasn't any direct connection with the debt that might be due to us from another country. That is why we have not mixed up the German indemnity in any way with our own debt.

[*The press put its finger on a difficult issue here. Interest rates and payment terms fixed by the World War Debts Funding Commission under an act of Congress of February 1922 were much more lenient than those permissible under the statute, and therefore it was necessary in each case to ask Congress to ratify an agreement.*]

January 2, 1925

I haven't received any text or outline of the French Government's note. I wouldn't want to assume that there was one, suggesting terms of settlement of the French debt to the United States, and including a proposal for a ten year moratorium. I don't want to be ungracious enough to say that I told you so, but so far as any information has come to me it seems to bear out the supposition that I made either at the last or the next to the last [press] conference that Mr. Clementel hadn't made any definite statements that undertook to bind the French Government, suggesting that the suggestion was made about that they wouldn't do anything about their debt. So far as suggestions have come to me from an authoritative source, they are to the effect that that wasn't at all intended by him. I think I did suggest at the last session that I doubted very much if responsible officials of the French Government were making any suggestions of repudiation, and that while some individual might make some statement that squinted in that direction, we ought not to impute that to the French Government or the French people any more than we would impute some improper proposal to our Government or our people, that apparently was biased by some public official over here. I am very glad to be able to report that that is apparently the case. Mr. Clementel seemed to indicate that his report was improperly reported and that there were things in it that indicated a desire on his part to pay what the French owe the United States, and not at all a desire to repudiate.

[*The President was being unduly diplomatic. In December, 1924 Minister of Finance Etienne Clementel invoked the principle of "strict justice": the Allies should pay the expenses of the war according to their ability. His countryman Louis Morin put the case more baldly: "In the common cause some gave ships, others arms, others the lives of their children, others, finally, their money, and today those who gave only their money say to us 'pay back what we loaned you.'"*]

February 13, 1925

I don't know of anything I can say more about the return of alien property than what I said the other day. I spoke then more about the practical difficulties. Of course, when it comes to a question as to what our rights are, I suppose they are absolutely in our own hands. We have a right to return it if we wish. But the effect it might have on other nations that are interested in securing money from Germany to meet their claims, I think would be what I have indicated. I think it is entirely a domestic subject, limited of course only by the treaty that we made with Germany. Insofar as that may limit it, it is a little outside of a domestic question, but no other nation other than Germany and the United States has any legal right about it, as I understand it. I think that is set out perhaps in the last paragraph of the Paris agreement, which specifically says that it doesn't change any rights of the different signatories.

———

PRESS: Mr. President, can I revert to the German property settlement? You told us Tuesday that you hadn't read the text of Senator Borah's bill. Have you read it since?

PRESIDENT: No, I haven't read it. I have talked with Senator Borah and he and I seem to be in entire accord in relation to it. He would like to see the property returned, but he doesn't feel that it is a matter that can be taken up now, and I have the same view about it. We would like to keep intact that great principle of not having private property seized during a war. We undertook to assert that principle, of course, in the treaty that was made with Germany, by the provision that the German Government was to repay the German nationals for their property that we had seized. Now conditions change. There may be some way that can be figured out by which we can return the property. Perhaps Mr. Borah can figure out some method that will seem acceptable. Perhaps I can. We haven't been able to do so at the present time, and I don't think any suitable provisions (I notice suitable provisions here is in quotation marks, referring I suppose to language that is in the Knox-Porter resolution and which is incorporated in the German treaty), I don't think any suitable provisions have yet been arrived at under which we can return the German property.

February 24, 1925

There isn't anything that I can say about our European debts. As I have suggested before, I don't like constantly to talk about that. It gives the impression abroad that we are trying to coerce them, or something of that kind. It isn't helpful in our foreign relations, nor is it helpful in securing a state of mind that will result in making payments to us.

August 25, 1925

Now here is a question about the Belgian debt settlement. Of course our law provides for a settlement on the standard that was adopted in relation to the debt of Great Britain. We have made four or five other settlements on that basis and if anyone wants to have any different basis than that it will be necessary for them to show the Debt Commission, as I understand it, specific reasons why in their particular case any exception to the British standard should be made. I suppose everyone recognizes that Belgium is in a somewhat different situation in relation to the war than other countries. It was a neutral that was caught between the great conflict between the Central Powers and Allied Powers, and in a way that appealed particularly to the sympathy and consideration of the American Government and I think to the American people. It was therefore on that account that there was a desire to treat Belgium as generously as we could under the circumstances. Now, of course while we speak of the standards adopted in the British settlement, the basis of that standard was the ability to pay. We adopted that standard in relation to the British on account of their ability to pay and that is the fundamental standard in relation to each and every one of the debtors that owe money to the United States. That isn't varied by the Versailles Treaty or any other agreement that has been attempted to be made, and the Belgian settlement hasn't anything to do with the debt of any other country to the United States. The basis and standard, as I understand it, is established by law in relation to the British standard. Now this Government is waiting to see what any other country may propose and any reasons that it may have will be listened to as to why any different settlement should be made with them than the British standard. That is entirely outside of the Versailles Treaty or any other agreement or obligation which may have been thought to have been in effect.

November 13, 1925

The results of the agreement between the Italian Debt Commission and the American Debt Commission have already been fairly well commented on in the news columns and editorial articles. There isn't very much that I can add. Of course, in making these settlements the general result which is always arrived at is the fact that we do not get as much as we would like—to have the other countries pay more than they want to pay. I think I commented on the very fine spirit that seemed to be manifested by the Italian Debt Commission before, and hazarded the prophecy that where a spirit of that kind prevailed it was almost certain that the parties would reach an agreement. That has been done. And that, as I already said, is the most satisfactory thing, the fact that an agreement has been reached which closes up that question for discussion between the Italian nation and our nation. We have recognized, the Commission has recognized the difficulty that the Italian Government and people are under, the meagerness of their resources in comparison with their obligations. I think the debt that Italy owes to the United States and to Great Britain is almost equal in amount to the debt that the British owe to the United States. When you consider the difference in resources between the British Empire or the British Isles and the resources of Italy, it is quite apparent that the small country of Italy can not meet any such payments as could be met by Great Britain. That occurred to me as perhaps the most significant comparison that could be made.

December 11, 1925

I have two or three inquiries here about the return of the alien property. I do not think any full plan has been matured about that, but there is a hypothesis on which the Treasury Department and the interested parties are working to see if it can be put into effect and to ascertain whether it would be satisfactory to the parties interested. Of course this is all a part of our general creditor position. I think the amount that is due to us from Germany is about the same as the amount that is due to us from Belgium, and very likely it might be proper to consider the fact that Germany is a debtor to us and is also a debtor to substantially all of our debtors, so that anything that we might release would in a way be so much more that would go to those that are to pay us money and those that have already made an agreement with us and those that we expect will make an agreement in the future. So it might be, so far as we are concerned, about as broad as it is long. What we secured from Germany wouldn't go to others and if we released anything it would go to others and they would be the better able to pay us.

[*The absurd circularity of the debts-reparations situation eventually helped to move it off the world stage.*]

January 22, 1926

Here is another inquiry about loans to finance foreign government monopolies, such as rubber, coffee, etc. Now, you always want to keep in mind that every application made for a loan is decided on its own merits. It is impossible to lay down any general rule that would be applicable to all cases and which would fit all circumstances. It has been the policy of the administration to refuse to approve loans that were contemplated being made to foreign governments for the purpose of supporting a trade monopoly. Now it may be that some application might be made for a loan of that kind that would appear not to be inappropriate for our banking concerns to make. We haven't had any such applications up to the present time and as near as I have come to laying down a general rule, borne out by past experience, it is that so far as we know the Government does not look with favor on loans made for the purpose of supporting government monopolies maintained in foreign countries on materials that enter into the general consumption of our own people.

February 19, 1926

I have a question here about the Italian debt settlement. I don't know that there is much more I can say about that in addition to what I have already said. I have no doubt you will recall that until the formation of the present Italian Government there didn't seem to be any disposition or any power or ability to meet the payment of the debt. After that government was formed it was taken up and they sent a Commission over here to confer with the Commission that had been appointed by this Government, which acts under the authority of a law of Congress. It is an expert Commission, made up of the best experts that we have in this country. It is bipartisan, so that it represented I think sufficient business ability and different political points of view to represent very fairly the sentiment of our country. They had at their disposal a large amount of information collected from original sources as to the capacity of the Italians to pay, and the settlement was made on that basis. If the men on that Commission with the information that they had aren't judges of the capacity of Italy to pay, I wouldn't know where to turn to get judgment on that question. It is desirable in order that Italy may arrange its finances, that there should be a settlement; and that it should be a definite settlement. If it is indefinite and indeterminate, to be reopened some time in the future, why then there isn't any basis on which you get a stabilization of international finances. That is desirable not only for Italy—it is desirable for us. And we have also taken into consideration, in all these debt settlements, the desirability to re-establish Europe and fix in a definite and determinate form the public finances of those countries. Some may think that our settlement with Italy is too liberal. I presume it will be recalled that the Congress ratified a moratorium to Austria of twenty years. Austria was not on our side during the war, but our country recognized that after the war was over the cause of humanity required us to help feed the Austrians, which we did. And when the question came up of paying that it was found that the Austrian finances were in such shape that nothing could be done at the present time, so we passed a moratorium of twenty years. The case of Italy comes before us in quite different fashion, being one of the countries that fought with us during the war, and we ought to be willing to treat them as well as we did the Austrians. It is also a question of the economic re-establishment of the world, which we think will be for our benefit. We are a great producer of raw materials and a great exporter. We export abroad tremendous amounts. I think our exports in that respect in 1924 of the two great staple raw materials which we export, cotton and foodstuffs, was $2,445,000,000 and in 1925 it was $2,602,000,000. That is 2245 and 2602. Of course our importations were large. In 1924 they were $1,096,000,000; for 1925 $1,238,000,000. The foodstuffs that we exported in 1924, the 1925 figures are not yet available, were $615,000,000 and cotton in 1924 was $842,000,000. Now it is greatly to the advantage of our foreign trade that these debt settlements be made. It results in stabilization of currency, stabilization of exchange. And we have here a settlement that has been made and ratified by the bipartisan commission of experts. It has my approval. It has been adopted by the House by a vote of 257 to 133 and is now before the Senate. I think it will pass because I am certain that it ought to pass. But suppose it shouldn't pass. The vote would be very large in favor of its passage. Where would that leave this country in future negotiations? Why, Italy would say, here is the approval of the Debt Commission, the approval of the President, the approval of the House almost two to one, and a very large vote in the Senate. We have done all that we can do and there is nothing more that remains for us. It seems to me that if the Italian debt settlement fails now of ratification it will simply relieve Italy from making any further effort to pay us. Of course, I am looking to the interests of the United States. I think that is my first duty and I don't want to bring any party consideration into this. I think that should not come in. But I assume it is generally understood in the country that the party I represent has been rather more diffident about extending favors than the other party. Now, if that is the case, I can't see that the other party should feel that they ought not to be willing to go as far as we are willing to go in making a settlement of this kind. That is not a matter of any importance, but a mere incident. Here is a party that has been criticized for not doing enough and those that have been criticizing us surely ought to be willing to go as far as we have been willing to go. But this is based on a bipartisan decision. It has no politics in it. It is an effort to settle our debt on a basis of all that we think Italy can do that is fair to the United States and for the general welfare of all concerned.

[*The President was shrewdly using the press conference to promote the Italian debt settlement in Congress.*]

May 4, 1926

You have already observed that with the exception of three or four comparatively small items about which nothing can be done at the present time the Debt Funding Commission has finished its work. They have settled debts that were in principal sum, $11,500,000,000, with interest of ten and a little over a half a billion, $10,621,000,000, making a total it has been contracted to pay into the United States Treasury of $22,143,000,000. I doubt if we are really able to grasp the magnitude of these transactions. They are the greatest financial transactions that ever took place between governments, and I want to take this opportunity to express my appreciation of the work of the Debt Funding Commission. It has had the advantage of a membership composed of representatives of both parties, some coming from the country and not holding official positions, some members from the House, some from the Senate, and three members of the Cabinet, the Secretary of State, Secretary of the Treasury and the Secretary of Commerce. I understand that the Secretary of the Treasury is the Chairman of the Debt Funding Commission, and without detracting at all from the splendid cooperation that he has had from the other members, of course the leadership in these settlements has necessarily fallen to him. And I think they have been brought about to a considerable extent by reason of the confidence that is felt in his financial judgment, not only by the people of this country but by the financial agents of the governments abroad. Without that feeling of confidence, it would have been impossible to have secured the negotiation of the settlements that have already been ratified by the Congress. It is altogether a very great accomplishment that I think our country may look at with a great deal of satisfaction. It will result in large payments into our Treasury. It will result likewise in the stabilization and rehabilitation of financial conditions of the interested countries abroad. While our settlements have been liberal, I think they have on the whole been just, the best that could be arrived at with the information and prospects that we have at hand.

July 27, 1926

There are no understandings in any of the debt settlements other than what are included in the terms which were signed by the parties and ratified by our Congress with foreign governments. This country hasn't any method of making any understandings except through the duly authorized channels of treaties, and all those treaties of course go to the Senate for ratification, and in almost all cases, I think practically every case, the Senate adopts a motion removing the injunction of secrecy, so that our treaties are public and of course the debt settlements were all public. They were public when they were referred to Congress, somewhat different in nature than a treaty because they partook of the expenditure of public money and for that reason were ratified by both the Senate and House. There is no way we could make any private understanding. No one has any authority to make it. The only method that a private understanding could be entered into with this country, would be by a treaty ratified by the Senate from which the injunction of secrecy was not removed. Then it would be private in the sense that it wasn't published. I doubt if we have any treaties of that kind. I have never heard of one. It is customary oftentimes to discuss treaties in executive session, but it was the uniform practice when I presided over the Senate that if a treaty had been ratified that the injunction of secrecy so far as the treaty was concerned was removed and the treaty became public.

August 31, 1926

I didn't see Mr. Brush's article or interview or whatever it may have been relative to foreign debts. It is sometimes easier for a person that is in private life and no longer charged with the responsibilities of the administration of public affairs to make a larger expenditure of the taxpayers' money than it is for those who have to be responsible for the collection of the money or the payment of it out of the pockets of the taxpayer. I have a good deal of respect for Mr. Baker's judgment and a high regard for his patriotism, but the matter of settlement or cancellation of our debts has been discussed a great many times. Our Government has taken an attitude on that which I do not think will be changed. All of the great powers, with one exception, have made a final adjustment and I think it is apparent that there is every expectation that France will adjust its debt settlement in accordance with the negotiations that have been made by its duly accredited Ambassador. So, as far as I am informed, I know of no reason for making any change in our policy. It has been pointed out time and time again that this money has to be paid by our taxpayers unless it is paid by the taxpayers of the country or the countries which borrowed the money. Mr. Baker I know is a perfectly sincere man and I don't want too much made of my suggestion that it is easier to make up your mind when you are not charged with public responsibility than it is when you are responsible for making the decision that settles the question.

[*Newton D. Baker was Secretary of War under President Woodrow Wilson. In April, 1926 the French Ambassador to the United States, Henri Bérenger, concluded with Secretary of the Treasury Mellon the Mellon-Bérenger Agreement, but the French Chamber of Deputies refused to accept it until July, 1929, after adoption of the Young plan, named after Owen D. Young.]*

October 14, 1927

I saw some reference to the statement made by Senator Glass relative to foreign loans. The Senator is a man exceedingly well versed in national and international finance, and anything that he says is entitled to a very great deal of consideration. I have had under consideration several times the question of entirely disregarding proposals made for foreign loans in this country, but it had all the time seemed to me that unless there was some contact between the State Department and those who floated foreign loans here it would be probable that the Congress would pass a very drastic regulatory law. So that it seemed to me best to proceed for the time being according to the present practice, which is merely advisory and really consists in inquiring whether, if the loan is made of such and such an amount to such and such a country, it would in any way interfere with the foreign relations that exist between that country and ours at the present time. The Constitution places in the hands of the President, and he exercises that authority chiefly through the State Department, the conduct of foreign relations, relations between this country and foreign countries. That is one element of them at the present time. Of course, our country doesn't undertake to make any suggestion about the desirability of a loan, or the financial soundness of it, or whether it is worthy or unworthy of investment in its bonds by investors in this country. That is a question between themselves and our bankers, a question ultimately for investors themselves to decide, whether they want to make an investment in foreign loans. So that, as I said before, our interest in it is chiefly a determination as to whether a loan made would interfere in any way in the foreign relations, the relations that exist between this country and the country proposing to make a loan.

[Senator Carter Glass of Virginia assailed the State Department for demanding clearance on loans by private American banks to foreign governments. He maintained the Department was overstepping its powers, an opinion shared by Senator William E. Borah, chairman of the Senate Foreign Relations Committee. While expressing confidence in Secretary of State Frank Kellogg, Glass said that a less able man might easily abuse such a power. Only Congress should act to curb such loans, he maintained.]

March 20, 1928

I am sending a message to the Congress relative to the Austrian debt. You may recall that 4 or 5 years ago we extended the time—put on what would be technically known as a moratorium for Austria, which runs into the early 40's. Now, Austria wants to do some financing, and has secured the consent of all the other interested governments

197

of Europe and wishes to secure our consent. That consent is being given by the other governments on condition that agreements are made for funding the present indebtedness of Austria to the other countries. We thought we should go in on the same basis. So that I am asking for legislation that would authorize us to grant the extension that is requested and to accept a funding settlement with Austria that will be as good as that which is given to any of the other countries.

October 2, 1928

There have been and probably will continue to be efforts to make some arrangement by which the taxpayers of America may pay the German reparations. That isn't looked on with any favor in this country, nor do we see that it has any connection with the debts that are due to our country. Those have all been settled, with some trifling exceptions, and all been ratified but one. I don't see any good result to be secured by discussing it in the press. It has been my policy for a long time to refrain from any discussion in relation to it, considering it as a closed incident.

December 21, 1928

We have had some suggestion that the European governments would make some representation to this government relative to American participation in a body of experts to examine the question of German reparations, but so far as I know no representation has yet been made to us, so that I couldn't make any decision about it until the representation comes and we are able to find out what it involves. We should, of course, look at any suggestions made in a sympathetic way. At the same time this is almost purely a European question. In fact, it is a European question. And while I don't want to have this country shirk any duty that it ought to perform I should certainly like it if European questions could be adjusted by the Europeans. Now, it may be that they are not able to do that in this case and we ought to step in and participate. If we do that, I hope there will be a little realization in some quarters that this country doesn't interfere in other countries unless it is obliged to, and that if the Europeans can't settle their controversy without calling on us for help and we respond I do not think that in European quarters we ought to be criticized for making a like response when we are asked to assist in Central America. I shall want to be convinced too that if we are asked to have experts participate that there is going to be an opportunity for the exercise of the judgment of the experts, and that those who go there representing other governments or those who go from the United States will all go free to exercise their judgment and not be given instructions beforehand that would hamper them in exercising their judgment. I mean by that that one side ought not to instruct its experts we can't pay more than so much and the other side ought not to instruct its experts we can't take less than so much. If they be experts, it means they are going to undertake in their own judgment what can be paid and should be free to make a judgment of that kind without being hampered beforehand with instructions.

January 11, 1929

There hasn't anything new developed relative to the German reparations problem. I presume the conference has in mind what the situation is; that the European governments that are interested, including Germany, would like to secure the services of two Americans to join with the experts that are to be appointed by the European governments, and we have reported to the European governments that our Government has no objection to their taking that course. It also needs to be kept in mind that it is the European governments that are making the appointments and making the selections. I think, as I indicated once before, I would be more pleased if the European governments would settle that question themselves, but if they feel that they need assistance of some Americans I don't think it would be becoming on the part of our Government to say that the people here that are willing to serve should not be permitted to do so, or rather that our Government wouldn't give its consent to their doing so. The last body of experts that was headed by General Dawes worked out what has proven to be an acceptable plan, and in its operation has been successful, so that I judge that one of the main things that is left to be considered is the final amount that Germany is to pay. If it is found that they could go on paying 2,500,000,000 marks, which is about $625,000,000 a year, then the only question to consider would be how long they ought to keep on paying it. If it is found there is some reason for varying that amount, why that is another question, and it is for the purpose of deciding what would seem to be fair between Germany, considering its ability, and the European countries that are interested on the other side, including Japan and the trifling amount that is due us comparatively, that this body of experts will be brought together. We are returning, as you will recall, the private property of the German nationals that we held as security for the payment due us as our bill for the Army of Occupation, which is some $200,000,000, and whatever may be found to be due by the German[-American Mixed] Claims Commission for damages which accrued to our citizens in the early part of the war, I think before we went into the war. Those two together are not very large sums, so that the amount due us is not large. That, however, would not be a matter that would be considered by a commission of experts—the amount of our bill. If there is anything to be done about that at this conference it would be done through our regular diplomatic representative, probably as, though there are Americans on the committee of experts, they do not represent the Government of the United States.

February 12, 1929

I had hoped, as I think I have already indicated, that it would be possible for the experts conference on reparations now sitting in Paris to agree on some member other than a citizen of the United States for their Chairman. It did not seem possible for them to do that, so that of course I indicated to Mr. Young that he and Mr. Morgan were to use their discretion about Mr. Young accepting the chairmanship. I understand he has done so. That seemed to be necessary. It wouldn't be of any value just to permit citizens of the United States to go over there to help unless their help is to be of such a nature as would be effective. While I would have preferred to have another person than a citizen of the United States Chairman, it seemed to be best under the circumstances for Mr. Young to serve.

[*J. P. Morgan was the second American member of the experts conference.*]

10 · The Old World and the New

IN THE 1920's most Americans thought Europe the root of all evil, an opinion which President Coolidge essentially shared. He had never seen Europe nor, for that matter, had most of his countrymen, except under the unfavorable circumstances of World War I. Perhaps that experience accounted for much of the anti-European attitude in the United States. Or perhaps it was a repayment in kind for the traditional anti-American attitude of most Europeans. Whatever the causes, the fact of dislike was undeniable.

Coolidge did feel that Europeans could be saved if they became more like Americans. First, they must pay their debts. And like their descendants in America, Europeans ought to live amicably with each other. They were, however, too removed from the United States to expect American help in settling their political problems. They were eligible to receive aid only on such extraordinary occasions as a world war.

Just as Coolidge and his fellow citizens failed to perceive the approach of the Great Depression, so did they fail to sense Europe's political, economic, and social insecurity. The 1920's, as everyone knows, marked a return to the hopes of prewar years—that the placid internationalism of the nineteenth century might be permanently re-established.

The two principal issues, along with debts and reparations, which compelled American attention toward Europe were the World Court and the Kellogg-Briand Pact. The World Court generated so much controversy in the United States that one might have thought it was the leading international issue of the day. The Court had so many well-intentioned supporters and adversaries that it was an issue difficult to consider on its own merits. Coolidge treated it cautiously. The Court became the focus of much anti-League of Nations sentiment; it fell into the clutches of such obstructionist Senators as William E. Borah of Idaho and Hiram Johnson of California. President Harding had brought the protocol of the Court to the Senate for approval in 1923. A running debate began which continued until January 27, 1926, when the Senate accepted the protocol with five reservations. The last of these denied the League of Nations Council the right to ask the Court for advice on any issue in which the United States had or claimed an interest. This was a crippling clause, for according to its protocol, the Court, when requested by the Council, was empowered to give advisory opinions. This same amendment also required that the Court be approved by all forty-eight nations belonging to the League. A conference was called in 1929 to find a formula acceptable to everyone including the United States. In spite of this effort, the Senate rejected the revised World Court protocol in 1935. American energy expended on the World Court, one must conclude, was a waste of time and a positive harm to world peace. That energy might better have gone into support of the League of Nations.

The diplomatic maneuvers between France and the United States which led to the Kellogg-Briand Pact were initiated by French Foreign Minister Aristide Briand. In a newspaper article on April 6, 1927, the tenth anniversary of America's entrance into the World War, he proposed to the American people a pact of perpetual peace between France and the United States. It was a clever proposal, embodying the hopes of such unofficial ambassadors of peace as President Nicholas Murray Butler and Professor James T. Shotwell, both of Columbia University, who called for "renunciation of war as an instrument of national policy," and Salmon O. Levinson, a Chicago lawyer, who proposed "the Outlawry of war." Briand utilized these sentiments for his own purpose: to enlist the United States in propping France's wobbly political position in Europe. In a countermaneuver Secretary of State Kellogg cleverly suggested that the original Franco-American proposal be developed into a grand multilateral treaty to include all the nations of the world. Coolidge, who thought the original proposal silly, the work of a few "volunteer" diplomats, displayed a mild interest in the international version. He thought it might conceivably contribute to world peace. Taking perfunctory credit for the Pact, which was signed by the United States and virtually all of the other great powers on August 27, 1928, he promptly turned his attention elsewhere.

August 21, 1923

I have a number of interesting inquiries here and one of the first is relative to the reports of observers returning from Europe, whether they point to the necessity of any change in the American attitude toward European affairs. So far as I get any information from there, it doesn't point to the necessity of any change. Those returning confirm the wisdom of the attitude that has been maintained since I have known about things in Washington. They realize the difficulties over there, perhaps more acutely by reason of immediate contact with them than we can here, and I think they can see that there isn't anything that America can do at the present time other than proceed with the course that it has mapped out.

[This is Coolidge's first press conference statement as President.]

August 28, 1923

An inquiry about whether it would be helpful for the press to discuss the policy of the United States for the purpose of the abolition of war. I think that candid discussion of any question is always helpful. That is the great service that you perform, of reasonable and candid discussion. You all have in mind that Mr. Bok has pending a proposal to give an award of $100,000 to the person who can successfully propose some plan of this kind. It happened that I was near his place in Maine early in July. He came to call on me at the hotel. I was attending a conference of Governors and I had an opportunity to go over to his house and spend a few minutes one afternoon with him. He went over somewhat of his plan and the main desire of it, the main element of it at least, was a public discussion of these questions, in order that the public might better be informed as to what our foreign relations really meant, their dependence on it, the effect that friendly or unfriendly relations have on their personal economic condition. He thought that if that could be thoroughly understood by the people of the United States, it would be of great public benefit, and with that in mind, I think that the discussion in the public press along lines of that kind will also be productive of a great deal of public benefit.

[In 1922, Edward Bok sought to bring peace to the world in not more than 5,000 words. He offered a $100,000 prize to the author of the

best proposed peace plan, $50,000 to be paid immediately and the balance either when the plan went into operation or received substantial popular support. Among the 22,165 entrants were William Jennings Bryan and Franklin D. Roosevelt. Winner of the contest was Charles H. Levermore, secretary of the New York Peace Society, whose plan was entitled "Progressive Cooperation with the Organized World, Sustained by the Moral Force of Public Opinion and by Developing Law." Levermore received only the first $50,000.]

October 9, 1923

An inquiry about Senator [Royal] Copeland [Dem.] of New York, suggesting that in a series of speeches he is urging the calling of an international economic conference, and inquiring whether I have given any consideration to this subject. I haven't given any particular consideration to it. It is a matter that has been up for discussion in Washington now and then for two years. But, up to the present time, there hasn't seemed to be a condition existing abroad that made action of that kind practicable; and, of course, it is fundamental that while you might like to do something in this direction, or that direction, or the other, there isn't any use of starting in on it unless there is at the outset a good reason to expect that it might be successful, and that is the condition in this respect. The matter that they are discussing in Europe, and about which they are moving armies, is an economic question in a way, and with the present condition of mind over there, it hasn't seemed that it could be decided at a conference. They have had various conferences in Europe, and had up this matter, especially, for discussion and consideration, and they haven't been able to reach any conclusion.

[The President was referring to the reparations negotiations and Franco-Belgian occupation of the Ruhr.]

October 12, 1923

I have another inquiry, I don't know whether I covered that, about the proposal of Lloyd George for an entente between the United States and Great Britain to maintain the peace of the world. That, as I have explained, is an unofficial proposal made by a prominent man, but not made by the Government of Great Britain in any way. Should it be made by the Government of Great Britain, why we would take it up and consider it then. Coming, as it does, in this way, I think we will have to regard it as a speech and I don't care to make any particular comment about it.

October 23, 1923

I have another most interesting inquiry. It has quite a long preamble, but there is one very significant thing in it, "The United States has never interfered in the internal affairs of other nations, except by precept and example"; and inquires whether it is the hope of the

United States that people will eventually be at peace everywhere under democratic forms of government. I have partly answered that question in what I have already said—that we demanded the right at one time to have such a form of government as we want for our people, and we have to concede that same right to others. I don't know of any case where the United States has interfered directly with any other government, because they had a form of government too democratic, or not democratic enough, in accordance with our views. I think the inquiry is very well answered when it sets out the sentence that I have just read, which says that we have never interfered in the internal affairs of other nations, except by precept and example. That, of course, is the notable exception, and I might go on with a discussion of this inquiry, the monarch threat, so on and so forth, and you all will see the implication and the application of it, that our country expects to maintain its present form of government. We wouldn't want any country to interfere with our form of government, and we don't want to take any action that would interfere with the rights of other countries. While the United States Government has no opinion, I have no doubt that thoughtful people in our country have hope that governments, similar to our own, will ultimately, and could ultimately, be established. No doubt, they have been gratified to see republics springing up, and there has been an absence of gratification when anything like a reaction occurred, tending to bring people back under any form of government that wasn't an expression of their own will and their own wish. Anything like a dictatorship, or any manner of government of that kind, of course, is not a condition that is gratifying to the American people.

November 16, 1923

An inquiry also about my answer to a recent question which was interpreted as favoring a monarchist regime for Germany. I suppose it is well known that the long expressed policy of the American Government, especially as set out in the Monroe Doctrine, is that of favoring everywhere a republican form of government. That doesn't mean that we can always interfere, even when we should want to interfere, nor does it mean that the Government as a government can always express the opinion that would probably be entertained by each member of the Government, and known to be entertained by all the people of the United States. That question arose from an inquiry about a report of the return of the Emperor of Germany into that country. I suppose one of the things for which we went to war was to drive him out of power and prevent hereafter what the Emperor at that time was doing. That was supposed to have been effectively prevented by the Versailles Treaty, and those who are parties to that treaty have the authority, of course, and ought to have the authority, to enforce its provisions, and in that they would have the sympathy always of the United States, I am sure.

May 24, 1924

I doubt if there is much hope of getting an agreement among the Republicans on the Foreign Relations Committee on the subject of the World Court at this session. They would not need all to be in agreement, I think, if they were to get action. There are two, four, six, eight, ten Republicans and one Farmer Labor, and two, four, six, seven Democrats. It won't be necessary for the Republicans all to agree. I have stated my decision on the matter, as you know, in my message to Congress, in several conferences and in one or two addresses I have elaborated my ideas. Secretary Hughes has made elaborate speeches on it. So it has not seemed necessary to make an address on the World Court. My position is favorable to the plan presented by President Harding.

I know the Foreign Relations Committee are working on it. I had a conference the other night with several of them in which they told me of several different plans that were before the Committee, and I told them that I had taken my position and virtually gone to the country on it. . . .

January 30, 1925

I don't think I can make any comment relative to the proposals of the French and German Governments for a security pact [the Locarno Agreements] for the guarantee of European peace. I don't know any way that America could cooperate in that. It seems to me that it is almost entirely a European political subject in which we can't take any very helpful part.

September 8, 1925

I don't know as there is anything more to say about the World Court. I judge that the suggestion that the United States should adhere to it has been gaining strength. I expect that after due consideration the Senate will pass a resolution of adherence.

[*Sensing the World Court's "extraordinary unimportance," as an officer of the State Department described it, Coolidge was not going to jeopardize other legislation by pushing the issue.*]

October 9, 1925

I can't comment on any of the phases of the Security Pact Conference that is now being held at Locarno. At Cambridge on the third of July I expressed the general hope that a pact of that kind might be entered into on the part of European countries, and I am still of the opinion that that would be very helpful and I would be glad to reiterate the hope that this conference may be able to agree on the principle and form of a pact of that kind. Now, as I say, as to the particular phases of it and the different questions involved, I haven't any information that would warrant my expressing any opinion except in the general hope of the success of the Conference. I think it is exceedingly important that some agreement of this kind be made in order that there may be a cessation of the uncertainties and the constant preparations for defense and the armaments that are going on in Europe.

[*Because of the connection between debts and reparations, Coolidge closely followed the proceedings at the Locarno Conference.*]

October 16, 1925

As I have said, I have several inquiries here about the pact that has been signed at Locarno. Quite naturally we haven't yet the official report and I don't know whether we have a very accurate report of just what the document contains. If it is what I understand it to be, the security pact between the great nations, I regard it as one of the most important events that have occurred since the adoption of the Dawes Plan. I think the adoption of that plan was the first instance of the interested nations being able to make any agreement for a very long time previous to that, I think running back practically to the signing of the peace treaties. Now this has indicated that they can agree on other very important and material things. This ought to be what it purports to be—a real covenant of security that will relieve France and Italy, Great Britain and Belgium, and also definitely commits Germany to a peace program. I suppose it goes without saying that we understood that that had already been done before, but to have an agreement of this kind in which all those nations were able to join is an accomplishment of value that it is almost unable to estimate. I think it will have a very beneficial result on the financial situation. It ought to relieve those countries of the necessity of maintaining great armaments and I should expect it would have a very helpful effect on the proposal to have a Disarmament Conference in this country. As I say, I can't be certain about that until I have seen the official text, but it all works in that direction. We have had the Dawes Plan. We have had the conference at Paris of the representatives of those governments over there. They were able to agree. We have had the settlement of a good many European debts to this country. We have had the putting into operation of the Reparations Plan. And all of these things are I think a most helpful and promising accomplishment. It indicates step by step a very remarkable progress that is being made, and I can't think of anything that would be of a more hopeful nature and hold out more promise of benefit to the world in general than action of this kind.

[*The Locarno Agreements turned out to be a mixed blessing. With the Dawes Plan they facilitated payment of German reparations and, thereby, the war debts to the United States. They also led to Germany's admission to the League of Nations in 1926. But the convening of the Preparatory Commission for a forthcoming general disarmament conference produced much international rancor and put France's armaments (maintained chiefly against Germany) in a bad light. The Locarno Agreements, moreover, had an unsettling effect on the long-term fortunes of Europe, for the signing of treaties guaranteeing Germany's western borders but not its eastern boundaries established, in effect, first- and second-class border situations. The eastern borders of Germany, of course, were allegedly the cause of war in 1939.]*

October 20, 1925

. . . I might restate too the well-known and what I hope is becoming the historic attitude of our Government, of desiring to do everything that we can, without jeopardizing our own interests, to help the European situation. We have realized all along that it would be useless to have any thought over there that there must be a constant reliance on us. I think I have stated in some of my addresses that we couldn't help people very much until they showed a disposition to help themselves. I think that disposition is becoming more and more apparent abroad every day, and it is a rising of a condition that is exceedingly gratifying to those that want to help and those that want to see the European situation progressively developed.

February 2, 1926

There are two sets of people in the country at the present time that I think have the wrong impression of our vote to become members of the World Court. One set thinks it doesn't mean anything and won't be helpful. I think it will be very helpful. It will be regarded all over the world as a helpful attitude, and an expression of the sentiment of desiring to cooperate, and a desire to put America on the side of having differences settled by orderly procedure and as near as they can be in accordance with international law, friendly conferences and settled rules, rather than to resort to force and have the question settled because one country or the other has a larger army and navy. There is another opinion that is being expressed: that this is merely preliminary to our country becoming a member of the League. I don't regard that as the case at all. You will recall that in my message to the Congress I differentiated the very marked difference between adherence to the protocol that established the Court and adherence to the Covenant of the League. They are two very separate and distinct things. One of them doesn't at all imply the other. I don't regard the action that has been taken as at all indicating that there is any difference in public opinion in this country in relation to any suggestion that America should become a member of the League. I rather regard it as an implication to be taken in the other direction, that we wanted to become identified with the Court, and a rather definite expression of the fact that we don't want to become identified with the League. One is a judicial institution; the other is a political institution. Their aims are different; their methods of procedure are different; and because we wanted to belong to the Court is no indication at all, but rather the contrary, that we want to belong to the League.

March 23, 1926

I have only seen a report in the press to the effect that there might be an invitation from the League of Nations that we should send some representative to discuss with them the matter of the reservations that were put on by the Senate in its ratification of the protocol of the Court. I don't think any such invitation has come. If it does come, why of course it will be taken and considered then. I haven't come to any final conclusion about it. The method that the State Department is adopting to deal with our entrance into the Court is that of sending a copy of the vote of the Senate to each interested nation and requesting them to send to the Department the note that is specified in the reservations signifying their consent to our adherence on the conditions that are expressed in the reservations. I think I saw in the morning press that one nation, Cuba, had already sent in its note, and I presume that that would signify that other nations would be rapidly sending in their consent. I don't know what would be in the mind of the League, but as the reservations undertake to emphasize especially the independence of the Court from the League, and perhaps strengthen it, I assume that perhaps the League thought that it was a matter that might interest them in some way and there has been a discussion as to whether they would hold a conference to consider it and have someone present representing this country to explain the reservations. So far as I can see at the present time, that would hardly be necessary. The reservations seem to speak for themselves and I think are quite plain. In general, they do emphasize, of course, the independence of the Court from the League.

April 2, 1926

I think that the invitation has been received from the League about a conference with nations to consider the reservations that we have proposed to our proposal to adhere to the statute of the Court. Of course it was a most courteous thing for the League to do, to extend that invitation to us, as it was a discussion of some matter in which we have some interest, and quite properly they would inquire whether it was a matter that we wanted to discuss. As far as I have been able to determine, I don't see any necessity for any discussion on our part. The reservations speak for themselves. So that I don't expect or anticipate—unless some reason appears that I don't expect to appear on further study—that we should consider it necessary to send any representative. We are dealing, as I have indicated before, directly with the nations concerned. We are adhering to the Protocol, which is the technical name of the Statute that created the Court and which is the action of forty-eight different nations. The League has nothing to do with it and can't do anything with it if it wanted to. The only persons that can make any change in it are the forty-eight nations, so that it would be our attitude that we would deal with them, rather than to undertake to deal through any other channel.

May 4, 1926

Here is an inquiry about a Third Hague Conference. The value of a conference of that kind depends not merely on the attitude of our Government, but it depends on the attitude of the other governments that it is proposed to have attend the conference. I don't know of any present desire on the part of other governments to promote a conference of that kind at this time, the reason being that there are so many pressing questions in Europe that take up the attention and exhaust the energy of the present governments over there that I doubt whether they would be interested to take on a Hague conference at the present time, though of course I well understand that there are a good many things that we would be interested in that might be taken up at a Hague Conference—perhaps progress made there in consideration of arbitration, perhaps something might be done looking toward a clarification of international law. But with present conditions in Europe, and the other things they have to attend to, I shouldn't expect that we could get a favorable response on any effort on our part to call a conference at this time.

[*The First Hague Conference met in 1899, the Second in 1907. Plans for a Third were shelved with the outbreak of the World War.*]

July 27, 1926

There has been quite a good deal of discussion in the press about the attitude of foreign countries toward us. I doubt if we need to pay too much attention to that. I have seen reports, I don't know how trustworthy they are, of alleged difficulties that some of our tourists have had abroad. Two kinds of tourists go abroad. One kind are of a somewhat bumptious nature. If that kind of tourist gets some education abroad and finds out that there are other people in the world that are entitled to some consideration and respect as well as Americans, I don't think that will do any great harm. There is another kind of people that go abroad that have an appreciation of the amenities that are usually practiced, and if they do not find things to their liking abroad of course their remedy is to come home and stay here and spend their money here. But the main point that I wanted to emphasize is this: That as one holding the office that is responsible for our foreign relations and one who wants to maintain friendly relations with all other nations, I always regret that some of our people make assertions that are not always warranted by the facts, the main effect of which is to stir up animosities in foreign countries against us. When anything of that kind occurs I always hope that the people abroad will realize that it is a somewhat irresponsible utterance and doesn't really represent the feeling of this Government and probably doesn't represent the public opinion of this country. Now, it is a poor rule that doesn't work both ways, and when some irresponsible person abroad makes some statement that is likely to irritate us, why I have to apply the rule here that I hope others will apply to us and realize that it is not an expression on the part of foreign governments, probably doesn't represent their convictions, probably isn't an accurate representation of the public opinion abroad.

September 3, 1926

I don't know that there is anything I can say that hasn't already been said about the World Court. I feel quite certain that when the other nations come to examine the reservations they will see that the purport of them is merely to put this country on a parity with other countries that are members of the League and have a seat in the Council. I understand that they have already agreed to four reservations and the one that is under consideration is the 5th. As I understand the rights of members of the League who may be members of the Council, in order to have an advisory opinion it has to be by the unanimous action of the Council. That means that one nation in the Council can object to having an advisory opinion and the advisory opinion is then not called for. So I understand the 5th reservation is merely for the purpose of putting the United States in the same position as other countries, which I think when it is understood and studied by the other countries in interest will be regarded as entirely fair. If other countries have the right individually to prevent the asking of an advisory opinion, why I see no reason why the United States shouldn't have the same right which it would have under the 5th reservation. The speedy action that has been taken on the first four reservations I should think would indicate that there would be little, if any, difficulty in the 5th reservation.

May 31, 1927

I knew that some parties in New York, I think one of them is Professor Shotwell, are making a study of a possible treaty to be negotiated between this country and other countries on the subject which is generally referred to as outlawing war, and I had directed that they take the matter up with the State Department, which I think is being done. I wouldn't want to hazard any definite comment on it until I find out from the State Department just what is being proposed and what the view of the State Department may be. I have referred to that subject several times in my messages to the Congress. It is one which I have been very glad to observe is being studied and which I should be very much pleased to find had been put into a practicable form.

[*This was Coolidge's first comment on what became the Kellogg-Briand pact. Professor James T. Shotwell of Columbia University gratuitously had involved himself in a complicated politique—nominally a proposal in April, 1927 by French Foreign Minister Aristide Briand for a pact to outlaw war between France and the United States. France was in a difficult position. By the end of the World War she had lost her old ally Russia. In the postwar years she possessed only the loosest of ties with Great Britain. The Germans were restive. France sought allies wherever she could find them. After signing up the lesser states of Europe—Belgium, Poland, the Little Entente (Czechoslovakia, Rumania, Yugoslavia)—the French obliquely approached the United States. Their tactic was to exploit the idea of outlawing war, popular in America. Foreign Minister Briand's original proposal to Secretary of State Kellogg was negative. The outlawry pact provided that in the event France went to war (with Germany, for instance), the United States would remain neutral. Such a pact also had admonitory value. The French could display it to the Germans as a mark of special American favor. All in all it was a tricky French maneuver, coming after France's failure to ratify the Mellon-Bérenger debt-funding agreement and shortly before the Geneva Naval Conference to which France refused to send a delegation.*]

June 17, 1927

There are no developments, so far as I am aware, in the French proposal relative to outlawing war. I think the Secretary of State has already announced that he has sent some message or a note to France relative to it. Has he not made an announcement of that kind?

PRESS: Yes, sir.

[*Secretary Kellogg, who heartily disliked Briand's new proposal, sought to forestall it by doing nothing. But public opinion was aroused. By chance, Charles A. Lindbergh had chosen May of 1927 to fly nonstop from New York to Paris; his flight greatly increased Franco-American amity. Kellogg on June 11 instructed the Ambassador in Paris, Myron T. Herrick, to inform Briand that the American Government would be pleased to enter into diplomatic conversations regarding the French proposal.*]

Rapid City, S. D., June 24, 1927

I don't know whether Ambassador Herrick will come out here while he is in this country. I think it is somewhat doubtful, though he may. I haven't any plan about that at the present time. I do not think he is coming here with any plans for a new treaty between this country and France relative to the suggestion of outlawing war. I never heard of any such thing and I think it is entirely improbable that such is the case. There have been no developments about that. I think you had a report from the Office of the Secretary of State relative to the nature of the response that he made to France that our country would be glad to know what plans they had and that they could be developed when Ambassador Herrick returns to France and when the French Ambassador returns to America.

[*Herrick was to bring back to the United States a French draft of the proposed treaty, dated June 20 (the day the Naval Conference opened in Geneva). It already had been cabled to the State Department. Briand did not want to postpone negotiations until the end of August, when the French Ambassador would return to his post in Washington.*]

November 4, 1927

I don't know of any recent action that has been taken relative to the suggestion that came from France last spring about a treaty with that country to make our peace relations with them more certain and any warfare more improbable. That was to be taken up on the return of their Ambassador here and our Ambassador over there. Mr. Herrick, as you know, has been ill, and hasn't been able to go back. I think he will be expecting to return in about three weeks. Then the matter will be ripe, I should judge, for further discussion.

[*Coolidge and Kellogg were not going to be rushed; they sat on the treaty draft all summer and into the autumn. Herrick was not diplomatically ill; he died at his post in early 1929.*]

November 8, 1927

I had a short talk with Mr. Steed, Wickham Steed, the editor of the *London Review of Reviews* when he was here. I didn't have a chance to go into much of the development of the suggestion that he is making relative to some position that should be announced by the United States as to what it might do in certain contingencies, so I have never come to any definite conclusion about it. I told him I thought it could be assumed that our main desire was to keep out of controversies that affected other nations. But of course on the other hand our country assumes to have certain rights, commercial intercourse, and so on, that our people might not like to have interfered with. Where the line would be drawn between those two possibly conflicting sentiments, it would be hard to say. So that I haven't developed his proposal sufficiently to come to any final determination about it. It is a very interesting proposal. Mr. Steed seemed to be a particularly well informed and very brilliant man.

[*Steed proposed that the United States issue a unilateral pronouncement, similar to the Monroe Doctrine, that "the United States abhors aggressive war, and that it will never weaken the hands of other nations which may band themselves together for the purpose of deterring*

213

an aggressor or of compelling him to desist from aggression." It was a great time, of course, for plans, and the President had to be diplomatic. Such plans usually sought to involve the United States in some kind of extra-League of Nations or super-Locarno pact.]

November 25, 1927

I have given some thought to the suggestion for the outlawry of war. Any treaties made on that subject are somewhat difficult under our Constitution. Those difficulties were quite clearly set out some months ago by Dr. David Jayne Hill in an article that was, I think, in the *Saturday Evening Post.* I don't know that they are insuperable, but they are certainly very great, because our Constitution places the authority for a declaration of war in the Congress. Of course, that makes it quite obvious that any treaty that might be made would not take away from Congress the power to declare war. Such a treaty, however, would amount to a declaration of a policy that might be helpful in promoting a sentiment for peace. I don't know that we regard our own country any differently than other people regard theirs. I suppose that most of our people would say that this is a peaceful country as indicated by the very infrequent occasions in which it has resorted to war, emphasized by the many treaties that we have for arbitration, the moderate size of our Army, and considering all our conditions the very moderate size of our Navy, and our general indisposition to interfere in the affairs of other countries. Still, if there is more that could be said that would indicate a desire for honorable peace, it might be desirable to say it. I do not think it is likely that anything of that nature could be well dealt with in a conference. It would have to be taken up by individual nations.

[Stenographer's note: The President was asked if he had seen a certain proposal for putting an embargo on arms against aggressor countries.] Well, I have seen some reference to that. I haven't given that study enough either to come to a definite conclusion about it. It would depend very much upon the form, the details that it might take; also it would depend on what it was to be applied to. If it was to apply merely to arms and ammunition it would be taken differently in this country, than if it meant to be carried to the extent of non-intercourse, which would practically mean that we would join any other country that started a blockade on some foreign power. Whether that might involve us in an act of hostility would be something that would need to be explored. And then of course the question of what is aggression has always been one that is very difficult to determine. It is thought, I believe, that they have some formula now to the effect that it is to be the nation that refuses to arbitrate. That, I assume, would have to be modified some, because it has always been understood there were some questions of national honor and integrity that no nation ought to be

214

called on to arbitrate or, at least, should not be held up to criticism because it refused to arbitrate such a question. I am not undertaking to go into any details or discussion, but merely indicating some of the questions that would have to be disposed of in order to come to a definite conclusion. There isn't any short cut to peace. There is no short cut to any other salvation. I think we are advised it has to be worked out with fear and trembling. I don't believe there is any way in which you can escape from that conclusion and that condition.

December 13, 1927

I have referred to the State Department a suggestion that came to me that something might be secured relative to the World Court by further negotiations. I haven't in mind exactly the language of the replies that were secured by the Department when it notified the different countries that were signers of the treaty that our country was willing to adhere to it in accordance with the resolution passed by the Senate. Whether there is anything in those that would give any encouragement to further negotiation, I therefore could not tell. So far as I know, they were not of a nature that encouraged the thought that further negotiation might bring about positive results, and so far as I have made inquiry of men in the Senate who were very friendly to the World Court proposal they have uniformly indicated to me that they would not be willing to support any modification of the position that the Senate had already taken. I thought the general result of the conference that was held by the other members of the Court was quite a strong indication that they would not wish to have our country become a member of the Court if it was going to involve any modification of the present rules governing the action of the different countries that have established it, in relation to it.

January 31, 1928

I haven't any information of any developments as to negotiations between the United States and France for a treaty to outlaw war, other than what has already been given to the press, our general position being that we would like to make treaties of that kind, thinking that it would be more advantageous if they were made with the several great powers than to undertake to make such a treaty with one country alone.

[*In a skillful countermove Kellogg proposed to Briand that perpetual peace was desirable for the world, that France and the United States should not seek it just for themselves but for all nations. Kellogg's riposte was intended to embarrass France, which had security pacts with several European countries and could not guarantee peace with everyone. He was also following the old axiom of diplomacy that the more nations brought into a treaty the more worthless it is likely to become.*]

February 7, 1928

There is very little that is new, as I understand it, in the arbitration treaty that was recently signed with France. I regard all treaties of that kind as of importance, as signifying the peaceful intent of the countries involved and the declaration made in the solemn method of a treaty of the desire to adjust all differences by negotiation, conciliation and arbitration. In a way, they provide a method before controversies arise by which controversies may be adjusted.

[*On February 6, France and the United States had signed a new, somewhat revised, bilateral treaty of arbitration. The preamble called for "condemnation of war as an instrument of national policy." Briand apparently hoped to head off Kellogg's recent maneuver by claiming that the arbitration treaty had expressly carried out the Secretary's proposal for multilateral agreement. Coolidge and Kellogg, enjoying the Foreign Minister's embarrassment, refused such an interpretation; hence the President's declaration that the arbitration treaty was merely routine.*]

June 29, 1928

I haven't received any specific communication from Secretary Kellogg relative to his recent note concerning the outlawry of war. It is my expectation that during the summer we shall be able to get a treaty drafted and ready to lay before the Senate at its next session.

[*During the spring of 1928, Kellogg began to take his antiwar proposal seriously, believing that a grand multilateral peace pact would indeed benefit the world. The French dragged their heels; the Quai d'Orsay found the whole affair farcical if not embarrassing. Eventually France realized that the United States might take more interest in European affairs if everyone signed what was beginning to be known as the Kellogg-Briand Pact. Kellogg pushed his pact with typical American enterprise, and all but forced the European powers into a ceremonial conference of signature at Paris on August 27, 1928.*]

July 13, 1928

I have a telegram from Secretary Kellogg stating that Germany has accepted the multilateral treaty without condition and France has notified him that they will send a note within a few days, probably Saturday, stating her willingness to sign a treaty, which is all very encouraging progress on that important proposal.

July 20, 1928

I had learned from Secretary Kellogg that various governments interested in the proposed treaties were considering meeting in Europe, so that they might all be signed at the same time. I think the suggestion has been made that such a conference would be held in Paris. The State Department has that proposal under consideration, but while it looks on it with favor hasn't come to any definite conclusion.

I am not familiar with all the details of it, but so far as I am informed I am inclined to think that such a conference might be very helpful in giving it a setting and emphasizing the importance of the proposed treaties.

PRESS: Has any one suggested holding it in Washington?

PRESIDENT: I think not. It is so much easier for one man to go to Paris than it is for all the countries concerned to come over here that I think it is more probable that if such a conference is held it will be held in Paris, rather than in this country.

[*Coolidge's references to "treaties" might have been a slip of the tongue, or he might have been out of touch with the negotiations, which never involved a series of bilateral treaties.*]

July 27, 1928

I don't know just what the plans of the State Department are, either, as to the early conclusion of the peace treaties. I haven't any idea whether there will be any opposition to the treaties in the Senate. There is usually some opposition there to everything, but I understood that the responsible leadership of both parties in the Senate had been participating in these treaty matters and that the action of the State Department had their approval.

August 10, 1928

I haven't any information from the State Department about any other countries adhering to the peace treaties, except the expression and the hope that others will adhere.

It is too soon to say what could be done as the result of the peace treaties relative to our national defense. It would be better to wait and see whether the peace treaties are signed and ratified by the Senate before we begin to discuss hypothetical conditions that may arise as the result of their adoption. This of course is to be kept in mind—that these treaties that are being made are treaties in which they agree not to attack each other and have very little to do with national defense, so that so far as our country is concerned the peace treaties would have little effect on the Army and the Navy, because our Army and Navy are maintained entirely for defensive purposes and not with the idea of attacking anybody.

I don't know the purpose that the British had in submitting the proposed peace treaty to the League of Nations. Perhaps it was with a view of interesting the different governments that are signatories of the covenant of the League of Nations to join in this treaty. Not knowing what the purpose was, it is not possible for me to comment on it. There is a provision in the League covenant that requires all treaties that members of the League make to be filed at the Secretariat of the

217

League, but I think it does not apply to the treaty until it has been made. And there are certain limitations I should say in the covenant of the League concerning the kind of treaties that can be made. Perhaps this was submitted with the idea of finding out whether the League had any objection to the members of the League, certain members, entering into a treaty of this kind. I can't conceive of any objection that could be raised. The claim of the League has been that it is an instrument of peace, though some opponents of the League have not always viewed it in that light. I should suppose the members of the League, whether it was proposed to include them in this treaty or not, would be delighted to see the great powers joining in a treaty of the kind that is proposed.

October 26, 1928

I haven't seen any reference to any address made by Wickham Steed, an Englishman, so I don't know what he may have said or may not have said. I doubt very much if he quoted me relative to what this country might do or might not do in case a blockade was declared by the League of Nations, because I am quite certain that I have never made any statement relative to it and quite certain further than that that this Government has never indicated what it would do or would not do relative to any blockade that might be declared by the League.

[*No sooner was the treaty signed than questions arose: what would the United States do to support the Pact, how would the Pact relate to the League Covenant? During the 1920's many Europeans feared the United States would not support a blockade established by the League under Article 16 (the sanctions article) of the Covenant.*]

November 23, 1928

I have had no discussions concerning any reservations to the peace treaty. I do not think any reservations ought to be attached to it. I can hardly comprehend the nature of any reservations that any one might think would be desirable. I think the treaty itself carries all the reservations that are necessary to protect our rights and protect our interests.

[*Although the treaty itself carried no reservations, the preliminary correspondence of the nations prior to signature, notably the note of Secretary Kellogg of April 23, 1928, did contain reservations to provide for any contingency. As if these were not enough, the British had excepted from the treaty "certain regions of the world," unspecified. The Senate, not content with the reservations of others, wished to add a few of its own.*]

December 7, 1928

I do not know whether or not the Committee meeting of the Foreign Relations Committee of the Senate this morning was public. However, I think the attitude of the Committee was favorable to the treaty. The thing that bothered the Committee most was whether the provisions of the treaty required a specific act of the United States if the treaty were violated, and of course the Secretary's answer to that was that it did not. I think I have already stated that if the treaty were violated it would leave the United States in the same position that it would be without the treaty, and Congress would determine as usual what action would be taken. A positive violation would occur if a nation attacked the United States and a negative violation would occur if a nation attacked another nation, not the United States. I am getting a great many letters favorable to the treaty, about 200 today, and am sending them over to the State Department. Mr. Kellogg told me that they had a special staff and certain stenographers for taking care of these letters. I think Mr. Kellogg told me he is receiving about 600 letters a day. . . .

PRESS: Are the letters coming in uniformly favorable?

PRESIDENT: I haven't seen one that is in opposition. Of course some of them are in the nature of propaganda, evidently having been made by people that were asked to write, but a great many of them are voluntary expressions of their own desire to see a treaty of that kind. I hope I haven't violated any of the niceties of Senate procedure by revealing the Secretary's statements before the Senate Committee on Foreign Affairs, but if that is the case I have suffered so much in the same respect that perhaps they will reconcile themselves to it.

[Coolidge's distinction between positive and negative violations revealed the nature of the pact's provision for enforcement: the "moral force of public opinion." Nations were to discover that public opinion was in part an invention of the merchants of toothpaste and tobacco, that its larger manifestations were difficult to predict or measure, that it was subject to national prejudices, that, in short, it could not act as an international force for peace and indeed might do the opposite.]

January 15, 1929

I think it is likely that the Senate will reach a vote on the treaty very soon. It is an especially important subject. In fact, I don't know of anything that has come before the Senate while I have been President that is of greater importance than this treaty. It would do more than anything else of which I know to stabilize and give expression to the peace sentiment of the world and greatly increase the probability of permanent peace. It would be a very complete answer on our part to the criticism that our country is sometimes under, especially to any suggestion that we had any motives of aggression toward any other country. I think the Senate understands the situation very well and that they want to ratify the treaty and are especially desirous of avoiding any action on the part of the Senate that could be interpreted either here or abroad as varying the terms of the treaty by making any amendments or reservations in relation to it. And with that situation before the Senate and before the country, I feel quite certain that the Senate will act favorably on it.

January 18, 1929

I was naturally pleased that the peace treaty was ratified. As I said at the last conference, the indications were that it would be ratified all right, and I think the importance of the treaty will grow among the people as it goes into operation. Twelve or fifteen nations have already adhered to it. I think ours was the first nation of those which signed it which has ratified it.

[*The treaty had passed the Senate on January 15 by a vote of 85 to 1. The dissenter, Republican Senator John J. Blaine of Wisconsin, approved neither of the British nor their exemption clause. Coolidge had signed the American instrument of ratification on January 17. Meanwhile nations not present at the Paris ceremony of signature in August, 1928 were adhering to the treaty. Coolidge's hope that the treaty would go into force among its principal signatories before his Administration went out of office on March 4 was not realized. President Herbert Hoover proclaimed the treaty on July 24.*]

January 25, 1929

I haven't seen just what suggestion Senator Borah has made relative to an international conference to codify maritime law, particularly the laws of sea water. I am of the offhand impression that that would be theoretically a fine thing to do. As a practical matter I wonder just what chance there would ever be to get any Senate to ratify a codification of any kind of laws. I think anyone that knows our Senate knows that such a ratification would be impossible. The maritime laws relative to sea warfare, of course, relate almost entirely to the rights of neutrals in time of war, and all the developments of the last war would seem to indicate that in future wars neutrals are probably not going to be accorded much of any right. Whether anything could be done by international agreement to clarify that or not, I don't know. It is a matter that I have thought of some and talked over some with the State Department. There never has seemed to be any time that it was feasible to call a conference on it. We have some work progressing in the Pan American Conference for the codification of international law, and I think that is going on very well. But the difficulty about that will be in ever securing approval of it by the Senate.

February 12, 1929

I haven't seen the Capper resolution relative to giving the President authority to put an embargo on the sale of arms. Such comment as I have seen on it indicates that it may go somewhat farther than I would think it was wise to go. The President already has power to embargo arms and ammunition against the western hemisphere when there are domestic disturbances within any of the nations, and against any other country where we have extraterritorial jurisdiction. We have that in China, for instance, and formerly had it in Turkey, but I think that has been eliminated. I think that something of that nature might be helpful. It would be extended, of course, to include cases where there was not only a domestic disturbance, but where there was international conflict. There has been a bill in the Congress by which it was proposed to enact a law absolutely prohibiting in the future any export of arms and ammunition to any country or countries that were at war. There are some objections to that. The smaller nations that do not make arms and munitions would feel that that would be a handicap on them. If they were at war with some other country, they couldn't secure arms and munitions, and the country that manufactured arms and munitions could secure them. I would look with sympathy on a proposal of that kind as far as the principle is involved, but I should want to have the details of it carefully investigated before making any specific commitments in relation to it.

11 · Vexations of Imperial Power

A T THE TURN of the twentieth century, the United States took on several outlandish possessions which demanded considerable attention for the next four decades. Washington statesmen also had to attend to that imperial purchase of 1867, Alaska, which was something of a nuisance to govern. And in the Latin American countries they faced the delicate political, economic, and moral issues of rule and intervention.

Curiously, in his press conferences Coolidge said little or nothing about the Hawaiian Islands. But the Philippines commanded his attention. During his presidency the Islands were in their usual muddled political situation. In 1921 the Harding Administration had sent out General Leonard Wood as Governor General. Wood brought order to Philippine finances, bucked up a sagging administration, and restored health and sanitary conditions. But in the process the not always tactful general incurred the ill will of the Filipino politicos, who on the whole were an extremely uncooperative group. While their rallying call was independence, they did not in fact really want it; they feared its economic and military consequences. Wood saw through their pretense. Meanwhile, his health was declining, but the old fighter would not give up the job at Malacañan long enough to return to the United States to report to the President. Consequently, Coolidge, inadequately briefed about conditions in the Philippines, dispatched Colonel Carmi Thompson on a thinly disguised inspection tour. Wood finally returned in 1927 and died in a Boston hospital.

Coolidge appointed Henry L. Stimson as the new Governor General, and Stimson proceeded to oil the waters.

Closer to home, the President had to cope with Alaska, which repaid many times over Secretary of State William H. Seward's purchase price of $7,500,000. Yet the territory presented Washington with minor but persistent annoyances. Coolidge interpreted the strange factional fighting there as a struggle of interested parties to get on the federal payroll. His problem was to appoint federal officeholders in the midst of this petty power struggle.

During Coolidge's era most nations to the south were in a state of political somnolence. The gravity of their social and economic problems was not fully evident until the Great Depression; in the early twenties, with the notable exceptions of Nicaragua and Mexico, the political lid stayed on, and Coolidge could turn his attention elsewhere. Panama and Puerto Rico (spelled *Porto Rico* in Coolidge's time) gave him little trouble. Haiti, a loose protectorate of the United States, continued in semidarkness. Coolidge thought little about it. Cuba did not belong technically to the United States, but the provisions of the Platt Amendment of 1901, written into the Cuban-American treaty and the new Cuban constitution, allowed for American intervention if necessary. The United States did not give up the amendment until 1934, well after the Coolidge era. Cuba, during his administration, remained quiescent. Dictator Gerardo Machado was in his "democratic" phase, behaving reasonably well. Not until 1933 did his excesses bring on a crisis which raised the issue of intervention.

Nicaragua was a troublemaker. After the Nicaraguan presidential election of 1924, the United States had pulled out from Managua its "legation guard," a force of about one hundred Marines which had helped keep order ever since the administration of President Taft. Revolution broke out three weeks later, and the political situation became so critical that Coolidge dispatched Marines to establish neutral zones. When, early in 1927, fighting between Nicaraguan factions threatened to involve the American forces, the President sent down troubleshooter Colonel Henry L. Stimson with a mandate to settle affairs. Stimson persuaded President Adolfo Díaz and General José Moncada to disarm their troops; in return the United States would guarantee the first free presidential election in Nicaraguan history. The election brought Moncada to power, and thereafter the situation remained relatively quiet except for the activities of General Augustino Sandino, a patriot Robin Hood who hated both Moncada and *imperialismo yanqui*. Nicaragua was a source of serious concern to Coolidge. Contrary to the claims of some American journalists, the President was no imperialist. He desired only peace and quiet in that small Isthmian country.

The Mexican problems, dating back to the revolution of 1910, were far more complex. Until the late 1930's the country was often in turmoil. In Coolidge's time, the Mexican government had succeeded in getting on a fairly even keel, but the original inspiration of the revolution, a sort of nineteenth-century political liberalism, had changed into radical social aims. Mexicans expected a better livelihood, the breakup of large and frequently foreign-held estates, regulation or confiscation of foreign oil holdings, refunding (with considerable shrinkage) of the largely foreign-held government debt, and tight rein over the Catholic Church. In the midst of this burgeoning social revolution, American nationals were in a defensive, if not losing, position. For several years the strain of American-Mexican relations fell on Ambassador James R. Sheffield, who did not particularly care for Mexico or Mexicans. Finally Coolidge replaced this unsuitable envoy with the Morgan financier Dwight W. Morrow, who skillfully arranged a temporary solution to the more pressing problems.

August 21, 1923

An inquiry about Mexico. A report has been made by the two Commissioners, Mr. Warren and Mr. Payne. That is in the hands of the State Department being digested and considered. When that work is finished a report will undoubtedly be sent to me with recommendations as to what attitude ought to be adopted toward the provisions of the report and the recommendations that are in it. After that has been determined, should it then be possible to resume relationship with Mexico, I think the procedure would be the appointment of a chargé d'affaires. Sometime later the question would be taken up of the appointment of an Ambassador to represent us and, of course, the reception of an Ambassador here to represent Mexico. Now I don't want to be asked about the details. Those you get more properly from the State Department. Nor do I know just when they will have finished their study of the report and their digest of it, so that they will bring their recommendations to me. But I think very shortly.

[*The United States had declined to recognize the Mexican government of General Alvaro Obregón which took office in 1920 after displacing President Venustiano Carranza. A subcommittee of the Senate Committee on Foreign Relations, headed inappropriately enough by Senator Albert B. Fall, who was deeply involved in oil scandals, recommended using diplomatic pressure for the protection of American property and the security of United States citizens in Mexico, and recognizing Obregón's government only if it guaranteed American rights and settled damage claims. There followed the Bucareli Conferences, meetings between American and Mexican representatives in Mexico City. The American duo, Charles Beecher Warren and John Barton Payne, accepted the Mexican Government's general position that it had a right to regulate the oil industry according to the new Mexican social reforms. But they denied that such new rules should apply to property acquired before May 1, 1917, the day the Mexican Constitution went into effect. They also contended that title to such property did not depend on a "positive act" of exploitation. The Mexicans virtually accepted the American view. In addition the conferences defined the procedure for confiscating foreign-held land and arranged for two claims conventions between the two nations. The agreement was signed on August 15; on August 31 the United States formally recognized the Obregón regime.*]*

August 24, 1923

An inquiry also about the Philippine situation and the protest of the Filipino Cabinet Officers, who resigned as the result of controversy with General Wood. There is only one position that the President could take in relation to that, and it is the position of supporting General Wood, as he is the authorized representative of the United States. That doesn't mean that in doing that I should want to take an unsympathetic view or act in an unsympathetic way against any of the representatives of the Filipino people, or desire to do anything but what would be helpful to them, but Governor Wood is there as the accredited representative of the United States and, of course, must have that support which is his due. As that support necessarily should take the form of undertaking to help him adjust his differences, of course, that should be afforded to him, but, of course, it must take the form of supporting him in things in which he is right and helping him in any other difficulties.

[*Coolidge would not permit efforts to undercut his representatives, even General Wood, with whose policies he did not altogether agree. Wood probably had the right prescription for the Philippines: government honesty and tight administration. But the crusty General's approach was hardly admirable. Filipinos were not welcomed socially at the palace of the Governor General, who was full of the imperial prej-*

udices of the turn of the century. The thwarting of his hopes to lead troops in France in 1917-18 and to win the Republican presidential nomination in 1920 had disillusioned him. In some ways he sought to make his Philippine administration a magnificent final testimony to his leadership. Filipino opposition to his rule baffled him.]

September 4, 1923

I have a suggestion here that, on account of the very great calamity that has overtaken Japan, the United States might consider turning over to them the Philippine Islands. That, of course, is somewhat a novel suggestion. I don't know how serious the suggestion is, but I do know that the United States Government and the people of the United States ought to give every possible assistance and every possible relief to the people of Japan. And I think you can perform a public service, demonstrate the friendship that Americans feel for Japan, by stressing the need of an immediate response to the appeal that is going to be made through the Red Cross for funds to carry on the work of relief in the stricken area. It is apparently one of the greatest calamities that nature ever inflicted on mankind anywhere in the world. Greater loss of life, and apparently, greater destruction of property than any other experience that mankind has had anywhere in history. So that you can't make any too strong the determination of our Government to put all its resources that we reasonably and properly can into the relief. I have called on the Navy Department, I have called on the War Department, called on the Shipping Board. Of course, I have been in conference with the Red Cross, and I have issued my proclamation. The Red Cross will make its appeal today for immediate subscription of $5,000,000. Ships will go there, food and supplies through the action of the War Department will be sent there. We shall do everything we can do in the way of relief. I don't know about the Philippines. They haven't proven a source of income to our Government. I don't know whether they would prove to be a source of help to the Japanese Government. I am interested in bringing that to the attention of you because it shows an inclination to take up the work and shows that America is glad to do everything possible for the help of the Japanese people.

[The great Japanese earthquake of September produced this strange pronouncement.]

September 11, 1923

The Minister of Panama [R. J. Alfaro] called this morning to discuss generally the policy of Government business operations within the Zone. Our country has, under the Treaty, all the powers of a sovereign within the Panama Zone. We don't always care to exercise every right that we have there, but we are always careful to state that we claim these rights and shall use them if they are necessary, coupled also with the statement that we do not want to do anything there for the purpose of securing a slight income to the United States Treasury that would be thought to be detrimental to the people of Panama or contrary to the wishes of the government of that country. That was the message that I gave to the Minister. He expressed very great satisfaction in having that message and said he would transmit it to his government, and that it cleared up every possible question that he had in mind.

November 2, 1923

Also an inquiry about the Monroe Doctrine. Whether it would be repugnant to the country if monarchies were created in the western hemisphere. I don't know as I could discuss that in a way as to shed any more light. The general prescription on all of these questions is to read the original document, whether it be a note or the Monroe Doctrine. Of course, it is well known that there was a statement by President Monroe that he didn't want any European or foreign establishments set up that might be inimical to American institutions. That is capable of a great many different interpretations, on which you are at liberty to use your ingenuity.

November 27, 1923

An inquiry about Philippine independence. I haven't any clear and definite information about that. There is a bill known as the Jones Bill that it is my impression, I think I am right, promises independence to the Philippines some time in the future. I suppose my own position is the well-known position that has been reiterated from time to time by the Government of the United States, of a desire to see the Philippines under self-government as soon as we felt warranted in withdrawing. I think it is generally recognized that our presence there is not so much an advantage to us as a very large bill of expense, but that it was an obligation which we had undertaken when we received the Philippine Islands from the Spanish Government and that we couldn't cast them adrift. We are anxious, by maintaining educational institutions, to show them the way toward good government, and by the example that we are able to set there of providing a sound government for the Philippine Islands, one that will be able to maintain the freedom and independence of the people there. As soon as that can be done, we will then feel at liberty to withdraw.

PRESS: Mr. President, are there any signs that that time has arrived or will arrive in the near future?

PRESIDENT: I think they are making very good progress. I haven't detailed information. I have never been to the Philippines, nor am I a particular student of them, but I get the general impression that they are making very good progress there—very encouraging progress.

[*The Jones Act of 1916, known as the Organic Act of the Philippine*

*Islands, reaffirmed the United States's intent to recognize uncondi-
tionally Filipino independence as soon as possible. The President,
like most Americans, knew very little about the Philippines, but was
certain that his country was uplifting, Christianizing, and civilizing
the Filipino people. Americans were not reticent in contrasting their
rule in the Philippines with that of the British in Egypt and India. It
remained for another generation of Americans to recognize that the
accomplishment in the Philippine Islands was a fragile one indeed.]*

January 4, 1924

In view of the sale of arms and munitions to Mexico, will the President please state the administration's policy? I don't know that any
policy is involved, other than to consider each case that might arise
and trying to consider and decide it on its merits. I don't think it involves anything further than that. Any friendly government might
request opportunity to purchase a few muskets and a few rounds of
ammunition. Of course the matter would be considered on its merits.
It would be quite a different proposition in selling a large amount
of material that our Government thought it was expected might be
used for war purposes between one nation and another. This is more
a matter of domestic policy than the carrying on of warfare.

*[As evidence of American good will, the Coolidge Administration in
1924 allowed sale of munitions to the Obregón government, which was
then engaged in putting down a revolt during the succession to the
Mexican presidency of Obregón's good friend General Plutarco Elías
Calles. The Coolidge Administration would have reason to regret its
friendliness in 1925-27, when some of the munitions sent to Obregón
turned up in Nicaragua in the hands of the enemies of General
Adolfo Díaz, whom the United States had sponsored as president of
Nicaragua.]*

January 18, 1924

No final decision has been made about the extension of coastwise
shipping laws to the Philippines. A good many difficulties are in the
way. I should be exceedingly loath to take action in that respect that
was very much opposed by the Philippine Government, or by the
Filipino people. I recall that some of our own difficulties in colonial
days resulted from the fact that our people were very much embarrassed by the restrictions that were put upon their shipping. While I
am exceedingly anxious to build up the American Merchant Marine,
I shouldn't want to do so in a way that would imperil the friendly
feeling of the people of the Philippines for America. I don't think that
would be profitable or helpful. We want their friendship, their commerce, and their cooperation, and in order to secure that, of course,
we would have to take very largely into account their desire. If it is a
wise thing to do, deliberation and discussion on their part will reveal

that to them, and they would join in wishing to have it done. I am very loath to impose upon them something they don't want to have.

February 19, 1924

Here is an inquiry about the thirteen Pan-American conferences that are scheduled for the coming year and in the early part of 1925, on science, education, child welfare, and other matters that cover a wide variety of subjects. It is the policy of the Government to encourage this tendency towards cooperation between North and South America. That has been a well-known policy of our country for many years, a notable expression of which was the Pan American Union which we maintain here under the direction of Doctor [Leo S.] Rowe, who I think is doing very splendid work in that direction. It is especially desirable from every point of view of which I can think. It is desirable in the first place to maintain the most friendly relations between North and South America. We are contiguous countries and our interests are substantially the same, being in the western hemisphere. And I go from that on to the commercial possibilities which at the present time appear to be greatest for our country in that direction. The European field is fairly well taken up. It is an old country. It isn't a developing country in the way that new lands are. Those of South America are new and open to development. The natural resources of South America have yet to be developed. There are opportunities there for all kinds of production from agriculture to manufacture, so that the opportunity for production there being great, the opportunity for exchange is great. It isn't one government usually that trades with another, but it is the people of one country that trade with another. The governments can help in that direction by the diffusion of proper information, and by rendering every possible encouragement, to the people of one country to trade with the people of another country. In that direction I think our commercial welfare lies to a good deal of an extent.

February 29, 1924

I haven't any official information about the Mexican situation that amounts to anything. So far as I have any information, it indicates that President Obregón is at present successful. I don't know whether the revolt is entirely stamped out. I do not suppose it is. We don't have sources of information that would give either the Department of State or the public an exact picture of what is going on all over the Republic of Mexico, but it may be significant that we are not at present receiving any official complaints of disorders wherever any of our American citizens seem to be interested.

March 28, 1924

I have some information about Philippine independence. I gave out quite a lengthy statement not very long ago, expressing my views

229

about Philippine independence. Our country is committed to the policy of ultimate independence, so that the practical question which remains is the method by which it is to be put into effect and the time. I think the pending proposal is that it should go into effect in 1935, if the Filipino people about that time will vote for that proposal. They have an election every three years. They will have an election in 1934, when that question would be submitted for referendum. I think that under present arrangements they have an advantage in relation to their sugar crop of $12,000,000 to $15,000,000, and in relation to their tobacco crop about $5,000,000, which will undoubtedly be lost to them under the proposal of independence. That is a practical question that they will want to consider, when they decide on what action they ought to take. Of course they have outstanding in this country the Filipino bonds, providing for independence. They would necessarily have to take those into consideration and make due provision for their payment and retirement. There is a general feeling that if the Filipino people want independence that it is no material advantage to us or commercially to us to hold them under present arrangements. The people give voice to those two proposals and say therefore, "Why hold them?" To my mind that doesn't quite fulfill the requirements of our duties toward the Filipino people, or toward the world in general. I don't suppose the United States was willing to take on the obligations of Philippine Government or become responsible for the welfare of the Filipino people at the time it was taken over, but it seemed necessary that it should be done. Otherwise they would have been cast adrift and become the support I was going to say—anyway there would have been an invitation to occupation or aggression by other countries, so that we felt we had something of a duty to perform towards them. That duty is not all performed at the present time. The United States practically recognizes that that is the case, so that the practical question is to find the time when they may be ready to take up their duties and obligations of self-government. Some think that can be done as early as 1935.

I don't know as I can give you any information that would be helpful or pertinent about the bill relative to Porto Rico. The delegation from Porto Rico came in to visit me, perhaps you recall, some time ago. I made some comments then to them, which I later put on paper and transmitted, and I think gave to the press. I am not certain about that. The fundamental question there is a question of administration, and it is the difficulty of having an elective legislature and a Governor that serves by reason of appointment from here. I think it is recognized by students of government that an arrangement of that kind, even when all parties proceed with the greatest possible tact, has in it necessarily elements that are quite likely to lead to some kind of conflict between the Governor on the one hand and the local legislature on the other. At the present time they are getting on remarkably well, but if some means could be provided by which the Governor could be elected by the people of Porto Rico, it would eliminate that difficulty. Now, I don't know just what this Porto Rico measure of self-government does provide for, but if anything is to be done, something of a fundamental nature in that direction I think would be more helpful than anything else.

[*Like the Philippines, Puerto Rico had an Organic Act, passed on March 2, 1917.*]

November 21, 1924

I haven't any plan for the immediate withdrawal of the United States Marines that are now acting as a legation guard in Nicaragua. I haven't any very great detailed and precise information about that situation. I knew that there had been some trouble and it was my impression that we had sent some Marines in to guard the Legation, and that the difficulty was in relation to a presidential election. As I have heard nothing about it from the State Department for some time I had taken it for granted that the situation was cleared up. I think that is the case, but I haven't definite information.

[*Nicaragua had a population of less than 700,000, 72 per cent of which was illiterate. The republic, about the size of New York State, interested the United States because it offered the most practicable alternative route to the Panama Canal. Under the Bryan-Chamorro Treaty, ratified in 1916, the United States held exclusive and perpetual rights for building a canal across Nicaragua. American investments were small, almost nothing compared with those in Mexico. United States citizens owned plantations, mining and logging companies, and managed Nicaragua's customs service, railroad, and National Bank.*]

January 13, 1925

I am expecting that the American guard of about 100 marines will be speedily withdrawn from Nicaragua. Of course the Government there at present, and certainly in the past, has been rather solicitous to have them remain, thinking that although they are a small force on account of what they represent they give a stability and security to the government. But quite naturally Nicaragua might come to a time when it is able to provide its own security and not rely on us for that purpose and a time when we feel that American interest will be secure under the protection of the Nicaraguan Government without any military protection from our own Government. We think that time is approaching and are planning to withdraw the guard. I don't know just how soon, but I know that that has been determined to be our course.

[*After a moderately fraudulent Nicaraguan election in 1924, the*

United States contemplated withdrawing the Marines on January 1, 1925. The government of President Carlos Solórzano asked that they remain a few more months, to give him time to organize a police force to sustain his regime.]

February 6, 1925

I didn't have any information about reported frauds and irregularities in the recent Porto Rican elections. I don't think that either of the Porto Ricans who were in here this morning mentioned it. They were talking more about the economic conditions. I was more interested to see what we could do to improve them. Many of the people of Porto Rico are laborers, a low class of labor, and compensation is small, and if anything could be done to improve the economic condition of the Island is something to interest me more than past frauds in elections. So the matter of elections was not mentioned. I don't think I had heard anything about it.

March 13, 1925

Here is another interesting question—I touched on this general subject slightly in my Inaugural Speech—asking whether I will not discuss the possibility of early withdrawal of the American occupation of Haiti. Of course, we want to withdraw. We had made some plans to withdraw. We have there a few marines—sent there for the purpose of maintaining peace and order and protecting American interests, and, incidentally, perhaps more than incidental, for protecting also the Haitians. But the Government of Haiti sent a very strong request that we continue the occupation, and that we have done.

[*After President Guillaume Sam had slaughtered 167 hostages, on July 28, 1915 the Haitians rose against his regime. The populace of Port-au-Prince seized the President, literally cut him into small pieces, and paraded these trophies around the capital city. At this point President Woodrow Wilson dispatched Marines to impose a military occupation. President Philippe Sudre Dartiguenave, elected in August, 1915, signed a treaty on September 16 under which the Haitian Republic became in effect a protectorate of the United States. The treaty, which contained articles similar to those of the Platt Amendment for Cuba, was not terminated until 1934, when the Marines left. In 1918 Haiti received a new constitution, written by President Wilson's Assistant Secretary of the Navy, Franklin D. Roosevelt. In the election campaign of 1920 FDR described it as "a pretty good constitution, too."*]

May 1, 1925

Here is an inquiry about Ambassador Sheffield and the situation in Mexico. I had a letter from the Ambassador last week I should say, saying that—no, I don't know that it would do any harm to give this out, I suppose it is public—that Yale University was going to confer a degree on him. I think there is no impropriety in announcing that. It has been decided. He is going to be present to take it. And of course he wants to come up to have that degree conferred on him. And that when he was up here of course he would like to come to Washington and talk with the State Department and myself. I didn't get from his letter that there were any unfavorable developments in the Mexican situation, but rather that conditions were very promising there. There are always problems in Mexico, but I judge from the tone of his letter that he thought things were working along exceedingly well, as far as American interests are concerned.

[*Actually, Obregón's successor, Calles, was beginning to cause difficulties. He refused to be bound by the Bucareli Agreements, and in December, 1925 the Mexican legislature limited to fifteen years any oil rights acquired prior to 1917.*]

July 24, 1925

I haven't seen Senator Borah's article on the proposal that the United States keep out of affairs of American Republics. I have before me this editorial in relation to it. I suppose that if that is what he has proposed, that that was one of the fundamental desires of this country, to keep out of the affairs of American republics just so far as we can. We never interfere with them except in the case of last resort, and whatever action we are taking now in American republics is because of the request of the duly authorized government there that we do so. Even that we don't like to do. So if that is his suggestion, that we keep out of the affairs of American republics, the suggestion is wise and timely and is in accordance with what I understand to be the policy of this country.

[*William E. Borah succeeded Henry Cabot Lodge, who died in 1924, as chairman of the Senate Committee on Foreign Relations. He was a powerful and quixotic figure to whom both Coolidge and Secretary of State Kellogg accorded gingerly deference. His latest biographer, Marian C. McKenna (Borah, Ann Arbor, Michigan, 1961), has described him charitably as "a destructive statesman" with a "passion for wreckage." In 1925, as Coolidge realized, Borah was moving away from the Administration's view of Mexican affairs—taking a position against American economic rights there.*]

November 20, 1925

I don't recall having received any protest from Mr. [J. W.] Frame, of Alaska against the conduct of two Federal judges there. It may be that some protest of that kind has been sent to this office. If it was sent here it would be referred in due course of business to the Department of Justice for investigation and report to me. That leads me to remark about Alaska, that I think protests that originate up there against those who are holding office perhaps would need considerable investigation in order to determine just how much merit they have. It is my information that one person in every 11 of the white people that live in Alaska are on the Federal payroll. Business is not brisk up there. There are some fisheries there and some mining, but we are spending $11,000,000 a year so that I think the best line of endeavor that there is in Alaska is to get on to the Federal payroll. Now I presume it is unconscious, but a condition of that kind would stimulate an activity on the part of those that aren't on the payroll to criticism of those that are, in order that a change might be made to their advantage, so that whenever there are protests against Federal officers up there they have to be viewed with that in mind.

January 12, 1926

Everything that has developed in relation to Mexico has already been given to the press. We have to have a great deal of patience with that country. The government there has its difficulties and the people in this country ought to realize that Mexico is a different country from ours. The people have a different outlook on things. They haven't had the advantages that we have up here, and there ought to be a general public expectation that we would in every way that we can be helpful to that country, and instead of trying to oppress them in any way or anything of that kind, that such actions as we take are taken with a view to being helpful. We do wish that they should keep their agreements when they make a treaty with us and that the terms of the treaty should be observed, and as I stated at another conference, I am sure the government of Mexico recognizes that as a sound policy and expects to abide by the terms of its treaties. We have to recognize that they have a perfect right to pass laws affecting their internal affairs, their domestic affairs, whether it is in relation to property or in relation to persons. The question comes up of course when they attempt to pass a law that is retroactive and affects rights that have already been granted to Americans. It is under those conditions that we have interests that we have to protect and I haven't any doubt that the government of Mexico wishes to protect them and cooperate with us in their adequate protection.

[*The Mexican legislature had passed its retroactive law in December, 1925.*]

February 12, 1926

I haven't had any specific complaint about the administration of affairs in Porto Rico. I get those occasional complaints that always come from a situation like that which exists between the Government here and Porto Rico and the Government here and the Philippines. Complaint that arises partly by reason of the method of government, the local legislature elected by the people and the Governor that is appointed by the people. That is what makes a situation that needs to be handled with great tact in order to be successful. If anyone doubts that, I think they would be convinced if they would examine the outlying provinces of other countries and compare the difference in conditions—those that are under the American Government and those that are under the government of other countries. I don't say that in any way of criticism. Other governments I know are doing very well and the best they can, but I say it rather in praise of our own system and the results that it has been able to secure.

[*Coolidge erroneously stated that the Governors of Puerto Rico and the Philippines were appointed by the people. They were, in fact, appointed by the President.*]

April 2, 1926

I think it has already been announced that Colonel Carmi Thompson will undertake to go to the Philippines for me. It is possible he may stop at Hawaii, and perhaps at Guam, though that hasn't been finally determined on. It seems to me that there was a somewhat sentimental propriety in sending him. He is, as you know, the National Commander of the Spanish War Veterans. It was through their activities that we came into possession of the Philippine Islands. He also is a very warm friend of General Wood. He has known him and been associated with him, and of course it goes without saying that it is entirely a friendly mission. General Wood has been stationed there for nearly five years. He has had little opportunity to come to the States and I thought it would be a somewhat graceful thing on our part if we could send someone down there to confer with him and give him such reassurance as he may need and indicate to him personally the desire of the Government up here to support him in every way. Then I would like to have a survey—it couldn't be quite called an investigation—of what we are doing, what progress we are making in the Islands, what progress the Filipino people are making—because that is synonymous. I want to know how education is progressing, what is being done in the way of sanitation, policing; also the financial condition of the Islands as relates to their government and the economic condition as it relates to private enterprise there, and in general to make a survey and inspection to see what we can do to better conditions there.

May 18, 1926

I didn't discuss with Senator [Albert B.] Cummins [Rep.] any question of the adjournment of the Congress. He came in to talk with me about some of the Alaska appointments. There are two factions in Alaska, so that if an appointment is made out to one faction the other faction always opposes the confirmation. I am quite confident that the appointments I have made up there are as good as can be made, if I am to appoint people that live in Alaska. These are judicial appointments, two judges I think and one District Attorney and one Marshal.

Now, it is never possible to get perfect men to hold office, because there aren't any such. Sometimes they are better and sometimes they are worse. But so far as I can learn by diligent inquiry the appointments that have been made are as good as can be made, if I am to use people that live in Alaska. The other appointments have been reported on favorably by the Committee on Judiciary. Now, if these appointments can not be confirmed, the only other recourse that I shall have would be to go outside of Alaska and appoint some people that would go up there from the states. That might be a temporary relief, but I should expect that after they had been up there for three months they would be subject to the same attack that is being made at the present time on appointments. We spend quite a good deal of money in Alaska and one of the chief sources of income to those who live up there is to be in the Government employ. I think one in eleven white people that live there are employed by the Government and of course that makes a considerable motive on the part of the other ten to try and show that the person who is in ought to be displaced, so that one of the other ten could have the place and the revenue that is now accruing to the person that holds the office. Those are some of the difficulties that I have in the administration of affairs in Alaska, though I think affairs are going on up there in fairly good shape. But there are the two factions and this contention between them.

July 23, 1926

I am very sure there is not the slightest foundation for any report that General Wood has resigned as Governor General of the Philippines.

PRESS: In that connection, have you received any word that some complaints have been made about Mr. Thompson chumming with Quezon?

PRESIDENT: No.

August 17, 1926

Here is an inquiry relative to the status of the correspondence with Mexico relative to their land laws. About all I can say about that which can be understood without entering into a long explanation about rather technical matters would be that Mexico has made large concessions to the demands of the United States on these questions, but that there are still a number of questions that have not been definitely determined. I am informed by the Secretary of State that so far as he recalls he has had only one specific complaint—he has knowledge of only one complaint—that has been made in relation to the taking of church property in Mexico, I mean specific complaint that this property has been taken and not a general complaint about the taking of church property that was lodged with our Ambassador there and our Ambassador made representations to the government relative to it and was informed that it would be adjusted. It is very hard to say whether American citizens have suffered indignities in Mexico. That is rather a broad term. Some of them have been expelled from Mexico. The Mexico Constitution has that 33rd Article, which gives the Mexican Government authority to expel anyone. That is known in Mexico as "33ing" people. It gives the government absolute authority to expel anyone they may desire to expel. That is sometimes resorted to. Whenever it appears to be used without any action on the part of the person against whom it is used that would justify it, it has been the practice of our Ambassador there to intercede, sometimes successfully and sometimes unsuccessfully.

[*The leaders of the Mexican revolution often had been at odds with the conservative Catholic clergy. Calles, distrusting the church as an* imperium in imperio, *was determined to have a showdown shortly after coming into the presidency. An antirevolutionary pronouncement by the Archbishop of Mexico City in January 1926 gave him his excuse. In a few months the president put into effect several anticlerical articles of the Constitution of 1917. In retaliation the Mexican bishops ordered a political and economic boycott of the government and on July 31, 1926, suspended all church services.*]

White Pine Camp, Paul Smith's, N. Y., August 27, 1926
I expect Ambassador Sheffield and Mrs. Sheffield and perhaps their son will come up here to visit me before I go back to Washington. I think he has been in Washington to see Secretary Kellogg and I was advised that he is going to go to Atlantic City with his wife and son, so I don't know just how soon he will come up here. I would like to see him and talk to him sometime about the Mexican situation and get, of course, his firsthand views about it. Mr. Sheffield, as is well known, is a very able man, a trained lawyer, has made an excellent Ambassador and has managed a very difficult situation in Mexico with great skill and discretion, and any representation that he might make to me regarding what policy ought to be adopted in Mexico would have very great weight with me. I asked him to go there at a considerable sacrifice, and for a man who had the large legal practice that he had in New York I feel that he has performed a very distinct public service in making a sacrifice of that kind. Last year when he was here he came up to call on me in Massachusetts while he was going by there on a boat trip he was having. He had had a serious operation, from which I understand he has entirely recovered.

[*Sheffield was certain that Mexico "is one of the countries where the gun is mightier than the pen." To a friend he commented on "the corruption and inefficiency" and "the futility of attempting to treat with a Latin-Indian mind, filled with hatred of the United States and thirsting for vengeance, on the same basis that our government would treat with a civilized and orderly government in Europe. . . . I have sought no credit for anything I have done but I have tried to be a red-blooded American South of the Rio Grande just as I have tried to be North of the Rio Grande and whether I go back in a pullman car berth or in a pine box, I shall not change my point of view as to my duty as American Ambassador." Coolidge supported him. "Of course," the President told ex-President Taft, "they don't like him particularly in Mexico, but how could a man decently act in such a way that they would." (Sheffield to ex-President Taft, March 5, 1927, Sheffield* MSS *deposited in Yale University Library; Sheffield to Senator James W. Wadsworth, Jr., March 4, 1926, Sheffield* MSS; *Taft to Sheffield, April 13, 1927, quoted in Claude M. Fuess,* Calvin Coolidge *(Boston: Little, Brown, 1940), p. 411n.)]*

September 3, 1926

The only reports I have ever had in relation to Ambassador Sheffield are those that praised his conduct. I have never had any criticism. So that if you see any reports of that kind, why I think you can set them down as the natural result of a man representing this Government who has had to insist that the rights of our citizens be respected when there were some people that thought it would be to their advantage not to respect those rights.

September 8, 1926

PRESS: Would you care to say whether or not our lives and property have been generally respected or have suffered in Mexico?

PRESIDENT: Well, you can't generalize about that. There isn't any information about that that hasn't already been made public. Mexico has been in a condition of uncertainty and there have been quite a number of years of burglary and revolution, but for the past three or four years that has been getting less and less, so that I don't think there is much complaint now about a condition of disorder that has characterized Mexico in some years past. The present government keeps a very fair condition of order. Of course we are not able in this country to prevent considerable lawlessness. We have constant outbreaks of burglary, highway robbery, and things of that kind. I don't suppose anyone would say it is because the Government is lacking in authority. We make every effort to apprehend anything of that kind and punish it. But I think generally speaking over practically the whole of Mexico there is a very good condition of order. Our citizens down there have been murdered in the past since 1913, a good many of them. But there is practically no complaint about that now. The complaint is rather about prospective, rather than present, interference, with the rights of our citizens. There has been a good deal of recession on the part of the Mexican Government in the claims that it has made of the privilege of interfering with the rights of our citizens. We still have some unsolved questions touching the rights of our citizens to hold property and conduct business there, but the general statement that I would make in relation to that is that the Mexican Government has receded very materially in the claims that it had put out as to its right to interfere with the business of our citizens in Mexico. On the domestic difficulty that they are having there, over the religious question, which is a religious question touching all denominations alike as I understand it, though it is referred to more particularly as a Catholic question, because I suppose 95 per cent of the Mexican people are Catholic, 95 per cent of those that have any church affiliation are affiliated with the Catholic Church, there is no difference whatever and we deal with that as we would deal with any other question that might affect the rights of property of our citizens. When those are affected beyond the practice of the Government relating to religion or the carrying on of business or anything else, we try to protect the rights of our people.

December 3, 1926

PRESS: Is General Wood coming home?

PRESIDENT: It has been expected that he would come home for a visit some time this season. He hasn't been back for five years. I thought perhaps he would be back last winter, but he didn't seem to be able to get away. The Vice-Governor, I think he is called Vice-Governor, was over here last winter. Now we have been expecting that General Wood would come back this winter. He has recently been ill. I understand he is making a good recovery. Whether that would interfere with his coming over, I don't know. I hardly think so. He ought not to stay in the Philippines as long as that. The climate is difficult. The duties are difficult. A person accustomed to our temperate climate ought to have an opportunity to get out of a climate as warm and trying as that of the Philippines for a considerable length of time, much oftener than five years. I speak of that as an indication of the devotion that General Wood has shown towards his duties and his intense loyalty in their discharge.

December 28, 1926

I don't know as there is much of anything that I can say about Nicaragua. It has been apparent to me that the press has been considerably misled in respect to American activities in that country. There is a revolution going on there and whenever a condition of that kind exists in Central American countries it means trouble for our citizens that are there and it is almost always necessary for this country to take action for their protection, protecting their safety and protecting their property. That is what is being done at the present time. This Government is not taking any sides, one way or the other, in relation to the revolution. It never takes sides in those matters. Admiral [Julian L.] Latimer is there with a landing force of Marines and they have not molested Sacasa, the head of the revolutionary movement, or any members of his Cabinet. Sacasa and his Cabinet are still at Puerto Cabezas where they are treated the same as other Nicaraguans. I understand that the American Lumber Company has furnished Sacasa with a house without any cost to him and tells him he can continue to occupy the house as long as he desires. The landing force has not molested him in any way. Of course, as I have stated, the marines are there simply for the protection of American and foreign lives and property wherever it may be necessary. I think that is the extent of the action that this government has taken.

[*After Coolidge withdrew the little Marine legation guard on August 4, 1925, Nicaraguan politics "went to hell in a hack." The strong man of Nicaragua, Emiliano Chamorro, locked up such of President Solórzano's Cabinet as he could lay his hands on. After a series of fast shuffles ending with the flight of Vice-President Juan B. Sacasa and the enforced "leave of absence" of President Solórzano, Chamorro emerged as the new president on January 16, 1926. Apparently he had paid Solórzano $30,000 to persuade him to resign. The United States refused to recognize the new president, continuing to address him as "General" Chamorro. For a few months Chamorro had the upper hand, that is, he had it in the Nicaraguan treasury. In the course of his conflict with the American Government he made the error of becoming too vocal, advertising his sentiments: "To Hell with the United States, with the State Department, and with its diplomatic representative here!" But early in the summer a new American Chargé d'Affaires, Lawrence Dennis, put unmerciful pressure on Chamorro. Moreover, the Nicaraguan treasury had been emptied. Chamorro resigned on October 30, 1926, and the United States proceeded to replace him with Adolfo Díaz, a former president of the country. Díaz tactfully gave Chamorro $20,000 and sent him on a sightseeing tour of Europe. Former Vice-President Sacasa, who had gone to the United States to ask for support, suddenly proclaimed himself constitutional President of Nicaragua and Commander-in-Chief of the revolutionary forces. He recruited General José Moncada, a better commander than Díaz, to lead his forces of a few thousand irregulars. The rebels, with the noisy support of many Mexicans, began to win. Coolidge threw in Marine reinforcements which established neutral zones in wide areas, but could do little or nothing to stop the revolution. There was constant danger that the Marines might become involved in the fighting.*]

March 11, 1927

I haven't given any particular attention to the details of the treaty that has been proposed by President Díaz of Nicaragua. Of course this country would consider carefully any suggestion that the government of Nicaragua desired to make to us, but from such casual consideration of it as I have been able to give to the reported outline I doubt very much if the Government of this country would think it desirable to enter into such a treaty. As I have expressed to the conference heretofore, we have some peculiar interests in Nicaragua, on account of our right to build a canal there and establish a naval station, and in addition to that we have a desire to help that country or any other Central American countries in any way that we can, but of course it has been my policy and I want to carry it out as far as I can to leave those countries as undisturbed as possible to work out their own salvation. That was the reason why I withdrew the Marines from Nicaragua in 1925. We are willing to respond so far as we can any time that we can be helpful, but to take on a permanent obligation of the nature that I understand is contemplated in the suggestion of President Díaz would be, I think, a little farther than this Government would wish to go.

[*Díaz, fearing the progress of the revolution, had offered to make Nicaragua an American protectorate.*]

May 6, 1927

I haven't any report today from Nicaragua. The only thing that I am certain about down there from reports that I have received is that Mr. Stimson is doing his best to compose the differences and find some method by which peace can be restored. Perhaps the method that he may employ is not so very important, if it results in bringing about an amicable condition. I think perhaps it would be well not to take too literally what the contending sides may think it is necessary to give out as publicity, but keep in mind that the main effort of this country is to restore peace and prevent further bloodshed. I have great hopes that Mr. Stimson is going to be able to bring that about.

[*Coolidge had sent Colonel Henry L. Stimson to Nicaragua as a special presidential agent to achieve a settlement. Stimson, who knew absolutely nothing about Nicaragua, went down posthaste and entered into negotiations with Díaz and Moncada. The problem was to disarm Moncada, who was obviously winning the revolution. The two men met on May 4, 1927, at Tipitapa. According to Stimson, they "sat down under a large blackthorn tree near the dry river bed. He spoke English with unusual simplicity and directness, so no interpreter was needed. In less than thirty minutes we understood each other and had settled the matter." Moncada proved tractable: "Agreed to constabulary under American control. Admitted explicitly that no Nicaraguan could pacify country without help of U.S." (Diary of Henry L. Stimson, May 4, 1927, Stimson MSS deposited in Yale University Library.) Stimson, without authorization from Coolidge but confident that he would receive it, guaranteed free elections under*

241

American sponsorship. In return, all soldiers would immediately lay down their arms and receive ten dollars for each serviceable rifle or machine gun. If Moncada's troops refused, the Marines would force them to disarm. In a few days the war was over. Moncada was elected president in 1928.]

May 20, 1927

I don't know as there is any comment I can make on the resolution that some representatives of Porto Rico brought in yesterday relative to their desire to have Governor [Horace M.] Towner continue in office. Of course, I was pleased to receive the information that he was giving general satisfaction to the local government of the Island. I don't just know why the delegation should be sent up here for the purpose set out in their resolution, but considering the fact that some of our officeholders are not averse to visiting Porto Rico on occasion perhaps it is not difficult to imagine that officeholders in Porto Rico would not be averse to coming up here. It is very much more pleasant to have them come telling me that they are contented with the situation as it exists, than it is to have them come making complaints about their government. Perhaps their visit may be taken as an indication of a very happy condition on the island, indicating satisfaction on their part with the general way that their government is proceeding. I suggested to them that it is always necessary to use care in the raising and expending of the revenue of the government. The resources of the Island are limited, of course. They have been embarking on a considerable policy of public improvements, the building of a rather ambitious capitol or state house, the construction of a system of highways, increasing their educational facilities, all of which calls for a considerable outlay of money. I suggested to them also the great desirability of a general knowledge on the Island of the English language. They are under an English speaking government and are a part of the territory of an English speaking nation. I thought that it would be very much easier for them to understand us, and for us to understand them, if they had a good working knowledge of the English language. While I appreciated the desirability of maintaining their grasp on the Spanish language, the beauty of that language and the richness of its literature, that as a practical matter for them it was quite necessary to have a good comprehension of English.

May 24, 1927

I was naturally very much pleased with the report of Colonel Stimson, former Secretary of War, on his return from Nicaragua. He told me that he would prepare a short statement and give it to the press, which I think he did and which covered the vital points that he reported to me. He is very certain that peace has been entirely re-established and all bands of any consequence that were engaged in warfare in Nicaragua have delivered their arms to the United States authorities there, both those that represented the government and those that represented the revolutionary forces. It was a very excellent accomplishment on the part of Colonel Stimson and one to which he is entitled to great credit. I am personally very appreciative of what he did there and it was a great service to the people of Nicaragua and a service that the people of this country may view with a good deal of satisfaction, I am sure.

June 28, 1927

I don't know of any change in the policy that has been recently pursued toward the Philippine Islands as a result of the visit of General Wood. The General met with an uncomfortable and somewhat painful accident on his way over, an injury to his ribs, but not anything serious. I was very glad to see that his general health was so good and very much encouraged with the report that he gave me in relation to conditions in the Islands. The general result is I think that there has been an acceptance on the part of the Filipinos of the present policy toward the Islands, and I think that change has resulted in the feeling of stability. I have all the time advised the Philippine people to show their capacity for self-government by a careful administration of the fundamental law of the Islands, which is the Jones Law, the Organic Law we call it, and apparently they are wholeheartedly undertaking to pursue that policy. I think General Wood pointed out to you that some 99 per cent of the administration of the Islands is in the hands of the Filipinos. They hold almost all of the offices and carry on almost all the government. They are in that happy condition of having virtually self-government without the responsibility for protection and national defense and so on that usually has to be shouldered by people who have self-government. . . . General Wood and I discussed very briefly the establishment of some central bureau that would have charge of all our insular possessions. That is not exactly a new thought. It was included in the reorganization bill which the Congress never got around to act on. There they were placed under the Secretary of State. I recall that Secretary Hughes said he wasn't anxious to undertake the administration of insular possessions, but of course if it seemed best to put it in his department he would undertake that service. I have never given the matter a great deal of study. As far as I had thought of it at all, it had seemed to me that the Department of the Interior, which is the department that has always had charge of our territorial and disconnected possessions like Alaska might be the logical place to put the administration of our insular possessions, the only difference being there that those territories that have been in the Department of Interior have been a part of the United States in a little more intimate and a different way than our insular possessions are,

243

because it is always understood that those territories that were under the Department of Interior would very soon come into statehood, which they all have now, with the exception of Alaska.

[*The Bureau of Insular Affairs in the War Department supervised the Philippines.*]

July 8, 1927

I shall of course accept the resignation of Ambassador Sheffield. When he was at White Pine Camp last summer he indicated to me that he didn't wish to remain in Mexico more than three or four months, but he has been willing to stay on until this summer vacation. He is now on leave of absence. . . . I don't imagine that a successor will be appointed and qualified for some time.

PRESS: Some months?

PRESIDENT: I didn't say some months. It will be some time, perhaps.

July 29, 1927

There haven't been any developments so far as I am aware about the invitation that was presented to me by President [Gerardo] Machado [of Cuba] to attend the Pan American Conference which is to be held in Havana next winter. I told him I would take it under consideration and expressed the hope that I might be able to attend. Of course, it involves some question about the President going out of the country and so on, which it might be necessary to give some thought to and which, when it is investigated, may not prove to be very serious.

September 20, 1927

I have appointed—I haven't put the appointment on paper, but have made arrangements to appoint and have secured the approbation of the government of Mexico to the appointment of Dwight W. Morrow, of New Jersey, to be Ambassador to Mexico. [Stenographer's note: One or more of the correspondents left the room hurriedly at this point.] I hope that is not going to cause any considerable exodus from the room. I can well understand how anyone would like to go out to congratulate the country. I am very much pleased that Mr. Morrow is going to make the sacrifice that is entailed by accepting an appointment of this kind. He of course is retiring from his firm, of which he has been a member for thirteen years. He is a lawyer by profession, is very much interested in public affairs and has made a study of them. He is wonderfully well equipped I think to take a mission of that kind. It is one of our most important foreign missions although perhaps not one that would be so much sought after as an appointment at St. James or at Paris.

PRESS: Is he going at once?

PRESIDENT: I do not know just how soon he will go. I suppose in a very few days.

[*Dwight W. Morrow, a classmate of Coolidge's at Amherst College, was bored with his partnership at J. P. Morgan and Company and anxious to engage in public service. In 1927 Coolidge considered Mexico the government's most important ambassadorial post.*]

October 7, 1927

So far as I know, the United States Government is neither favoring nor opposing any particular candidate for the office of President of Nicaragua.

November 4, 1927

Senator [Manuel] Quezon and Senator [Sergio] Osmena—he is a member of the Senate—called on me yesterday with the Secretary of War to pay their respects. I was pleased to learn that Senator Osmena's son, who is a student, I think, at Cornell, is very much improved. We talked rather generally about things in the Islands. They advised me that they had no particular person to recommend as Governor General and hoped that someone would be appointed who had a knowledge of affairs in the Islands, and someone with whom they could cooperate to carry on the government of the Islands. I suggested to them the desirability of having the legislature pass on the appropriations that have been recommended by the Governor General and also pass on the appointments that are pending, I believe, before their Senate. In that they agreed with me and said they were to be up here for perhaps a month or so. I told them I hoped I might be able to see them from time to time, as I was anxious to get all the information I could respecting the needs of the Islands and what we could do to better conditions there, that I was especially interested in good roads and a good system of education and in the agricultural development, that I thought it would be very helpful if they would confer with the Secretary of Agriculture to see what he might advise about sending an agricultural adviser who was familiar with tropical agriculture down to the Islands to help them in that respect. They agreed with me about that and I understand that is one of the things they are going to do. They reported that the economic conditions of the Islands were very good and they thought on the whole improving.

[*Leonard Wood had died on August 7, in Boston, during a brain operation.*]

November 8, 1927

I have here a communication from one of the important newspapers of the country making a suggestion which I will pass on to the members of the conference for whatever they may think it worth. It is in relation to a book which has been published, entitled *The American Policy in Nicaragua,* by Colonel Henry L. Stimson, former Secretary of War. I think that was first published in periodical form. Now I understand it has been gathered together in book form. It wasn't very long. I think there were three articles. Colonel Stimson submitted

245

them to me and I looked them over with a great deal of interest and notified him I didn't want to make any suggestions regarding any changes in them. I merely state that, so you will know that I had some knowledge about it. The suggestion is that it would probably be helpful to the correspondents here in Washington in discussing the Nicaraguan subject if they would read that book. This editor thinks very highly of it and thinks that work would be helpful to the other members of the profession.

[*Stimson's articles appeared first in the* Saturday Evening Post *and then in book form. They remain a perceptive account of the Nicaraguan revolution and of his mediation.*]

November 15, 1927

I haven't any knowledge of any movement on the part of the Government to apply what might be called a colonial policy to the Philippines. I doubt very much if General [Frank] McIntyre is committed to anything of that kind. I have set out several times my policy in relation to the Philippines, one in a letter that I sent to Mr. [Manuel] Roxas two or three years ago, and then again when I vetoed the Philippine legislature's bill to have a referendum taken on the question of immediate Philippine independence. In general my policy, of course, is to work out their situation under the present Organic Law usually referred to as the Jones Law. I have often expressed the thought that the ability of the Filipino people and their local government to comply with the terms of that law was to quite an extent a measure of their capacity for government. Now, I am open minded, of course, about things in the Philippine Islands, and if some better plan could be proposed I should examine it with a great deal of care. But I think the Jones Law on the whole is a very good law. It would work out much better than it is working out, if it was received sympathetically by all the Filipino people and all the members of their government, and if they would adopt toward it an attitude of cordial cooperation. It is doing very well as it is. You will never get any law that is absolutely perfect or any administration that is absolutely perfect, and we need to look upon the Filipino people and their aspirations with the very broadest kind of sympathy. I have conferred several times with ex-Secretary Stimson, had him come down from New York once on purpose to go over the Philippine situation as he found it. Of course, I have kept rather in close touch with it myself, had reports and letters and a conference that I had last summer in the Black Hills with General Wood. This matter can't be considered from a personal angle. It has to be discussed in relation to principles, rather than in relation to personalities. Perhaps the less attention we give to personalities, while giving every possible approval and support and expressing the approbation of those who have done well in the Philippines, the sooner we shall arrive at a wise solution of the problems out there.

[*General McIntyre was chief of the Bureau of Insular Affairs in the War Department. Stimson had visited the Philippines in 1926. He had been a close friend of Wood during the Taft Administration when he was Secretary of War and Wood Chief of Staff.*]

December 2, 1927

Colonel Judah was in to call on me this morning. He is starting for Cuba, I think next week, returning to Chicago this afternoon to finish up some private matters there. He is going to Cuba at once to make such preparation as our representative there may find necessary as a preliminary to the Pan American Conference, which is to be held about the middle of January.

PRESS: Will you permit a question as to whether or not you will go to Havana.

PRESIDENT: I am expecting to go. There is never anything terribly certain about the President's movements. I have indicated several times it was my expectation to go. My plan is to go down to Key West and cross over on one of the Navy boats. The Secretary of State will go with me, and if I am going on the Navy boat possibly the Secretary of the Navy. Some of the members of the Commission, or representatives at the Pan American Conference, will probably also go at the same time. Some of them may perhaps precede us to do whatever is necessary in the way of preliminary work. I don't know that any of them will find that necessary. Mr. Morrow, who is one of the delegates, is in Mexico City, so he would not join us here, but would join us at Havana.

PRESS: Have you any idea how long you would stay?

PRESIDENT: Oh, I would make a very short stay. Perhaps arrive in the afternoon and address the conference the next day, and start back that afternoon or the day following. That is necessary because of my official duties here and in order that I may keep the social schedule that has been laid out for the winter at the White House.

[*Noble B. Judah later served as Ambassador to Cuba.*

Coolidge's reference to "one of the Navy boats" hardly shows the proper respect for a battleship.]

December 9, 1927

I do not think the question of whether a man might be called a military man or not is one of very great importance in relation to the Governor Generalship of the Philippine Islands. I suppose what is meant by that is the attitude of mind of the man. Some civilians may have what I would designate as a very military type of mind. Some men who may be officers in the Army and the Navy might not have a military type of mind at all. I think this—that the Governor Generalship of the Philippine Islands would probably be better administered, as any civil office would be, by a man who didn't have a predominantly military type of mind. That wouldn't by any means eliminate plenty of men we have in the Army and Navy, and I would not think that Governor General Wood was a man that had a predominant military type of mind.

December 16, 1927

There has been so much already written about the flight of Colonel Lindbergh to Mexico City that it would require more invention than I have to add anything new or fresh to what has already been said. I suppose what the conference wants, though, is something that they can hang on the words of the President. It is quite evident that his flight there has had a very pleasing effect. It has evidently pleased the people of Mexico very much. The government of Mexico has accorded him a most painstakingly cordial reception, and the President of the Mexican Congress have done everything they could to honor him. I have no doubt that his going there will increase the friendly relations between the people of Mexico and the people of the United States. I have no doubt that the Central American Republics would be very much pleased to have Colonel Lindbergh fly down there. I have no information whether he contemplates anything of that kind. I think I have seen it referred to in the press, but that is the only information I have about it. There is a further interest connected with that, which I referred to in my Message to the Congress, my desire to establish as soon as can be an air service between this country and the countries south of the Rio Grande. I think that Colonel Lindbergh's visit to some of those places would increase the already great interest in having something of that nature done.

[*Colonel Lindbergh's trip facilitated the Ambassador's task of improving Mexican-American relations. Contrary to the aloof Sheffield, Morrow liked Mexico and admired the Mexican people. According to his biographer, Sir Harold Nicolson, Morrow "applauded their food, their climate, their agriculture, their hats, their ancient monuments, the bamboo cages in which they kept their tame parrots, their peasant industries, their patriotism, their volcanoes, even their finances. Here at last was a North American who neither patronized nor sneered. His boyish enjoyment of his task was infectious. In the sunshine of his zest, under the warm breezes of that creative credulity, even the most morose suspicions melted." In a series of conferences the remarkably tactful Morrow and Calles managed a détente to most Mexican-American problems, including the oil question. The Ambassador, a Protestant, also took a hand in settling the Mexican Government's quarrel with the Catholic Church.*]

December 20, 1927

Mr. Stimson, recently appointed Governor General of the Philippines, came in this morning. He is conferring with the Insular Bureau of the War Department and the Secretary of War. He is going to meet with the Committees of the House and the Senate that have especial charge of legislation dealing with Philippine questions and he expects to start for the Philippines in the very near future. As I understood it, he had no new or changed or particular policies to announce. He will go out there to undertake to execute the Organic Law of the Islands and cooperate with the Philippine officers in doing what he can to provide a good government.

[*Stimson's success in Nicaragua, his friendship with General Wood, and his acquaintance with the Philippine Islands made him a natural candidate for the Governor Generalship. He went to the Islands in the belief that this assignment would mark a valedictory to public service. Instead, he returned home to become Secretary of State under President Herbert Hoover and subsequently (1940-45) Secretary of War under Franklin D. Roosevelt and Harry S. Truman.*]

January 10, 1928

I had a short conference with Colonel Stimson this morning. He is lunching with me at 1:00 o'clock. He is very much encouraged at the prospects of his work in the Philippines. He seems to have assurances of cooperation from the Filipino people who have been over here and with whom he has talked, and it is evident that his appointment has been very well received by the Filipino people who are in the Philippines. What he is especially desirous of working out is a method by which he can be assured of an opportunity to secure adequate assistance. He was very much gratified that he had assurances that that can be worked out through some action of our Congress here and through the cooperation of the Filipino Government.

[*In the Philippines Stimson desired to appoint American civil officials without submitting their names to the Senate or making their tenure at the pleasure of the Filipino legislature.*]

I don't quite understand this question—oh, I misread it. It is a suggestion of Senator [William H.] King [Dem., Utah] that we ought to press as fast as we can the settlement of claims that our people have against Mexico. I think the question is perhaps asked under a misconception of the situation, because it says that the settlement of those claims should be given right of way over other questions we have with Mexico.

PRESS: That is what Senator King said yesterday after he had seen you.

PRESIDENT: Oh, yes. Well, the situation about that is this—that we have reached an agreement with Mexico some time ago relative to the investigation and adjudication of these claims. I don't know what their amount may be, perhaps no one can tell in advance. They are considerable and run over a series of years. But we have under our agreement appointed a Claims Commission—I don't know but what there are two Claims Commissions, one anyway—and that work is in process of going on at the present time. What I want to get clear in the mind of the Conference is that this matter has been taken out of diplomatic channels. There is nothing further to be done about it through diplomatic channels. It has been transferred into judicial channels. That is we have set up a Court before which those that have claims may appear and prove their claims and have them allowed, and that work is going on. The time limit that was on that expired some time ago and it was renewed by the Mexican Government and this Government, and those claims are being pressed as rapidly as we can, and I think that is the desire of our Government and the Mexican Government. Many of these claims are for amounts that are not large in comparison with the whole, but they are large so far as the individual that is pressing them is concerned. They oftentimes might represent all the accumulations of the individual for a good many years, and perhaps represent all the property that such an individual might have, and it is important that they be taken up and disposed of promptly. That is what our Government is trying to do.

PRESS: Do the arrangements for the adjudication of those claims provide any means for payment after their settlement?

PRESIDENT: I am not sure just what is the case. I don't know whether they provide for any particular method by which they shall be paid. In general they would of course be paid out of the treasury of the Mexican Government.

[*The history of the claims of American citizens against the Mexican Government is not yet closed. Land claims—for confiscation of American-owned ranches—never had general attention but were settled on an individual basis. American oil and bond claims were settled during World War II. By the 1960's the Mexican Government had almost wiped out the entire indebtedness except for certain railroad bonds scheduled for payment by 1974. Several factors led the United States Government to sacrifice large claims of its nationals upon the Mexican Treasury. The Mexican Government clearly did not have the capacity to pay for all confiscations. Many claims, moreover, went back to the days of Porfirio Díaz, when Mexican properties were often obtained by fraud or collusion. Finally, the changing international climate of the 1920's and 1930's dictated a* rapprochement *with Mexico: the Good Neighbor policy developed into an important weapon against the Axis powers of Europe and Asia.*]

250

January 20, 1928

There is nothing I can say about the Pan American Conference that occurs to me, that has not already been said. Naturally our Government is pleased with my reception at Havana. One of the most pleasant opportunities that I had there was going out to the country place of the President, which gave me an opportunity to drive through quite a number of miles of Cuban territory where I had a chance to observe the people and see something of the progress they are making. As I left there it seemed to me that the conference was in a position to do very much excellent work.

[*Early in 1928 the Sixth International Conference of American States assembled in Havana, with Charles Evans Hughes as chief of the American delegation. Coolidge went down on a battleship to give a fulsome address. The high point of the conference came after the President left, when the delegate of El Salvador, Dr. J. Gustavo Guerrero, offered a resolution: "No state has the right to intervene in the internal affairs of another." In a stirring speech, Hughes called upon international law to justify the American interventions in the Caribbean area, and the conference ended on an uneasy note.*]

March 16, 1928

We haven't matured any plan about what can be done in Nicaragua. We had expected to secure some legislation by the Nicaraguan Congress that would enable us to carry out the terms of that agreement that was made with both the contending parties down there by the President of the United States. We thought that would be the most feasible method of procedure. I don't know that it is absolutely necessary, but we felt it was very desirable. The [Nicaraguan] Senate, I think, passed a bill that was satisfactory—it did not pass the House— so that we shall have to consider the situation and see what other plan can be adopted. When we went in there we were advised by the Nicaraguan Government that they were not able to protect life and property, which meant that their constitutional guarantees were practically in abeyance. We have at least been able to restore order under which the inhabitants of that country in almost every instance have been able to return to their usual vocations. We have stopped the warfare. We have collected the arms that both parties had. Some 13,000 rifles were turned over to us. So Nicaragua has a year of peace anyway to its advantage and what is necessary now is to provide some method by which the inhabitants can express their desires for the filling of the offices that are necessary to fill in the coming election and start out again under the terms of their constitution. We are trying to help out in that direction and I rather think we can.

[*After Stimson and Moncada had made their agreement and Díaz approved it, the Nicaraguan Congress balked. If the 1928 Nicaraguan election were not under United States supervision and the Nicaraguans instead held an election according to their own questionable procedures, Díaz's party would certainly win. Ultimately, the Americans persuaded President Díaz to consent to the necessary election code, and thereby to court his political suicide.]*

July 24, 1928

The situation in Nicaragua seems to be progressing very satisfactorily. The operations of Sandino apparently have entirely ceased and the different bands of bandits have pretty much surrendered. It is reported, as I understand it, that Sandino has left Nicaragua. There is no absolute certainty of that, but that is my information. There is no active or armed opposition to what the country is trying to do, so far as we know at the present time.

["General" Augustino Sandino, one of Moncada's lieutenants, refused to disband his followers. He was a colorful figure who enjoyed harassing the Marines and mocking Coolidge. He left certificates with fellow Nicaraguans from whom he had requisitioned supplies: "The Honorable Calvin Coolidge, President of the United States of North America, will pay the bearer $—." Inserted on the certificates was the amount of the levied goods. His private rebellion was a nuisance to all concerned. From early March until November 1928, a force of 5,480 Marines and the Marine-trained Guardia Nacional tried unsuccessfully to capture him. During a truce in 1934 the Nicaraguan army betrayed and shot him.]

August 14, 1928

I haven't received any further information, as I recall, about the situation in Nicaragua which would indicate that everything is proceeding as harmoniously as could be expected there. When I begin to get reports on matters it usually means that there is some question up for my decision. When I do not get reports it means everything is going all right.

November 6, 1928

The press has noted somewhat the very important events that have taken place in Nicaragua, but they have been buried up so in our election here and probably will continue to be for several days, so that I do not know that comment of mine on it would be likely to get very much space. But the outcome down there has been particularly successful and particularly agreeable to the United States Government. I think it demonstrates clearly that we were pursuing the right course. I suppose everyone knows and recalls that the Marines had been in there for a number of years. I was anxious to withdraw from a contact of that kind and took the Marines out. They hadn't been out only about 30 days when revolution started and even then we withheld any action in relation to it as long as we could. Finally our citizens and their property were in so much jeopardy that at the earnest solicitation of the government of Nicaragua we sent Marines there to protect our interests. There was a very terrible warfare going on between the people of the country, the loss of life was very great, and in order to compose that I sent Colonel Stimson down, who made the plan which we have been carrying out and which was successfully consummated last Sunday. They held a peaceable and orderly election which apparently is an expression of the will of that country. Our policy there, of course, has been very similar to our policy in Mexico and China, of trying peaceably to compose our differences.

November 9, 1928

As has already been announced from Palo Alto, Mr. Hoover is thinking of making a trip to South America. I have wired him to advise me what he would like to have the Government do to assist him. He says he would like to have the warship *Maryland* assigned for the journey and that his purpose in making the journey is to evidence the good will and desire for mutual cooperation between the United States and South America and to familiarize himself with the common problems. He says also that the matter hasn't been finally determined. I am having the State Department make the usual inquiries as to whether the places he is expecting to visit would be agreeable to receive him. He spoke to me about this the last time I saw him as a matter that he would like to do after election. I told him I would be very glad to afford any cooperation he might require.

February 8, 1929

I do not contemplate any trips to foreign countries after the 4th of March. I think I have been invited to go to different foreign countries. I don't know just which ones. I think several South American countries with whose representatives and citizens I have happened to come in contact have expressed to me a desire to have me visit their countries.

Now that I am thinking of that, I recall especially the delegation that was in the other day from the Argentine, a delegation of 15 or 20 people, and the man who had charge of presenting them to me expressed a very ardent desire that I should visit that country, and hoped I might come in the immediate future. But I have no plans for anything of that kind. I always tell people that I have so many places still to go to in the United States that I don't know when those will be so much exhausted that I will arrive at a time when I can visit other countries.

12 · Coping with China and Russia

CHINA was in turmoil during most of Coolidge's presidency, and many Americans yearned for the United States to intervene to set things right. Coolidge, responsible for protecting the lives of American citizens, had reservations as to how far he should go, for it took almost one soldier or sailor or Marine to protect each American in China. By the end of his presidency the United States had recognized the Nationalist regime of General Chiang Kai-shek.

Events in China ran briefly as follows. By the middle of the 1920's the Nationalists were beginning to move northward from Shanghai toward Nanking, which they reached in 1927. They occupied Peking in 1928. The takeover was not bloody, for Chiang Kai-shek fought only a few of the opposing warlords, and bought or balanced the others. Meanwhile Chinese everywhere, whether under Nationalist or other regimes, acutely desired national unity. The new national sentiment in large part was directed against foreigners; notable outbreaks occurred in Shanghai in 1925 against the British and in Nanking in 1927 against all foreigners resident in the city. During the Nanking incident Western warships in the river threw a protective barrage of shells around the property of the Standard Oil Company on Socony Hill, to enable foreigners concentrated there to escape over the compound wall and down to the ships.

As for relations with the Soviet Union, nothing seems stranger today than the policy of the Coolidge Administration toward that nation. Here was one of the admittedly great peoples of the world whose government—so far as the State Department was concerned

—stood outside the pale of civilization. Nonrecognition had its supporters, and President Coolidge was one. The President was no prude about foreign governments, but neither he nor his Secretaries of State, Hughes and Kellogg, could abide the USSR. Slaughters of the early Bolshevik period deeply shocked Americans in a way that genocidal and thermonuclear mass killings would not shock them later. The American Government also knew that the Soviets, in their drive for world revolution, would employ any means to subvert bourgeois government and to extinguish democracy. The result was nonrecognition, a policy challenged only by a few political mavericks like Senator William Borah.

August 31, 1923

An inquiry about the recognition of Russia. There is no change in the American policy, which, as I understand it, is that of awaiting evidence of the existence of a government there that, in accordance with our standards, would warrant recognition, one that has such a form and has adopted such policies that we should be warranted in saying to the American people—this is a government that meets these standards and these requirements and you will be justified in making commitments accordingly, and expecting, that when those commitments are made, the usual support from your own government.

December 18, 1923

Here is an inquiry about the offer of the Russian Government to enter into negotiation for a restoration of diplomatic relations. That has been answered by the State Department in a statement that has been given out to the press within an hour, and the answer in general effect is that no action is necessary on the part of this Government for the Russian regime to comply with the conditions that were laid down in my message. That can be done entirely by them without negotiating with us, and should be done as a foundation for any negotiations. I suppose you recall, generally, the restoration of property, recognition of the debt, and the cessation of propaganda against our institutions. Those were all the result of acts taken there, and can be remedied by acts now to be taken there.

January 22, 1924

I don't think I have anything especially to say regarding the reported death of Lenin, other than what would occur to anybody,—that he cast a good deal of influence over the destinies of Russia for a considerable length of time and it would be very unbecoming of anyone in the Government of the United States to undertake to make any criticism of a man in his position having passed away. Let us hope that the work he did, though it is difficult to see just how it did, worked for the benefit of Russia and for the betterment of civilization.

I don't foresee any change, answering an inquiry here, that may be brought about in the Russian policy of the United States by reason of his passing away. That would depend upon what happens. If the policy there should be changed, it would change our policy. If it doesn't change, ours will not. My attitude toward that was set out, of course, in my message to the Congress.

January 25, 1924

Here is another inquiry about the recognition of the Russian Government by the British Labor Government. That has not been done yet, though I saw a report in the morning paper, I think, that it was expected that the Labor Government would recognize the Russian Government. I don't know that that would have any effect on the action of the United States Government as to its recognition of Russia. The executive end of the Government you know gets foreclosed sometimes by the legislative end, even on those things that the executive end alone has constitutional authority to act on. I think there is pending in the Senate an investigation of the question of whether the Russian Government ought to be recognized. Something may develop there that will produce information that would be controlling. The investigation is in such hands that I know that whatever develops there will be pertinent to the subject. So that I think at present I am disposed to wait and see what that investigation may develop. I don't know of any developments that have taken place since my message to the Congress that would in any way change the position that I took in the message. My position there was plain.

February 15, 1924

Here is an inquiry about the Russian situation—whether the American attitude has produced, or shall begin to produce, results such as the stoppage of propaganda and the recognition of private American claims, etc. I haven't any information that would enable me to answer that either one way or the other. I don't know of any effect, either favorable or adverse. The situation, as I understand it, is exactly as it has been for some time, barring certain changes in personnel, etc., in Russia. Whether the action of some of the European governments which are reported to be about to recognize, or have recognized the Russian regime, will materially affect our attitude or not, I don't know. I don't see now that it will, unless they bring about a change in the attitude of the present Russian regime. It is possible there may be some effect in that direction. Should that be so, we would govern ourselves accordingly. I don't know of any change in the situation over there. I don't know of any present activity in the way of propaganda, nor do I know that propaganda has ceased. I haven't any information on one side or the other.

September 19, 1924

Here is an inquiry asking for my opinion whether there will be any diplomatic intervention in China to prevent further spreading of the civil war. Of course, the Government has been taking such action as we thought necessary to protect American lives and property. We have an Ambassador or a Minister in China?

PRESS: A Minister.

PRESIDENT: Minister Schurman was in the other day, Dr. Schurman, and he didn't seem to think that there was imminent danger of further spreading of the war in China at this time. He seemed to be of the opinion that the battles that had already been fought were about as decisive as those Chinese battles are. I inquired of him as to the loss of life and the destruction of property, which he said were both exceedingly meager, almost no loss of life in battle and no destruction of property as they had no heavy artillery. So that so far as I know at the present time American rights are being protected. It seems apparent that a decision in China of affairs of this kind can hardly ever be regarded as final, but as final as those things usually are. That isn't a very definite statement, but those things are quite indefinite in China. So as far as I know there isn't any occasion at the present time for any action, other than what we have already taken.

[*Jacob Gould Schurman had been President of Cornell University. Since the collapse of the Manchu dynasty in 1911, China had no real central government. Representatives of China abroad were clever at giving an impression of unity, notably at the Paris Peace Conference of 1919: China was, in fact, a geographical expression.*]

January 13, 1925

There is nothing that I can say about the Russian situation that is materially different from that which I have said in the past. If you will recall my message of 1923, in which I spoke of this, and some other comments that I have made on it in different addresses, I have been hopeful that a situation would develop there so that that great country could take up the burdens of civilization with the rest of us. I laid down some rules which were amplified in a note that Mr. Hughes sent in relation to Russia, somewhat less than a year ago. I think that the Russian people have made some progress since then. But their progress is slow, and it hasn't been so rapid as I hoped it might be.

March 27, 1925

I haven't made any decision about the new Minister to China. There are several names under consideration. One of them is Mr. [John Van A.] MacMurray of the [State] Department. My hesitation about him is to decide whether he would be of more value here in

257

Washington serving in the Department, or of more value in China. He is an expert on Eastern affairs in the State Department—not the only one, but he is regarded as the chief expert.

[*Coolidge did appoint MacMurray, an Assistant Secretary of State.*]

June 5, 1925

I think that some of the Marines are at Shanghai for the purpose of protecting American lives and property, and they will be used to whatever extent it is necessary that they should be used for that purpose. That is the only purpose that America ever lands any Marines on foreign soil and they would have no other purpose in the present situation. You can get more detailed information I think from the Secretary of State's office, or from the Secretary of the Navy, than I have. I know that we have some war vessels in the harbor at Shanghai, and I think one or two others on the way there. Though we know—I know of nothing serious that has happened to any American citizens or any American property, but on account of the disorder there it is considered that they are in jeopardy and Marines have been landed in order that they may have proper and ample protection. That is all the action that I know of that is contemplated in relation to China or Chinese territory.

[*In the Shanghai International Settlement on May 30, 1925, a group of police under command of a British inspector fired into a crowd of some 2,000 Chinese, killing twelve and wounding seventeen. The incident inspired a tumultuous outburst of antiforeign feeling, with boycotts and strikes throughout China. The United States had a contingent of Marines and Army troops permanently stationed in Shanghai and Tientsin, and could send reinforcements from the Philippine Islands.*]

July 14, 1925

Now I think that is the real extent at the present time of the Chinese policy, based on those two things—carrying out the Washington Agreements on the one side and doing what we can to get China to protect foreign interests on the other side. Now that includes of course the consideration of the tariff and extraterritoriality and all other questions that were considered in the Washington Agreements.

[*The Washington Conference of 1921-22 promised to ease the treaties of extraterritoriality and to change the Chinese tariff. An international Commission on Extraterritoriality was to have convened within three months after the Washington Conference and a Special Conference on the Chinese Customs Tariff within three months after all the Washington powers had ratified a tariff treaty signed at the Conference. After Washington the French Government became involved in a dispute with the Chinese, thereby delaying ratification of the tariff treaty until August, 1925. The Customs Tariff Conference*] *met in Peking on October 26, 1925. The Extraterritoriality Commission convened, also at Peking, on January 12, 1926. Silas H. Strawn, a Chicago lawyer, represented the United States at both meetings.]*

July 21, 1925

PRESS: Mr. President, would you elaborate upon your policy of returning the Boxer indemnity, which was reported in the paper this morning.

PRESIDENT: That was provided for by the legislature in the last session and all I did was to issue an executive order carrying out the terms of the legislation.

PRESS: Don't you think it is going to be helpful at this juncture, if it comes about?

PRESIDENT: Well, yes, I think so. It is an exhibition, I don't want to boast about our own country too much, but I think it is an exhibition of good faith on the part of this country. Perhaps it would be more appropriate for someone else to say that, other than myself.

[The first remission of the Boxer indemnity case came in 1908 and a more generous one in 1924. Funds were to be used for a college in Peking and for sending to the United States some sixty Chinese students each year for further study in American colleges.]

September 22, 1925

I have a question here as to whether communists ought to be allowed to come into this country if they come in for commercial purposes. Well, I rather think that that question would answer itself. The only thing that the Government is trying to do is to see that our laws are observed. It isn't trying to enforce its own ideas or carry out its own desires about people that can come in or stay out. The fact that a person was going to come here and spend a large sum of money I don't think would make any difference in the law. I don't know of any provision in the law that says the right to come into this country is for sale, that the principles of the United States are for sale if you want to pay enough and you don't have to live according to the laws of this country. That isn't what I understand to be the policy of our land. I think I said something to that effect in my first message to the Congress. Personally, I think it is a good policy to permit very free discussion of anything that relates to our institutions. If anyone says anything about them with which I don't agree, of course I talk back and it is out of discussions of that kind that public opinion is developed and the soundness or unsoundness of institutions that prevail. But I don't know that that policy has anything to do with the duty that is incumbent upon the public officers of this country to try and enforce the law. When the law says that certain persons are excluded from the country, why then I suppose it is the duty of those who are charged with such enforcement to see that they don't come in. Of course it would be rather absurd to say that they could come if they agreed to spend considerable money after they got here, so I think that question would rather answer itself.

January 22, 1926

No information has come to me about any report from the Methodist Missionary Board in China that American gunboats are not helpful there and ought to be withdrawn. Such information as I have has rather been in the other direction. I think that the last session of the Congress made a specific appropriation for the purpose of building a special gunboat, or gunboats, to run on the rivers in China, some of them. These have to be of light draft and of special construction, and I think the building of those boats is now going on in China. I know of no such recommendation as this. There may be something of that kind in the State Department that hasn't come to my attention.

October 5, 1926

Nothing has developed in the Russian situation. I do not like to keep discussing that situation. It is not understood by the people generally perhaps that I respond to questions submitted, and it would seem to indicate that the President is constantly saying something about Russia. I have no disposition to say anything about it, and until something develops I think in the future you may expect that I will not make any comment about it. Of course, I am very glad to give at any time any information that may come, but I do not want to keep making comments unless there is information developed about which comment can helpfully be made.

December 14, 1926

Silas H. Strawn is not now in the employ of the Government, so far as I know. He went to China for us at a very large personal sacrifice and remained there much longer than he expected to remain. On account of the unsettled conditions in China he and his associates were not able to come to any final conclusion, as I understand it. They stayed until all of the representatives of the Chinese Government had been withdrawn or left the conference. That was no fault of theirs. It was due to the unsettled state of affairs there. As nothing could be done without them, Mr. Strawn and the other representatives of the foreign powers of course were forced to discontinue their efforts. I do not know what Mr. Strawn is saying in his speeches. He is a very well informed man and would be very discreet, I am certain, in his utterances, so I do not wish to say that they are approved or disapproved. And of course they are not an expression of any official position of the United States Government. I am merely stating a fact about that. I shouldn't want any unwarranted inference drawn from it that the President had disavowed Mr. Strawn's statements. I am not doing anything of the kind. So perhaps I had better repeat again that I am neither undertaking to approve them or to disapprove them, merely stating what I understand to be the fact, that they are not the expression of the American Government. And, as I do not know what they are, I couldn't tell whether they represent the official position of the Government or not. I want to repeat again that he is informed and discreet. I do not know that any approach has been made to this Government by the British relative to the recognition of any new government in China. If you want to get more accurate information about that, of course apply to the State Department. They might have made inquiry there which wouldn't be reported to me unless the situation had developed far enough so it was proposed to take some action.

[*Before Strawn reached China civil war began. By April 10, 1926, seven of the ten Chinese delegates to the tariff conference had fled to foreign concessions, making it impossible to carry on meetings. The conference adjourned in July, 1926. The Commission on Extraterritoriality signed its report and disbanded on September 16, 1926. It recommended no relinquishment of extraterritoriality until the Chinese judiciary was guaranteed protection against interference by executive or military authorities. After returning to the United States, Strawn spoke both frankly and publicly about conditions in China.*]

December 31, 1926

I never knew of any preliminary movement on the part of this Government to re-establish diplomatic relations with Russia. I saw a report of that kind in the press. I judged it was without foundation. Of course, our diplomatic relations suffer somewhat, I suppose all countries do, from volunteer activities of people without any authority. We have a great deal of that in Europe. There are a great many Americans that go over there that undertake to say and do things that do not represent the position of the American Government and I think oftentimes result in misleading foreign people and foreign governments. I don't have Russia particularly in mind, but all the governments of Europe. That is something over which we have very little control, but something that happens right along. The organization of the American Government is quite different from that of Europe, which probably results in European governments and certainly European people oftentimes being misled.

January 21, 1927

I think the press already has all the information that has come to me relative to the situation in China. That country is undergoing a revolution and is split up into different sections, each of them contending against each other and each of them pretty much entirely denying the authority of the central government, so that at the present time there are so many factions that it is difficult to know whether the central government is in possession of much of any authority. What we are trying to do there, of course, is to afford such protection as we can for the lives and property of our citizens in accordance with our treaty rights and faithfully execute the treaties that have been made between the Chinese Government and ourselves. Because of the very grave danger of disorder I understand that Mr. MacMurray has been ordered back to Peking, or has remained there, I haven't had any report from Mr. Kellogg about that within 24 hours I should say. I have talked with him about dispatches that came from MacMurray. I don't think he indicated in any of them that MacMurray had started for home. But perhaps he had. We arranged some time ago that he might come home partly for the purpose of rest and recuperation and partly that we might have a chance to confer with him personally about all the different angles of the situation.

January 25, 1927

Our policy in respect to our citizens and their property in China is that which I have often outlined to the conference, of doing what we can to protect them. There are great difficulties because of the vast extent of territory and the fact that we have people who are located in many different parts of China. All we can do about it is to do the best we can. The American situation and that of Great Britain is quite different. They have concessions in China and we have not, so that their policy perhaps might be different from ours. We have at the present time some forces around Shanghai. It is there that there is located the principal number of our citizens in China. I think there are some 4,000 in Shanghai and those we shall attempt to do the best we can to protect from disorder and mob violence. A memorandum was handed to the Secretary of State not very long ago from the British and the Secretary has been considering making some statement that would more clearly define the policy of the United States relative to our treaty rights and so on in China. I think he may have such a memorandum ready within a day or two, so that you will have an authoritative and carefully prepared statement of the American position and policies. That hasn't anything to do with protection of our citizens and their property that is located there, but it has to do with the other matters which are not in the memorandum that the British made.

[*The Shanghai affair of 1925 greatly troubled the British Government, and the result was a statement of policy in December, 1926. "The political disintegration in China," the British note stated, "has . . . been accompanied by the growth of a powerful nationalist movement which aimed at gaining for China an equal place among the nations, and any failure to meet this movement with sympathy and understanding would not respond* [sic] *to the real intentions of the Powers towards China." Sir Austen Chamberlain proposed that the Washing-*

ton powers jointly declare willingness to negotiate outstanding issues "as soon as the Chinese themselves have constituted a Government." The British announcement was made without consulting Washington, where the note became known facetiously as "the Christmas present." Kellogg spoke out on January 27, 1927. The United States, he said, would negotiate with China either in concert with other powers or unilaterally; such negotiation need not await a new and broadly representative central government in Peking, which at the moment seemed remote, but only appointment by China of delegates representing "the authorities or the people of the country."]

March 25, 1927

Of course, it is difficult to say, but so far as we can foresee it would appear that we now have sufficient forces in China to take care of such Americans there as need to be cared for. Just at the present time the situation at Shanghai appears to be less tense, but considerable trouble, as has been reported in the press, has broken out at Nanking. The Navy Department has reported to me that their information is that one American there has been killed and the American Consulate attacked and the Consul and his staff driven out. There are some 125 or 150 Americans still within the city supposed to be at the University and their safety is naturally giving us a good deal of concern. I think we have sufficient forces there for rescue purposes and to do everything that could be done in that direction. The only advantage that could be secured by a larger force would be from sending a very large force.

PRESS: And that isn't being considered at all, Mr. President?

PRESIDENT: Well, I hardly think so at this time. That would not now help the situation that has developed with reference to the people in Nanking and we think we have a sufficient force to protect our people at Shanghai.

PRESS: Is there any evidence that the attack on foreigners at Nanking was instigated by the Cantonese forces, or was it the affair of the mob—people that got out of hand. Have we information on that score?

PRESIDENT: The information I have is that it was almost entirely by soldiers who are in the Cantonese uniform.

[*The Nanking incident had occurred the day before. Nationalist armies were moving north from Canton. In occupying Nanking, soldiers apparently belonging to the communist faction of the Nationalists (Chiang Kai-shek had not yet expelled the communists from the Kuomintang) attacked foreigners, destroyed foreign property, gutted the American, British, and Japanese consulates, and killed Dr. John E. Williams, the American vice-president of the University of Nanking. Another missionary, Miss Anna E. Moffet, was seriously wounded. A group of Americans took refuge in the Standard Oil Company compound at Socony Hill and escaped over the wall to the river when*

British and American naval vessels threw a protective barrage of shells between the refugees and their Chinese attackers.]

May 3, 1927

There is no foundation for the reports, so far as I know, that Mr. MacMurray, our Minister to China, has resigned. I think it probably wise to look with more or less suspicion on reports concerning the attitude of this Government toward China and its representatives in China which originate out of our country. I have happened to see a number of reports of that kind which had a foreign origin that didn't have any foundation.

May 31, 1927

I do not think any movements of Marines in China of any considerable extent are contemplated. Our main base now is at Shanghai. We may send some more Marines to Tientsin. That will depend on developments in north China and whether we think that our Legation and our Diplomatic and Consular representatives in that locality and the American interests there are in any peril. We have in general contemplation that we should remove the Legation from Peking if any general disorder develops in that neighborhood, because that is a long ways from the coast, comparatively over there, difficult of access, and therefore difficult to protect. It would be very much easier to take care of our interests if our Embassy and the people connected with it—I mean the Legation—was brought down where it would have better access to the sea.

PRESS: Can you say where the Peking Legation may be moved to?

PRESIDENT: I can't say yet. May possibly go to Shanghai, or some other location.

[*The Nationalists did not occupy Peking until 1928; meanwhile their headquarters were in Nanking. They preferred that city to China's ancient capital, which was more exposed to raiding by unfriendly warlords and pro-Soviet generals.*]

August 5, 1927

I don't know of any new developments in China that would change the views that I expressed in an address I made in New York on, I think, the 27th of April relative to our policy there. I do not know just how many Americans we have in China. We have been getting them out and having them go home in a great many instances, and in others bringing them down to the coast where we could give them protection. I judge from the question that is before me that there has been some suggestion that because there are only 14,058 American citizens there that we are not justified in keeping 13,200 American soldiers and sailors and Marines in that locality. Of course, we have to keep a sufficient force there to protect our people as best we can, and I haven't had a sufficiently detailed report of conditions in China for some days, so that I know just what is developing. I had understood that the situation at Shanghai had quieted down so that it has been possible to remove the barbed wire and other obstructions that fenced off the foreign quarter from the rest of the city. But I suppose that everyone knows that it was the presence of the forces of the various interested countries at Shanghai that prevented the taking and looting of the city, which was a service not only to the foreigners that happened to be there but a great service also to the Chinese people that were in the locality.

February 24, 1928

I haven't very much information about the shipping of Russian gold to the United States. I assume that is for the purpose of making payment on goods that have been purchased here. It is no different than any other commercial transaction, so far as I know. Trading has been going on constantly between Russia and the United States. Goods have been bought here and payment made for them, and our people have bought goods in considerable amounts in Russia. That makes necessary setting up some method for payment. I suppose this shipment of gold is for that purpose. It would not indicate anything new in the relationship, simply a continuation of what has been going on for a number of years.

July 27, 1928

I don't know just what the State Department is planning as to a recognition of the Chinese Nationalist Government. Those details are in their hands and they haven't sent me any information about it. I suppose that making the treaty with a government usually, if not necessarily, constitutes a recognition of that government. It might not, but generally does.

[*On July 25, 1928 the United States signed a customs treaty with the newly created National Government, allowing tariff autonomy to China on a most-favored-nation basis on the condition that the other tariff-treaty nations followed suit. The treaty constituted recognition.*]

November 6, 1928

Our policy there [in Nicaragua], of course, has been very similar to our policy in Mexico and China, of trying peaceably to compose our differences. We are succeeding admirably in Mexico, and the situation in China which was very ominous in the winter and spring of 1926 has also been composed, so much so that we now have under consideration the question of raising our legation there to an embassy. We were besought to take very strong military action against China, which I all the time refused to do, thinking that it was much more likely that they would be able to adjust their own differences if we refrained from interfering or doing any more than was necessary to protect the lives and interests of our people there.

INDEX

Agricultural Credit Corporation, 120-121

Agriculture, 8, 11, 99, 111-112, 114-117, 119-126, 128, 136, 139, 141-142, 158-159, 194. *See* McNary-Haugen bill

Air force, US. *See* Army, US

Alaska, 62, 222-223, 233-236, 243-244

Alfaro, R. J., 226

Alien Property bill, 16

Allied Reparations Commission. *See* Reparations

American Bankers Association, 176

American Bar Association, 185

American Brown Boveri Electric Corporation, 138

American Legion, 167

American Lumber Company (Nicaragua), 240

American Policy in Nicaragua, by Henry L. Stimson, 245-246

American Red Cross, 226

American Senate, by Lindsay Rogers, 14

American Sugar Company, 93

Amherst College, 35, 43, 49, 136, 244-245

Anglo-French Naval Compromise *(1928),* 171-172

Arbitration, 214-216

Argentina, 253

Army, US, 12, 15, 37-38, 41, 46, 55, 57, 76-78, 86, 107-111, 147-173, 214, 217, 226, 247-249, 254, 258, 264; and air force, 147, 153-156, 158-160, 162. *See* Flood control; Marines, US; West Point

Associated Press, 150-151

Atlantic Monthly, 130

Austria, 175, 193-194, 197-198

Baker, Newton D., 196

Balfour, Arthur, 178

Banks, 81-82, 117-121, 123-124, 126, 129-131, 138. *See* Federal Reserve System; Reparations; War debts

Baseball, 10

Bauer, Ralph, 26

Beach, Lansing Haskins, 37-38

Belgium, 179, 191-192, 204, 207, 212

Bérenger, Henri, 196-197

Berlin, Treaty of *(1921),* 182

Bethlehem Steel Company, 134-135

Black River Academy, 43

Blaine, John J., 220

Bok, Edward, 18, 203-204

Bonus bill, 103, 110

Books, reviewing of, 14

Borah, William E., 190-191, 197, 202, 220, 233, 255

Borah, by Marian C. McKenna, 233

Boston Elevated Railway, 7

Boston Post, 28

Boulder Dam, 84-85, 111, 143

Boxer indemnity, 259

Boy Scouts, 31

Bradford, Gamaliel, 14

Briand, Aristide. *See* Kellogg-Briand Pact *(1928)*

Broad Street Hospital, 15

Brookhart, Smith W., 97-98

Brush, Chauncey M., 7-8

Bryan, William Jennings, 204

Bryan-Chamorro Treaty *(1914),* 231

Bucareli Conferences, 224-225, 233

Burton, J. R., 96

Butler, Nicholas Murray, 202

Butler, William M., 10, 98

Butterfield, Kenyon L., 78

Cabinet, 8, 11-12, 16, 23, 25, 34, 36, 56, 59-60, 64, 73-74, 87-89, 92-95, 115-117, 120-121, 126-127, 131, 150, 152, 156, 167, 195

Calles, Plutarco Elías, 228, 233, 237, 248

Calvin Coolidge, by Claude M. Fuess, 238

Calvin Coolidge, by Michael Hennessey, 42

Canada, 74, 116, 119, 148

Capper resolution, 220-221

Carranza, Venustiano, 225

Catholic Church, 10, 224, 237, 239, 248

Cecil, Robert, 66-67

Chamber of Commerce, US, 109-110

Chamberlain, Austen, 262-263

Manchu empire, 257
Marines, US, 223, 231-232, 242, 252-254, 258, 264
Maryland, ship, 253
Massachusetts Agricultural College, 8, 78, 158-159
Massachusetts State College. *See* Massachusetts Agricultural College
Mayflower, ship, 91, 164
Mellon, Andrew W., 92, 97, 114, 126-127, 131, 196-197
Mellon-Bérenger Agreement *(1926),* 196-197, 212
Mencken, Henry L., 14
Mercersburg Academy, 35, 37
Merchant marine, 135, 137, 228. *See* Shipping Board
Methodist Missionary Board, 260
Metro-Goldwyn-Mayer, 12-13
Mexico, 10, 71-73, 101, 223-225, 228-229, 231-234, 236-240, 244-245, 247-250, 253, 265
Meyer, Eugene Jr., 117-118, 182
Michaels, Charles, 28, 76, 166
Michigan Sugar Company, 95
Mind of the President, by C. Bascom Slemp, 27, 31
Mitchell, William, 147, 159-160
Mixed Claims Commission (German-US). *See* Reparations
Moffet, Anna E., 263
Moncada, José, 223-224, 240-242, 251-252
Monroe, James, 227
Monroe Doctrine, 205, 213-214, 227
Morgan, J. P., 200
Morgan, J. P. and Company, 156, 224, 244-245
Morin, Louis, 190
Morrow, Dwight W., 156, 224, 244-245, 247-248
Motion pictures, 12-13, 15
Mott, Lucretia, amendment to US Constitution, 15
Muscle Shoals, 99-100, 111, 143
Mussolini, Benito, 143

Nanking incident, 263-264
Nation, 20

National debt, 76, 102-112
National Geographic Society, 49-50
National Woman's Party, 15
National Zeitung (Berlin), 32-33
Nationalist Party. *See* China
Naval Academy, 12-13, 143
Navy, British, 155-157, 263-264; German, 155; US, 15, 23-24, 31, 41, 55, 86, 99, 107-109, 139-140, 147-173, 214, 217, 226, 247-248, 254, 258, 260, 263-264. *See* Army; Disarmament; Marines; Naval Academy; World Disarmament Conference *(1932-34);* Washington Naval Conference *(1921-22);* Geneva Naval Conference *(1927);* Anglo-French Naval Compromise *(1928);* London Naval Conference *(1930)*
New York Life Insurance Company, 74
New York Peace Society, 204
New York Times, 28
Nicaragua, 223-224, 228, 231-232, 239-243, 245, 246, 251-253, 265
Nichols, Malcolm E., 173
Nicolson, Harold, 248
Norbeck-Burtness bill, 120-121
Norris, George W., 100
Novarro, Ramón, 12-13

Obregón, Alvaro, 225, 228-229, 233
Osmena, Sergio, 245
Outlawry of war. *See* Kellogg-Briand Pact *(1928)*

Pact of Paris *(1928). See* Kellogg-Briand Pact
Painlevé, Paul, 160
Panama, 223, 226-227. *See* Panama Canal
Panama Canal, 226-227, 231
Pan-American Union, 229
Paris Peace Conference *(1919),* 178, 257
Payne, John Barton, 71-72, 224-225
Pease, Arthur Stanley, 49
Permanent Court of International Justice. *See* World Court